The Pipe
and Christ

by William Stolzman

Tipi Press
Chamberlain, South Dakota

Seventh Edition
2002

ISBN 1-877976-00-8

Published by Tipi Press, Chamberlain, South Dakota 57326

Illustrations and cover design by Ron Zeilinger and
Nancy Gordon.

Printed by Tipi Press Printing, St. Joseph's Indian School.

To

The Young People

On The Rosebud Reservation

Table of Contents

Acknowledgements

God is the first to be acknowledged and praised. It was He who gave this wretched sinner whatever calling and talent he has. To Him be the glory of all that is valuable and true in this book.

To Moses Big Crow goes the second statement of appreciation. He is noteworthy as the grandson of two medicine men, singer for all the Rosebud medicine men, solidly Catholic, widely recognized as a Lakota leader, a nation-wide lecturer on Indian culture, vice-chairman of the Rosebud Medicine men and Associates, a bilingual consultant for the University of South Dakota, and the chief interpreter for the Rosebud Medicine Men and Pastors' Meeting. His blindness was an asset rather than a liability to his personal and spiritual sensitivity. He is most appreciated, however, for the support and companionship he gave me during my Lakota-Christian journey, which left us both spiritually richer and the closest of friends. **Mitakola, pilamaya.**

A humble and gracious appreciation goes to Arthur Running Horse. He is the medicine man who guided me through my first four vision quests. This most traditional, contemplative medicine man is also a leader in the Catholic Church. In the Medicine Men and Pastors' Meeting, he often was the one to initiate discussions, ever urging the group forward to produce something that would help the people of the reservation follow the spiritual ways given by God for the health and salvation of the people.

Warmest appreciation is extended to all the medicine men who took part in the religious dialogue. Frank Picket Pin for many years was the oldest medicine man on the Rosebud Reservation. One of the early Catholic catechists, he was for a good number of years companion and Lakota teacher of one of the great early missionaries, Father Digmann. Bill (Chief Eagle Feather) Schweigman, attended meetings regularly; his sharings were special. His grandson, Titus, became a medicine man during the course of the dialogue; to him congratulations are expressed. Charles Kills Enemy often missed meetings because of his travels. Nonetheless he regularly performed Indian ceremonies arranged by me for the inmates at the South Dakota Penitentiary; he shared many religious insights with me on those long trips to Sioux Falls.

A young medicine man with growing experience, who regularly attended the meetings, was Gilbert Yellow Hawk; his presence and participation were valuable and appreciated. Rudy Runs Above, a Rosebud medicine man who performs most of his ceremonies on the Pine Ridge Reservation, attended many meetings, and his comments, especially outside the meetings, were most helpful. Although frequently off the reservation ministering to relatives and friends, Shelbert White Bear contributed to this book through his many private conversations with me. Joseph Eagle Elk, because of sickness and other difficulties, was able to attend the meetings only for a time. His father, George Eagle Elk, was one of the most faithful and interested participants until his death. John (Lame Deer) Fire made 130 mile round-trips to attend the meetings until his sickness and death. He frequently shared many of his particular insights from his well-known book, **Lame Deer, Seeker of Visions.**

Leonard Crow Dog was able to attend only a limited number of meetings because of his role as religious leader in the American Indian Movement. His traditional and dynamic input into the meetings was greatly appreciated. Because of the support which the Medicine Men and Pastors' Meeting gave him during his trials and imprisonments, Leonard gave the meeting the buffalo robe he used for his vision quests and his ceremonies. No words are enough to express our gratitude. Norbert Running received his vision during our dialogue and joined to share with us some of his wisdom. Because of a critical comment from an older medicine man, he decided not to attend the meetings after that. His continued friendship and conversations with me were greatly appreciated. Robert Stead, who is well-known for his healings, attended only a few meetings, but left expressing his belief that such meetings would compromise and dilute Lakota powers. I thank him for the respect he continued to show me as a religious leader.

The Medicine Men and Pastors' Meeting had many Indian consultants who contributed much to the fruitfulness of the dialogue. In particular, thanks go to the following: Ben Black Bear, Sr. and his wife, Iva; Julie Walking Eagle, Lucille Running Horse, wife of Arthur Running Horse; Jane Marshall, daughter of Moses Big Crow; Ellis Head; Elizabeth Clifford; Charles Little Eagle; Joseph Black Tomahawk and his wife, Laura; Marie Two Charge; and Ben Black Bear, Jr., a Catholic Indian Deacon.

The members of the Society of Jesus, both on and off the reservation were a real support in this project. Their fraternal encouragement and theological inquiry kept the dialogue searching and reflective. Special thanks go to the following mission personnel: Robert Hilbert, S.J.; Bernard Fagan, S.J.; Richard Jones, S.J.; Robert Demeyer, S.J.; Kenneth Walleman, S.J.; George Haas, S.J.; Harry Zerner, S.J.; Albert Janka, S.J.; Joseph Gill, S.J.; and Harry Eglsaer, S.J. Many thanks must go to the Jesuit Council for Theological Reflection (JCTR) for supporting the dialogue with grants the four peak years of theological sharing and reflection. Carl Starkloff, S.J. and Richard Smith, S.J. are thanked for the special outside consultation they gave.

Special appreciation is expressed to Bishop Harold J. Dimmerling of the Diocese of Rapid City for his interest and support of the dialogue, and to Sergio Cardinal Pignedoli of the Secretariate for Non-Christians, in Rome, for his warm reception of project materials.

Sr. Aurea Kimball, S.S.N.D., and Father Robert J. Schreiter, C.PP.S., are warmly thanked for their support and help in the preparation of the manuscript of this book.

There are so many friends, supporters, and critics who have contributed to my education in the Lakota and Catholic religions. I could not begin to list them all. My thanks to each. May God bless each of you and your families. **Pilamaya, mitakuya pelo.**

Preface
Personal Story

The Lakota Indians live mostly in the southwest quarter of South Dakota, southeast of the Black Hills and the Badlands, in and near the Pine Ridge Reservation, the Rosebud Reservation, and Rapid City, South Dakota. While the eastern Sioux call themselves "Dakota," a word which means "the friends," the western Sioux call themselves "Lakota" and speak the western dialect which is called **Lakotia.** (1)

In the Lakota way, speakers introduce **themselves.** Only after that do they proceed to the matter at hand. In telling their personal histories and related incidents, they display their attitudes and feelings toward those events and, more important, the impact those events have had on them. Thus their comments are spoken from a definite context, with definite attitudes which give their remarks a special integrity, meaning, wisdom and depth. Thus the hearer is able to appreciate both the experiences, preferences, and limitations of each speaker. Through their personal introductions, the speakers respectfully recognize that others may know other truths because others have different experiences and relationships to what is being talked about.

In Lakota ceremonies, the personal introduction is ritualized. After greeting the people and telling them why the ceremony is called, the medicine man **hanbloglaka** (he tells his vision). If he has ceremonies four nights in a row, he will usually **hanbloglaka** before each one. He recounts the dreams, visions, and spiritual experiences from which he has received his spirits and his spiritual power. In this way the people's faith and understanding are sharpened, their fears and confusions are reduced, and their hopes and confidences are strengthened.

In this preface I will give my **hanbloglaka.** I will tell of those spiritual experiences which have been for me the doorway into my involvement in both the Lakota and Catholic religions while on the Rosebud Reservation. This story will hopefully establish my right and authenticity to speak on Lakota-Christian spiritual matters.

(1) A pronunciation guide for **Lakotia** is given in the Appendix.

-1-

A word of caution first. The things of which I speak are sacred and should not be bantered about in ordinary conversation. These visions are mine, and anyone who speaks of them speaks not from what he knows but from hearsay. The stories may fill you with wonder, desire and questioning. That is good. Real answers and satisfaction, however, come only from one's own pursuit and experience of the Sacred.

Some Indians, I am sure, will consider it wrong for me to put these visions into print. I deeply sympathize with their fears and anxieties, I have always tried my best to respect Lakota religious ways, and there are some private revelations of which I will never speak publicly. Some religious experiences, however, are meant to be told. Stories, like the coming of the White Buffalo Calf Woman, have been told for centuries for the spiritual benefit of all. My early spiritual experiences, I find, were meant for many to hear, but current ones are for myself alone. I know that if I use these visions wrongly, I will pay for it. For several years now, I have told them to mixed Indian and White audiences — but always in a strictly religious situation. Many medicine men have been in those audiences. My **hanbloglaka** has always resulted not in personal condemnation but in an increased respect for both the Indian and Christian religions. The account of these visions is not meant to humiliate or put anyone down, but to lift the spiritual hopes, dreams, and faith of the people.

Let it be clear that visions are not a sign of holiness. Visions are given to saints and sinners alike. The seeker only accentuates them; the fleer can only suppress them. Visions do not come from humans but from God. And He gives them for His own purposes: both to convert and sanctify people. Some people are fearful of visions lest they come from an evil spirit. Even if a particular vision is not from God, human beings have the ability to turn even sinful things into things of spiritual profit. Some fear their power which may cause problems for themselves or their relatives if misused. Rather than avoid such matters, the Lakota person inquires of older and wiser people in order to learn proper religious respect. Last of all, it is my experience that noteworthy visions usually come at the beginning of what is spiritually new. Therefore, if anyone wishes to say anything about these visions, let him say that they are those of a struggling beginner.

I can vividly recall my first spiritual experience at about twelve years of age. The place is so clear in my mind: beneath the fourth stained-glass window on the east side of my home parish church, St. John the Baptist, in Marshfield, Wisconsin. I had come into church after school as I sometimes did. I liked being there. Sometimes I ferreted into the nooks and crannies of that old building, but this day I tried to settle myself to pray.

I have never been good at prayer. I never seem to find the right words, or any words. I simply long to pray. I long to contact God in a personal way. Half-distracted and slumped in the pew, I longed to pray well. Suddenly I heard a voice, a booming voice. Its power shook me. In the very speaking I knew it was God Himself saying to me, "I want you to be a Jesuit."

Immediately, panic exploded within me. Rebellion surged from my depths. "No! I am no good. I am a miserable sinner. I don't want to become a priest. I am going to be a scientist. I intend to be better than my brother. People will respect me for my scientific knowledge. No, no, no. . ." I kept talking to myself until I became aware of my surroundings again. In the silence of the church I shivered. Bracing myself, I arose and quickly left the church, trying to push out of my mind those few unforgettable words: "I want you to be a Jesuit."

The next years passed quickly with high school activities coming and going with varying degrees of importance. One day I remember well. A very tiny sister suddenly approached me and said simply to my face, "Bill, I want to tell you this. The Lord will one day ask something of you, and your answer should simply be 'Thy will be done.' Do you understand?" I pretended ignorance and surprise, but inside I shouted, "Never!"

As college years passed, God's call became louder. I did not want God's vocation, and I thought He might tire and allow me to go my own way. However, I did something very foolish; I still tried to pray and received the sacraments regularly. I say "foolish" because a person who is self-directed cannot be spiritual; the two are incompatible. After struggling in mathematics and physics, I got my bachelor's degree in Physical Meteorology from the University of Wisconsin, Madison. I desired to attend graduate school, but my scholarship had expired, and my summer job was inadequate to cover expenses. I tried to get into an Air Force subsidized program but was rejected because of poor eyesight. I borrowed some money to cover education courses I needed to teach in high school. I would earn the money I needed for graduate school that way. All this time the Lord continued to pursue me.

For eight years I continued to rebel, and He grew impatient. His call became louder and louder. I remember one particular night when the call was so strong I could not sleep. I paced the floor, pounding my head with closed fist, crying out, "I will not serve. I will not serve. I will not submit to the authority of a bishop." The last sentence indicates my total ignorance of the Jesuits with whom I had no contact before I entered. But the first sentence! Those were the words of Lucifer himself before he was cast into hell! To this day, the remembrance of what I said frightens me, for this was the most grievous of sins - to close one's fist before the face of the Lord. No man was ever more wretched than I, none more deserving of hell for refusing so deliberately and tenaciously the will of God.

And hell the Lord gave me. From that point on, everything went wrong. I did so deplorably in school that I was royally raked over the coals before the School of Education reluctantly gave me my teacher's certificate. I had car accidents, money problems, women problems, and school problems. In the classroom in a fit of rage, for example, I hit a student and knocked out one of his teeth. The bad consequences of this were manifold. I was then so publicly ashamed of my faith that I would not attend church in my hometown but went instead to a neighboring town. I tried to sink into anonymity as I cried to the Lord for help, but no help came. Then one day I simply walked out of school, got into my car, and drove to the church in the next town. I knelt at the communion rail and said those words that the little sister had told me to say so many years before, "Thy will be done."

Oh the tears that flowed when I finally gave in to the Lord! Oh the spiritual tension that was released after so many years of resistance! After nine long years of struggle, a glorious feeling seemed to lift my entire being. It felt like I was walking two inches above the ground. Everything suddenly seemed to go right — for almost two years straight. Difficulties melted like butter in the sun. Within six months I was in the Jesuit novitiate. There I began to have other spiritual experiences, but I quickly learned not to talk about them even to my spiritual director.

One day during the second year of my religious life, I lay on my bed, not sleeping but simply waiting for time to pass. As I faced the wall, suddenly it split open like the lid of a cardboard box, and there, in a panorama before me, I saw every person and sin I had ever encountered in my life. As I excitedly looked from one incident to the other, I heard a voice behind my shoulder speak in a warm, soothing, male voice, "See, it wasn't really all that bad." That was all. I burst into tears. When I regained my composure, I knew I was free — free to accept or reject my calling as a Jesuit. Now for the first time, my pride and shame would not drive me away. With dispassionate freedom I said, "Yes." How else could I respond to a God who had so clearly shown His call and His love for me?

Many people have asked me, "Why did you become a missionary to the Indians?" I think they expect a stock answer, for when I tell them, they appear shocked. My answer to this question is intimately tied to my involvement in Indian religion even though I am a Catholic missionary.

My coming to the reservation to teach at Holy Rosary Mission, currently called Red Cloud Indian School, was not planned. When I entered the Jesuit order, I had asked for mission work, but what I had in mind was teaching physics in one of our foreign universities, either at Sogang, Korea or Salta, Argentina. I still clung to the proud ambitions of the past. I never gave a thought to the Indian missions. Near the end of my philosophic training in a modern hybrid affectionately called "Missouri Thomism," I received orders to teach at Marquette University High School in Milwaukee. This assignment abnormally distressed me. It was not that I expected a higher position; I did not yet have a master's degree in physics and was not academically ready to teach anything at a university level. Somehow, however, I knew that this was not the right spot for me. I was not now meant for that group of kids. I prayed for peace and that God's will be done.

On the very day I was packing to leave for my assignment, I received a letter from the central Jesuit office. It was apologetic. A man had dropped out, and they needed a replacement at the Indian school. They presumed I would be disappointed, but they cited the interest in the missions that I had expressed when I first entered. A sudden feeling of relief came over me. My worrisome heart suddenly collapsed; I was strangely at rest. With joy I went to teach for the next two years of my training at the Catholic Indian school outside of Pine Ridge, South Dakota.

Holy Rosary had many boarders then. As dorm supervisor, math teacher, work supervisor, athletic director, and recreation prefect, most days started for me at 6 a.m. and did not end until 10 p.m. The school in many ways was home for me and for many of the students. Things were in a process of change. Dr. John Bryde, then of the Society of Jesus, was leading the way in education toward a greater consciousness and appreciation of Indian cultural values. All of the Jesuit scholastics sought to combine in a meaningful way the secure discipline necessary to every educational institution with the respectful love characteristic of the Lakota extended-family. Watching and listening, I learned that it takes more than good will and energy to be a satisfactory missionary to the Indians. I had heard of many incidents where missionaries of good will had hurt Indians spiritually through a lack of sensitivity and adaptability to the Indians' ways. At the end of my two years of teaching, I debated with myself whether I should return to the reservation after ordination. I did not want to be another cross for the Indians to bear. I did not know if I had the qualities to be a good priest to the Lakota. Besides, by now I had a master's degree in physics. Was I to throw all that work out the window in becoming an Indian missionary? Many questions about the future filled my thoughts and prayers.

As the summer ended, a young Indian friend stopped by to see me. His father was sick, and they were having several nights of Indian ceremonies for him. He asked if I would come. Many things flashed across my mind. I knew there was no official approval for attending such ceremonies. While traditionally the mission was negative on Indian religion, there were undercurrents of respect and interest in many places. My attendance at this meeting would be, as far as I knew, the first of its kind. I didn't know whether the ecumenical spirit was then far enough advanced on the reservation to sanction my attending such Indian ceremonies at that time. But in a flash, the whole religious question somehow became irrelevant. My friend's father was sick, and I was being asked to come and pray with his family and the Indian people for his health. I was his friend. I said I would come.

The ceremonies took place at the family home. There they greeted me warmly. Two nights of ceremonies had already taken place; I was present for the last two. The ceremony went well. The medicine man said that the prayers were answered, and the father would get well. I was happy for this and for many other things. I returned to my normal routine at the mission. But then something happened that has changed my life ever since.

About a week after that ceremony, as I stood in the Jesuit dining room late at night, I suddenly heard a voice. It was not the same voice as before but another spirit, a lower spirit this time. He talked very fast, but I understood well what was said. He told me the medicine man was wrong, and that the father would die — die soon. I was to go and tell the family. I was to tell the father not to be afraid, for his children would do him honor. The oldest son would sway, first one way and then another, but he would do all right in the long run. The second son would become a leader. The two daughters would get good husbands and have good families. I asked why I was being told this. The answer was: in this way I would know if I was to return to the reservation and perform four vision quests.

I was dumbfounded. This was crazy. Everything was backwards. In my personal opinion, the only son with a real chance for success was the older son, and he would sway this way and that? The second son was a confirmed drinker and one of the worst hell-raisers at school, and he was to be a leader? The girls were thought to be among the loosest in school, and they would find good husbands and have good families? Everything the spirit said was opposite my opinion. And I was to tell a man that he was about to die - after a medicine man had just assured him that he would live? The spirit was right: if this message turned out to be the truth, it would be a powerful sign that I should return. If it was false, however, I also knew I would not dare show my face on the reservation again. No sir!! That message was too hot a potato for me to handle. As I left the dining room to go to bed, I decided to leave that message in the dining room right where I got it.

Early the next morning I heard a pounding at the front door. Outside stood my friend. He and his family were driving into town from their home, and as they passed the missions, the car mysteriously stopped. I offered my help, although inside I was near panic. I offered them a lift to town — keeping them moving in an ''away'' direction. But no! They wanted to return home for the pickup. I said that I would take my friend home while all the others waited at the mission. No, they **all** insisted on going back. (Inside myself I groaned to think where my God was pushing me.)

Nine of us squeezed into a mission car, and I took them to their home in the country. By now I was learning how to agree to the Lord's indications more rapidly, even if I did not like them. Along the way I tried to find the words and the courage to say what I knew needed saying. At their house I asked if I could speak to the whole family, even the old folks who lived nearby. We all got out of the car except the old man, who had to be forced to get out. He seemed to know that something he would not like was about to happen.

Inside they all sat around the room. I stood in the center and began: ''You all know me. I have been here several times, but today is different because I have been given a message to pass on to you.'' I proceeded in Indian fashion to give my spiritual credentials; I told them of the visions I had seen and the voices I had heard and the message I was to bring them. ''I was told to tell you that the medicine man was wrong, and your father will die soon.'' I can still hear the gasps and moans of the women. ''The spirits told me to tell him not to be afraid, for his children will do him honor. The oldest son will sway this way and that, but will turn out all right in the end. The second son will be a leader among his people. The two girls will find good husbands and raise good families. This is what I was told to say. This is all.'' The family sat in silence; they nodded their heads, and a few said **''Han''** (Yes). Slowly and sadly I shook hands with each in silence. As I left the home, the older son, with obvious affection, thanked me profusely for my words. I went to the mission, packed my bags, and left the reservation for my theological training.

A month later, I heard that the father had died. The older son did struggle for years, trying this and that, but he is settling down to a good life. The girls left the reservation, found good husbands in the city, and had good families. Two years later at the National Congress of American Indians, I could not believe my eyes. There was the second son. He was attending the university at Berkeley at the time and was involved in the foundation of the Indian activist movement there. He later returned to the reservation as a teacher in the new Indian Culture Center attached to the mission school. In a very vivid way, something spiritual had answered my prayers and shown this stubborn ''mule'' that he was to return to the reservation for at least four vision quests.

The liberal atmosphere of the late 1960's allowed me to personally revamp my theology program toward anthropology and the Indians. After ordination, the Jesuits at St. Francis asked me to make a religious-sociological study of the Rosebud Reservation. After that I was assigned to St. Bridget Church in the agency town of Rosebud, South Dakota. There I began to prepare myself spiritually for the series of vision quests I had been told to make. But I could not conceive myself as a renegade, going out and performing those vision quests on my own. As an ordained priest and missionary, I knew that I could not shed my priesthood when I went on the hill. Although alone on the hill, I knew that I stood there publicly before every Catholic Indian and priest on the reservation. I could not make a vision quest without the knowledge and support of at least my missionary peers. Similarly, out of respect for the Lakota religious tradition, I felt that as a publicly significant outsider, I should speak to and receive general approval from the medicine men on the Rosebud Reservation before I went on the hill. I wanted no negative statements made subsequent to that sacred action. Talking to the leaders in both the Lakota and Catholic religions, I found that most of the people on both sides were interested in mutual understanding and acceptance. In response to this mutual interest, I organized the Rosebud Medicine Men and Pastors' Meeting, which completed in a six year dialogue a penetrating discussion of all the major topics of the Lakota and Catholic religions. After a cautious beginning, these semi-monthly meetings were soon attended by twenty to forty Lakota and Whites, nine months out of each year. As chairman of these meetings, I wrote summary papers to assist the discussions. The Lakota liked these so much they directed me to work them into a book — this book.

From the earliest meetings, it became clear to me that the dynamic force within the Lakota religion is found in the Lakota spirits, just as the real motivator within the Christian Church is the Holy Spirit. I quickly learned that to enter any Lakota ceremony and to walk the sacred red path, one had to believe in the Lakota spirits associated with the Pipe Ceremony. Because of my theological training and materialistic upbringing, I found it hard to believe that the Four Winds and Grandmother Earth were real spiritual beings. I wanted to believe, but my past would not let me.

I decided my pitifulness in my first vision quest would be my struggle with belief. The first quest would be one night and one day. It would be dedicated to the **Wakiyan,** the Thunder Beings of the West, the first direction. I prayed that the night would be full of lightning, but that no rain would fall into the sacred area. I prayed I would **not** have a dream or a vision. Dreams, especially, are always subject to the question: Are these dreams creations of my imagination or truly of the spirits? I wanted the spirits to show me their physical presence and respond to prayer with physical signs I could experience with my physical senses. As I recall my naive boldness, I shudder. I was spiritually desperate. I asked for much, and much was given.

When the assigned day for my first vision quest arrived in August, 1974, dark clouds gathered in the sky. The wind blustered, and it seemed that it would storm at any moment. As I prepared myself for the sweatbath, the area was surrounded with lightning on all sides.

By the time we reached the hill, the lightning and wind came continually from the West. Wrapped only in a star quilt and holding my Pipe, I stood on top of the hill in the midst of an electrical storm. Strangely, I had no fear in my heart. Whenever I thought of the dangers of lightning, my mind confidently turned to the protective power of the tobacco ties.

I felt confident in my prayer on the hill. Earlier that summer I had finally overcome my intellectual prejudice against repetitive, heart-dominated prayer, such as the Jesus prayer, the rosary, and "speaking in tongues." I had told the spirits what I wished before I went up. Now I put all that aside and said within myself that I would only express my pitifulness and be most accepting and observant of anything they wished to give me. As I faced each direction, my continual prayer was simply, **"Tunkašila, onšimala ye,"** (Grandfather, pity me). Nothing more.

As I faced the West, the wind became more and more ferocious. The black flag in the West was long, and it whipped me and lashed me painfully. How hard and testing is the West! The wind became so strong that I seemed to lean 45 degrees into the wind to keep my balance. Finally when I could no longer stand, I descended into the pit and sat facing the West. The wind roared, the flags slapped, and the lightning flashed from the West overhead. Suddenly, "Yehhhhhhhhhhhhhhhhhh. . .," the most blood-curdling eagle scream I have ever heard! It was a thousand times louder than any eagle cry I had ever heard before. The wind immediately stopped! The sudden silence was shaking. There was only the snapping and crackling of the lightning in the West. . . and the lingering memory of that frightening eagle's scream. I sat and shuddered. It was the **Wakiyan,** the Thunder Bird, controller of storms.

The lightning then moved to the South. Something was wrong. This was contrary to the way it should be. It should have turned toward the North! Only later did I understand that this was a sign of the companion of the West, the contrary one, **Heyoka,** the Clown. With the wind quiet, I returned outside to pray. As the lightning moved to the South, the wind began to come from that direction. With it came a fine mist. As it touched my face, I could not help but think of tears. I did not want the mist to come into the square, so I prayed, and even the mist stopped. (This was amazing, for at the medicine man's house a mile away, the people were anxiously praying for me. They were having a downpour, and it hailed several times. In fact, the entire region suffered the worst hail storm in years that night.) On the hill, however, there were only wind, lightning, and thunder.

I began to hear voices coming out of the floor at the southern edge of the pit. There were thousands of voices resembling the drone of a crowd. I bent over and cupped my ear in order to pick up some words to discover if they were speaking to me in Lakota or English. After a few minutes the voices stopped. These were the voices of the dead who journey south to the place called **Tate Makoce,** what White men call the "Happy Hunting Ground."

I remained for quite a while in the pit, praying and feeling very close to the earth, to which the bodies of the souls had returned. Then I decided to go outside. As I got up to leave, the earth gave a great heave one direction and then the other. I was bounced back and forth from side to side in the pit — gently. It seemed as if Grandmother Earth was showing her presence and love by rocking me back and forth in the "arms" of the pit as a little child is rocked in the arms of its grandmother.

By now the lightning and wind had turned to the East. As I ascended from the pit, the earth was radiant in golden light. I looked up, and a beautiful full-moon was shining down from the

East on the landscape. Then I accidentally stepped on the corner of my blanket and momentarily glanced down. When I looked back — the earth was suddenly dark. Only a sliver of the moon could be seen. The moon was now, as through the rest of the night, less than a quarter. But only a moment ago she had shown herself to be full, filling the night with radiance!

It was getting toward dawn, and different physical signs had come and gone. But there was one that was constant throughout the entire night. Despite the thunder clouds, there was one star that was ever visible, high in the near West. I am a scientist, and my wonder at that star increased throughout the night. With my own eyes I saw that star remain in the same spot overhead, ever watching over me through that storm-ridden night. That star was so brilliant that it even outshone the morning star in the East. It was the last star to disappear — only after the sun was fully in the sky.

I continued to pray through the morning in the warm sunshine. Storm clouds could be seen over the distant hills to the North. As I watched the lightning, I wondered why those clouds were so distant from me. I thought within myself that their distance might be a sign that I lacked discipline and that I was right in planning to make my next vision quest in honor of the North. But these were **my** thoughts. I knew I was stretching it. But I was growing weary. The morning was long. I was becoming anxious. By noon I was beginning to despair. My heart sank. My soul panicked.

I turned to the West and changed my prayer. "**Tunkašila, onmaspe ye,**" (Grandfather, teach me). Hardly had the words come from my lips when I twice heard the love call of an eagle. Over my head, flying from due north to due south, as straight and as fast as an arrow, an eagle shot through the blinding sun and disappeared in the row of trees that lined the southern horizon. By this eagle traveling straight and fast on the sacred red path from north to south, I was taught by my Lakota namesake how I was to live. (Later when I came from the hill, an eagle swooped and circled the camp as eagles usually do. This reassured me of the special and unique meaning of that straight, rapid flight.)

The honey locust began to sing its song, and I then knew that the vision quest was finished. I praised and thanked God and the spirits during the remaining hours on the hill. Soon the medicine man came to accompany me down.

When we came to the sweatlodge, the medicine man said he thought it was too windy for a sweatbath. He feared that a fire would be dangerous at this time. During the previous year a sweatbath fire had caused a prairie fire in weather similar to this. He smoked the Pipe and told me to break my fast with the sweet food and drink he had brought. I was then told to dress and come out. Everyone was happy to see me. They shook my hand and embraced me. They had worried so much about me on the hill in that electrical storm. These people then prepared for the ceremony that would take place that evening. I stood aside, leaning against the shade, looking at the sweatlodge and saying to myself again and again, "I should be in that sweatlodge. I should be in that sweatlodge. I should be in that sweatlodge right now." Immediately, CCCRRRAAAAAAACCCCKKK! From the blue sky a terrible bolt of lightning struck. It split a pine tree standing next to the sweatlodge where I should have been. That tree, split from top to bottom, is still alive today, and it still shows the scar of that lightning bolt. It is, for me, a lasting reminder of the physical signs shown me by the spirits of the different directions to convince me of their real existence and power.

My prayers had been answered. In fact, every time I have gone to the spirits on the hill my prayers have been answered. Yet they are always answered in ways I have never expected. I have studied some psychology, and I know that a person can sometimes unknowingly program himself to see what he wants to see or symbolically hallucinate events from the past. Every time I go to the spirits I find their response to be a total surprise. I guess if there were no surprises, they would be giving me nothing new, and there would be no need for their coming. When I try to set up expectations for them, they refuse to come at all. I am convinced that their coming is found not in me but definitely outside of me. Spirits must be treated respectfully as persons. They are responsive to a person's faith and prayer. Without personal faith, trust, and confidence in them, a person remains an outsider to the Lakota religion. There is such a difference between being a stranger looking in and being one of the family.

These are but some of the things I have experienced on my spiritual journey. I have told them at the beginning of this book because I see this book as something sacred, written for spiritual healing and instruction. I hope the story of my struggles will encourage and help others on their spiritual way. It takes many hours of dedication and work to achieve one minute of success. Remember what the Lakota have said on many occasions, "When the spirits come they speak very fast." Be ready for their coming; they will come when you least expect them. Take no pride in anything spiritual; everything you have has been given you so that you and your people may live.

Mitakuye oyas'in (All my relatives).

Introduction

The Medicine Men and Pastors' Meeting

Through the years Christian Churches have regularly condemned and censured the practice of Indian religion. Today militant Indians are similarly rejecting Christianity. Yet in the midst of these conflicts some Indians have continued to perform ancestral religious ceremonies while still embracing Christianity. And a number of Christian pastors, especially since Vatican II, have increasingly shown respect for and have even participated in Lakota ritual.

There is considerable ignorance and confusion about the relationship of the Lakota and Christian religions. This book is written to help both reservation and city people understand more deeply the relationship of the Lakota and Christian religions. Many Indians and Whites struggle over questions like: What are the similarities and differences between Lakota and Christian purification rites? More generally, what are the major Lakota ceremonies and what do they mean to Indians? Are there related Christian ceremonies, and what are their deeper meanings? Are they really the same thing, or are they really different? Can a single individual practice both religions authentically without any real conflicts or contradictions? How would this be done? These are the types of questions thoughtful persons ask when they reflect upon or approach any two religions, especially from two different cultures.

These were the types of questions that a group of Lakota medicine men and Catholic pastors on the Rosebud Reservation considered in a six year dialogue directed toward mutual understanding and respect for the Lakota and Christian religions. This book comes from those discussions. It is designed to help individuals understand and appreciate the Lakota religion and how it can be related to the Christian religion.

The discussions of this Rosebud Medicine Men and Pastors' Meeting began with the topic of ceremonies because both the

Lakota and Catholic religions put a strong emphasis upon ritual. These are concrete, clear, visible realities, and they served as a solid foundation for the meeting's comparative studies. Associated with these ceremonies are many spiritual realities and values. The discussions of these more spiritual, abstract realities flowed naturally from the discussion on the rituals. From these discussions, summary positions papers were produced at the Rosebud Medicine Men and Pastors' Meeting from which were written the chapters in this book. They are of two kinds: comparative studies of Lakota and Catholic ceremonies, and theological discussions on questions arising from each comparative study. Through these the reader will find consistent similarities within each tradition and consistent, radical differences between each religion.

Faced with the radical difference between the Lakota and Christian world views, many people end up opting to follow one religion or the other. In the last chapter a fundamental Lakota-Christian paradigm will be developed through which individuals can understand how it is possible for the Lakota and Christian religions to "fit" together.

It took many years of discussion, prayer, mutual respect and participation before the conclusions of the last chapter were reached. A few historic notes may help you to understand how the Rosebud Medicine Men and Pastors' Meeting developed and how this book came to be written.

While working on the Pine Ridge Reservation, I was spiritually called to perform four Lakota vision quests. I had great difficulty with this calling because I had many theological questions and apprehensions. I also had a real ecclesiastical sense that since I was a Jesuit priest and pastor, I knew that I stood on the top of that vision quest hill as a public figure, answerable to the Indian people, Christian and non-Christian, and my fellow missionaries. I was going to do something very sacred, and I did not want any questions or "talk" to cloud the value of those experiences. I went to every medicine man and priest asking his advice and, in effect, seeking his approval for my vision quest. Many said that the medicine men would not talk about things **wakan.** But when I talked to them, I did not come with abstract questions; rather I told them of my search for spiritual things, and they in turn shared with me spiritual experiences they had had on their journey in the realm of the Sacred. These men were eager to share and to learn more. The medicine men and priests both expressed a desire for more sharings and discussions.

As a result, I asked if they would like to meet with others to help everyone better understand and appreciate the Lakota and

Christian religions and their relationship to one another. The priests had the most apprehension; they wanted the meetings to remain private. They initially wanted to meet only with those traditional practitioners they already were associated with in the Christian way. They feared that if the discussions were public, the people on the reservation would take them as a sign of the priests' approval of Indian religion. And the priests were not ready to give general approval at that point. Later when the meetings did become public, the people did take those mutual discussions as mutual approval.

The meetings began in January of 1973 with a gathering of six Lakota medicine men, five consultants and eight Jesuit priests. That year we met every few months, but within a couple of years the meetings increased to every other Monday, nine months out of the year. The meeting also grew in size until there were usually eight of the twelve medicine men of the reservation, seven of the eleven Catholic priests, and about six Lakota consultants. With Lakota relatives and other interested parties present, there were often as many as forty people at these meetings. Almost two-thirds were full-blood Lakota.

Ministers from other Christian denominations were invited, especially the Episcopalians, because 50 percent of the Indians on the Rosebud Reservation are at least nominally Catholic and 35 percent are Episcopalian. Only one Lakota Episcopalian minister attended a couple of meetings but then stopped, saying, "I'd like to come, but I don't think my congregations would approve."

I became the chairman of the Medicine Men and Pastors' Meeting, and I tried to arrange everything so that the religious spokesmen from both sides would culturally feel at home. The meeting place was in the basement of a parish house that was between the central mission complex and the Lakota community. This was a place of both religious and secular meetings for the community. Table and chairs were put in a circle so that in Indian fashion each person faced the entire group.

All meetings were bilingual so that each speaker could speak about spiritual matters in his mother tongue. Moses Big Crow became the vice-chairman and expertly translated summaries of the speeches. The Lakota medicine men have an esoteric language, commonly called "medicine men's lingo." When an ordinary Lakota interpreter tried to translate the medicine men's speeches, he became very confused and produced nothing but gibberish. Since Moses was the grandson of two medicine men and was a long practitioner of the Lakota religion, he was well familiar with the metaphorical language of the medicine men. Likewise, Christian theology also has a technical vocabulary.

Moses and I spent many hours searching their meanings and finding adequate translations for various "jaw breakers" in Lakota and "big words" in English. Some participants raised questions about the accuracy of his translations. All meetings were recorded, and line-by-line translations, even complete transcriptions of the meetings for a time, proved the accuracy of these summaries.

Starting with the first meeting, the same general format was followed through all six years of the meetings. Several days before the meeting, written invitations were mailed reminding the members of the date of the next meeting and recalling what topic was on the agenda for the next meeting. A few questions encouraged thought and prayer on this matter before the meeting.

The meetings were scheduled to start at 7:30 p.m. "Indian Time." This was an important time when general news was shared and friendships were renewed. Around 8 p.m., the chairman rose and expressed his greetings. After an opening prayer by one of the participants, the floor was opened for announcements, prayer requests, and general comments. Often these general comments helped communicate matters that the members found to be worthwhile topics for the agenda since the last meeting. After these had been accumulated, the members of the meeting turned to prayer.

The importance of these prayer services was stressed repeatedly by the Lakota participants, for the members of the meeting were, first of all, **wocekiye wicasa,** men of prayer and intercessors to God for the welfare of the people. Usually the prayer period took about half an hour. Occasionally it ran two and a half hours when special ceremonies took place, like "Giving Smoke and Water" to the relatives of a deceased person.

The discussion period followed the prayer period. Sometimes the chairman introduced the topic by recalling the context in which the subject was raised. Sometimes he read a summary in Lakota of the ideas that had been expressed in previous meetings on an unfinished topic. As fitting the Lakota way of thinking, every topic was presented concretely, rather than abstractly, in the context in which it had meaning in Lakota life.

The Lakota medicine men and the White pastors had different styles of speech. The older Lakota waited to be officially recognized by name, stood to address everyone, and spoke formally in the traditional Lakota oratorical style. Their speeches lasted from fifteen to forty-five minutes. The pastors responded to a gesture from the chairman, remained seated, gave short and precise statements or questions, and desired a rapid exchange of ideas concerning the particular meanings of words, phrases, and sentences. They always "attacked" the matter at hand directly. The Lakota would respectfully go around the subject and only occasionally touch the specific matter at hand. Bringing in many personal experiences, they presented many illustrations rather than direct arguments. Each person in turn put **himself** on the table. One man's experiences triggered another series of reminiscences in the next speaker. Through all of these speeches, an attentive listener could perceive a fabric of a particular texture and consistency being woven. Often I found that at the end of a discussion I did not have any quick, crisp, formula-like answers, but I did find myself with a profound holistic understanding of the situation.

The missionaries were handicapped by their education, for they felt they had to have a clear theological understanding of all the things of the Lakota religion before they could legitimately participate in them. The medicine men were regularly upset by the many pointed, theological questions the priests raised; their religious tradition discouraged making specific pointed, statements about what was **wakan,** that is especially sacred and powerful in the Lakota religion. They regularly invited the priests to go to ceremonies where the **spirits** would answer their many questions. If each side had held rigidly to their cultural approach to the Sacred, communication would have been impossible. However, the participants willingly bent the rules to generously share the blessings God had given each, and both sides turned out the richer.

I resist calling the Medicine Men and Pastors' Meeting a dialogue. The word "dialogue" is usually applied to the confrontation of two well-established sets of doctrines, where the participants try to reconcile the different formulations by examination of the inner meanings of words so that a common statement can be agreed upon. Then perhaps some sharing of religious activities may be possible in the future.

The Medicine men and Pastors' Meeting was special because most of the medicine men were at least semi-active Catholics, some were even leaders in the Church, and some of the other priests and I had experienced the spiritual compatibility of the two religions through our participation in Lakota ceremonies. So what the meeting was trying to do was to describe a spiritual synthesis that already existed within religious men.

Occasionally some of the Lakota participants became anxious whenever they thought the group was moving toward combining the rituals of the two religions in a new or different way. At that point the vice-chairman always reminded the group, "We are not here to put anyone down or to change anyone's way of doing things. We are here to **understand** one another." Every consideration of adaptation through the meeting was suspended by the chairman, who had seen too many examples of shallow adaptation in the years he had been working among the Lakota. Without a solid theological foundation spanning both religions adequately, he considered every thought of assimilation, acculturation, and/or inculturation premature and probably deformed. So the meeting was not trying to produce anything that was really new, but rather to find the words to describe what God had already spiritually harmonized within the religiously integrated lives of a good number of the Lakota-Christian participants. Certainly there were theological and pastoral questions, but it was assumed that they would be resolved in the course of the much wider discussions. The meeting's radical spiritual respect for the existing faith-life of the participants was, in my opinion, the root strength of those discussions.

Many difficulties had to be faced in the discussions. On the Indian side the primary ones were anger against the Church for their suppression of traditional religion for so many years. On the Christian side the primary difficulties concerned the continued negative reports from Indians concerning the long-censured **Yuwipi** meetings. A climate of mutual respect and spiritual interest and concern helped the participants express their concerns in a respectfully open way, and patient perseverence paid off with mutual understanding in the end.

When the Medicine Men and Pastors' Meeting first started, the Fathers only asked a few questions, but otherwise they said very little. After about three years, one of the Indian men suddenly bolted in his chair and said, "Hey! For three years we Indians have been doing all the talking and you Fathers have been sitting there just listening. I want to know what **you** think on this question." From that point the Fathers became a bit more active, but they always remained in a lesser role. When chided to speak, one of the priests recalled what his father had said to him when he was young, "It's better to keep your mouth shut and have people think you are stupid than to open your mouth and prove that you are." When they did speak, the priests spoke more quickly and succinctly than the medicine men. Their continued presence at the meetings was noteworthy. Sitting silently for four hours listening attentively to long speeches in a foreign language can be very exhausting and difficult. But the pastors regularly said that they were at peace with what was being said at the meeting concerning the Christian side by the chairman.

After each meeting the chairman and vice-chairman, I and Moses, met and went over the speeches line by line from the tapes. Regularly the vice-chairman would stop the tape to explain the context and deeper meanings of significant Lakota remarks, and the chairman would also stop to inquire on any matters that were unclear in his mind. Together we gradually collected and organized significant ideas presented at the meetings. Often there were gaps and questions left in the data, so we would visit and talk with the various speechmakers at greater length and depth in their homes. In this way, holes were filled, incongruities were resolved, and greater reflective depth was achieved in the private conversations than was possible in the larger meetings.

After a few years, I found that the discussions in the meetings were beginning to repeat themselves. So I thought it important to summarize the material already covered in the meeting so that the discussion could move forward more easily. The summary papers were presented to the members at the next meeting for their acceptance, rejection, changes, and/or additions. After some initial difficulties, the summary papers were prepared in this way. After all the materials from the meeting's speeches and the home visits had been heard, I summarized them as best I could in English. I then brought these to Moses who had also heard all the material; he would make his own corrections and additions from the Lakota side. Then we began a slow process of translating these materials in a circular fashion. I would read the revised English text, and Moses would dictate a Lakota translation, which I would transcribe. Then I would retranslate the written Lakota into a new English text. By comparing the initial English version with the secondary English text, I was able to spot many hidden peculiarities of the Lakota and English religious words and thought patterns. Words difficult to translate were pinpointed, and their peculiarities were noted in an expanded redraft. By re-working the circular translation process several times, Moses and I were able to arrive at a summary paper in both Lakota and English that could be translated quite literally from one language to the other without much loss or distortion of meaning either way. The summary paper was then mimeographed in both Lakota and English and distributed to all the members. At the meeting, while English-speakers read their part silently, I read the Lakota version out loud for the Lakota-speakers. In this way each group received the summary in the style each culture was accustomed to. Then I opened the floor for any corrections or additions, which were incorporated in the next draft and presented at the next meeting again.

After four years, I collected all position papers into one mimeographed volume in English, and Moses gave an oral translation of the same material on a set of cassettes, both of which were given to the members of the meeting for their suggestions and corrections, but they only expressed their appreciation. The medicine men realized that most Lakota youth are today learning more from textbooks in school than from oral tradition in their homes. Consequently, the medicine men asked me, as chairman of the meeting and writer of the position papers, to put all these materials in a book for the young people. I protested because the position papers were prepared from a general, pastoral rather than a precise, professional point of view, and to a large extent the papers expressed very much my own personal search for understanding and a self-compatible expression of my Lakota-Christian spirituality. In wisdom they responded that they did not want an impersonal book written by a scholar but by one who is spiritually searching. . .as the young people are searching.

Discussions at the meeting usually started slowly, but the momentum picked up as different men reinforced one another and added their own experiences. Too quickly 11:30 p.m. came around. Some full-blood elders regularly reminded the group that in the old days people discussed important things like this through the entire night and into the next day, if need be, to settle the matter at hand. But a number of the participants had regular jobs and many had to drive a good distance before retiring, so calling the meeting to a halt after four hours was one concession I had to make to modern society if I was to keep all the participants returning.

Of course, every meeting had to end the Lakota way — with a feast. The quality of the chairman's soup was quite famous. It was not a big feast, but it was a happy one. Brief prayers preceded and followed the feast. With many happy and weary handshakes, everyone headed home for a well deserved rest until the next time.

The size and scope of the meetings were such that only so much could be accomplished through that format. After six years it was clear to many participants that nothing new was being presented at the meetings. The meeting had talked itself out on the Lakota-Christian topic. Some suggestions were made to establish a new focus and format. Some medicine men suggested that the meeting should become larger with more community participation — to discuss social and moral problems. Some priests suggested smaller specialist-type meetings to discuss theological concepts in greater detail. The chairman's concerns were turning toward this book. In 1979 the Rosebud Medicine Men and Pastors' Meeting fretfully became a happy memory.

Chapter 1

Making-A-Relative Ceremony and Baptism

Although the making-a-relative ceremony only takes place occasionally and baptism only takes place once in a person's life, both are rites of initiation into a new Lakota or Christian life. Through a comparative discussion of these two ceremonies, the members of the Rosebud Medicine Men and Pastors' Meeting were able to share and point out many basic religious and social values held by their respective traditions which help newcomers grow in their Lakota and/or Christian identities.

The **hunkayapi** or making-a-relative ceremony is the Sioux religious adoption ceremony in which someone is formally made a member of an extended Lakota family. Baptism is a Christian ceremony in which a person becomes an "adopted child" of the Triune God. In the Lakota ceremony, the individual is initially seen as an outsider, an enemy of the people, or one in material need. In the Christian ceremony, the individual is first seen as a sinner, separated from God, and in need of His mercy. Each ceremony places the individual in a state of unity and harmony with a group: the first, with the Lakota people; the second, within the universal Christian community. So in some ways the **hunkayapi** and baptismal ceremonies are alike, but in some ways they are different.

It is said that **"hunkayapi"** is a Ree word, which is equivalent to the Lakota word **"takuyapi,"** (they are relatives). This points to the national origin of the ceremony. The medicine men had sketchy recollection of the ceremony's origin and thought the account given by Black Elk was the best; this is recorded in **The Sacred Pipe** by Joseph Epes Brown.

There are many ways to perform a **hunkayapi** or a baptism. In the **hunkayapi** ceremony, there are four necessary things: 1) The appropriate words by a good man, indicating the meaning of the ceremony to the **hunka** and the people. (The **hunka** is the person being adopted.) 2) The tying of an eagle plume on the head of the

hunka. 3) The singing of a proper ceremonial song for the **hunka.** 4) A give-away and feast by the sponsor sealing and celebrating the new relationship of the **hunka** within the community.

In the baptismal ceremony, there are only three necessary things: 1) The person performing the ritual must have the correct intention, namely that of Christ and his Church. 2) The water must flow at least over the head of the person being baptized. 3) The pourer says the scriptural baptismal formula, "I baptize you in the name of the Father and of the Son and of the Holy Spirit," while the person is ceremonially washed. In addition, the Church encourages today that baptism take place during Mass. The Eucharist testifies to the worthiness of the Christian to participate **now** in that heavenly wedding feast which is to take place on the Last Day between the Son of God and his bride, the Church. In folk cultures there is often a great banquet given in honor of the newly baptized child of God.

These are the elements needed to perform each ceremony in the briefest way. Unfortunately many people on the reservation do not understand or appreciate the religious and traditional aspects of these ceremonies, and they skim over even these. However, Lakota and Christian traditions have even more elaborate rituals which have deep meaning. We will examine these.

1. The Preparation. Before both of these ceremonies, the persons involved learn what to do and what is expected of them after the ceremony. This learning does not take place all at once, but rather over a length of time, especially in the context of life within the home and community. Slowly the people start changing their attitudes and gathering things so that the new relationship may come to flower at the ceremony.

For the **hunkayapi** ceremony, the **hunka**s are taught who their relatives will be and how to name them; for example, **misun,** my younger brother; **atewaye,** my father or one of his brothers. They will no longer be outsiders, foreigners, or enemies to them. They learn how to talk respectfully to them and be generous to them. They are to grow in knowledge of family heritage, and commitment to it. They learn what they can expect from their future relatives and how they can depend upon them. For a year, the family collects things for the special give-away, which puts a material, communal seal on the ceremony.

For the baptismal ceremony, the individuals (if they are not too young), their parents, and their sponsors or godparents are instructed in the Christian faith, particularly about the special relationship the newly baptized will have with the Father, the Son and the Holy Spirit. They are taught to obey our heavenly Father's will, follow the teaching and example of Christ, be sensitive to the guidance of the Holy Spirit, and keep the traditional ceremonies and rules of the Church. They are taught to have a loving attitude and dedication to God and all people, even their enemies, for every person is one of our heavenly Father's children. For adult baptisms, time and effort may be expended on religious activities such as retreats, prayer services, and fastings to gather divine grace in spiritual preparation for that baptismal day.

2. The Minister. In both the **hunkayapi** and baptismal ceremonies, one person is chosen to officiate. In the **hunkayapi** ceremony, it is usually a medicine man, but for a good reason, a respected Lakota man may be chosen who embodies the best sentiments of the Lakota community. In the baptismal ceremony, the minister is usually the pastor, but he may delegate some other ordained clergyman or appoint a local catechist, thus linking the baptismal ceremony to Christ through the recognized leadership of the Church.

The responsibilities of the leader of the **hunkayapi** do not end with ceremony. Honored by the family and respected by the **hunka,** this good person talks regularly to the **hunka,** advising and helping within the extended Lakota family. When trouble arises, this man is the visible expression of the religious-social link between the **hunka** and the relatives.

After baptism there is a natural desire to maintain an affectionate attachment to the minister and the place of one's baptism. However, the real, lasting, and spiritual relationship formed in baptism is with the one high priest, Jesus Christ. He is the Christian's prime teacher, helper and guide. "I am the Way, the Truth and the Life. No one comes to the Father but through me." (Jn. 14.6) The personal relationship with the **hunkayapi** leader is primarily material; it is initially very close, but it gradually fades as one grows older, and it will last only as long as he lives. The spiritual relationship that the individual has with Christ is to increase and become more intimate as the years pass. While different persons may be appointed to continue Christ's role as pastor to the baptized in the world, the **hunkayapi** leader is not replaceable.

3. Special Relationships. The **hunka** has a special relationship with the sponsor and the sponsor's family. The sponsor is the one who arranges all the material details of the celebration. The **hunka** will thereafter find a special home in the house of the sponsor as long as the sponsor is alive. When the sponsor dies, however, such obligations cease, and the ex-**hunka** is sometimes put into a pitiful situation again and may be made **hunka** by another family. If the **hunka** dies, however, there is recognized an enduring spiritual relationship with the deceased foster relatives.

In baptism, the sponsor or the godparents are to be a special link of the child to the Church. These people are to look after the spiritual and moral welfare of the one to be baptized. If there is any death or emergency, the sponsor or the godparents are to be near at hand giving moral and religious assistance. They represent Christ, who perpetually dedicates himself to the newly baptized. Some do not understand this. For example, a young man told me how he was baptized seven times. He always became friendly with any new minister that came in the area, and out of friendship, he always did what pleased them, namely, he requested to be baptized in their church. However, just as there is only one Christ, there is only one baptism, regardless of one's particular Christian denomination, and that covenantal commitment is eternal.

4. The Community. Even though the medicine men and pastors take a dominant role in the instruction and blessing of the **hunka** and the newly baptized after the ceremony, others share in the responsibility of taking care of them. **Hunkayapi** ceremonies usually take place at community dancing grounds or at community halls. The **hunkayapi** not only affects the life of the **hunka** and the new extended family but also every member of the Lakota community. The formal pledge of continued support by the sponsor reflects the tradition of generosity and respect for one's relatives that is deep within the heart and history of the Lakota community. Baptisms are normally performed in the local church. The new liturgy recommends that baptisms take place during the Easter Vigil or during Sunday Mass so as to communicate to the Christian community on earth that the new relationship of the baptized individual is not only with one's immediate sponsors but also with the entire Church of Christ.

5. Prayers of Protection. In the **hunkayapi** ceremony, the **hunka** is seen as being materially poor and pitiful. In baptism, the individual is seen as spiritually poor and a sinner. Their poor conditions are seen, in general, to be a consequence not so much of their own willful deeds but of their heritage. Regardless, through the **hunkayapi** ceremony, all past crimes, hurts, and deficiencies are to be forgotten. Similarly, through baptism, all sin, original as well as personal, is forgiven. In both ceremonies, prayers are said that all that is evil in their lives may be wiped away and that good may come. In baptism, the healing and protection that takes place are signified through an anointing with holy oil over the heart. In the Indian way, the medicine man brings spiritual healing and refreshment by fanning the **hunka** from head to toes with an eagle fan. Each religious tradition identifies

and defends against negative elements, but with different understandings and in different ways.

6. Attitude Toward Enemies. In the **hunkayapi** and baptismal
ceremonies, the positive attitudes toward the **hunka** and the
baptized transform negative attitudes held toward enemies and
sinners. In the Lakota language, the Lakota expression, "He is an
enemy," [**Toka he ca**], has the same root and is notionally related
to the sentence, "He is different," [**He tokeca**]. Through the
hunkayapi ceremony, an enemy or an outsider is taken into a
Lakota relationship, and is expected to take the extended family's
ways as one's own. Otherwise the **hunka** is disrespectful to the
relatives. Acting differently, the **hunka** deserved to be
increasingly treated as an enemy again. If the newly adopted
family members do not conform, they are sometimes driven out
until that time when they show that they have that proper respect
for relatives which brings peace to the extended family. Because
these persons of a different "blood" have publicly and religiously
been received as relatives in the spirit of pity and generosity, then
they will find a home, peace, security, and their material needs
filled as long as their sponsors live. . .even though by blood they
do not deserve this.

In the Christian tradition, there are two kinds of enemies:
physical and spiritual. The Christian is told not to worry about
those who would destroy the body but him who would destroy the
soul — and the body with it. One is to be generous toward one's
physical enemies through patience, cooperation, and prayers. In
this way, one's enemies may abandon their oppressive conduct
and replace it with similar loving and generous behavior, which of
itself draws one closer to God, who is Love. But there are spiritual
enemies, Satan and his followers, who will tempt the person away
from God's way. If the baptized persons go against the will of God
as given in scripture or against the laws of the Church, they sin
and variously separate themselves from them. But God and his
Church seek the conversion of the sinner and provide the
sacrament of reconciliation as a means of returning the repentant
sinner to the divine life of salvation, of which by one's own human
nature one is not worthy, but only through the mercy of our
heavenly Father.

7. Words of Power. These words of the **hunkayapi** leader and
the baptizer are essential to the ceremony. Recalling the religious
traditions which they have received over the centuries, each
explains the particular meanings of the different parts and aspects
of these ceremonies. Then a special Lakota ceremonial song is
sung, calling down the Lakota spirits to bless the **hunka**s, protect
them from harm, and strengthen the entire family. In saying the

words which Christ gave his disciples on ascension day, "I baptize you in the name of the Father and of the Son and of the Holy Spirit," the baptizer proclaims a forgiveness of sins and the establishment of a new blessed relationship in the Triune God and His family.

8. Signs of Power. There are signs of power which are also essential in each ceremony. In the **hunkayapi** ceremony, the sponsor ties an eagle plume in the hair of the **hunka.** The eagle represents God above who will lift the **hunka** to great height to **wakan** things through this ceremony. The best eagle plume is the single downy plume from the center beneath the tail feather. This plume is hard to get, and it tells how choice, high, and holy the **hunka** is. Just as the eagle plume is also flanked by four other plumes, they say, so too the **hunka** is surrounded by the sacred Four Winds. These are surrounded by other fluffs, which stand for the Lakota people. As life is light and happy for them, so it will be for the **hunka.** But the **hunka** in some ways must be stronger and wiser than the ordinary blood relatives.

In baptism immersion in or the pouring of water over the one to be baptized has great symbolism. It reminds the person of the story of creation, where it is said that in the beginning the Spirit of God moved over the waters, from which, at the Word of God, the earth came forth and all living things emerged. Water points also to the sustainment of life, for without water, living things evaporate and die. Water also reminds a person of the story of the Great Flood in which God destroyed evil and rescued the righteous family of Noah in the ark. By means of water, impurities are washed away for a definite purpose and for a future use. It is through water that God washes away the corruptive and inhibiting burden of sin and establishes a pure, new and closer covenantal relationship with His faithful. Thirdly, the water of baptism reminds a person of the water of the Red Sea through which God's people passed from slavery to freedom, and the waters of the Jordan where they passed from a life of struggle due to sin to the Promised Land of milk and honey. In addition, water is the gathering place of scattered people. It is by water that God called people through John the baptizer and others to receive God's Spirit and law within their hearts. Finally the waters of baptism remind a person of the blood and water which flowed from the side of Christ after he died for our sins on the cross. This water points to a new life that has been hidden in God and revealed only in the death and resurrection of Christ.

9. Signs of New Life. At some **hunkayapi** ceremonies, the face of the **hunka** is painted — sometimes with four marks and sometimes with three sets of four marks down the nose and each

cheek. The painting signifies that a change in personality is happening in a sacred manner. Blue is often used to signify life; it is often the color of the clowns [**Heyoka**]. These contraries are two-sided. What is meant and real is different from what is seen and heard. They are associated with the West, the first direction; they mark the beginning. From the West come the storms, which mark the spring time and the coming of new life.

In the baptismal ceremony, a white garment is placed on the newly baptized. The white color is the sign of Easter joy. It celebrates the risen life of Christ and the newly baptized person's participation in it. White is the color of the clouds; it is a sign of God's glory. It expresses, in a visible way, the new life of God's grace in the person's soul. White is a sign of purity, the state of a soul freshly cleansed by the sacrificial blood of the Lamb of God, Jesus Christ, who died that our sins might be taken away.

10. Signs of Responsibility. Corn was especially sacred to the Ree and played an important part in the first **hunkayapi** ceremony. Today, the Lakota sometimes still use it. At times they will parch ground corn and mix it with grease and sugar into a corn **wasna** or pemmican. Sometimes ears of corn are put upright on sticks and stuck into the ground. Sometimes corn seeds are planted as a sign, for it will produce much food that can be given to the relatives. The corn indicates the primary duty the **hunka** and the sponsors have to see that no relative goes hungry or starves. The leader sometimes takes considerable time to speak about corn. Corn holds on to Grandmother Earth very tightly with roots the shape of toes. Its stalk is pointed straight upward. Its leaves open again and again to Grandfather above until it reaches its full height and flowers, blowing its life-filled pollen sweetly to every direction on the Four Winds. Around the ears of corn are many husks. The outer husks, which are exposed to the harsh outer world, are stiffer, stronger, and protective of what is held tightly inside. The inner husks represent one's tender enfolding of one's relatives. These inner husks are used to wrap and serve the best foods in a sacred manner to one's relatives. Finally on the ear of corn are different colored kernels: blue-black, dark red, yellow, white, and speckled — the sacred colors. These are sacred things that the corn gives the Lakota people. It makes them into a great people when they eat it. "This corn is very **wakan**."

At the baptismal ceremony, the candle has a special place. Throughout the ceremony, the Easter candle is lit. The Church has long maintained the tradition that the church candles be made of beeswax. It recalls the story of Samson (Jdg. 14.5-18). One day a young lion attacked Samson, and he killed it with his hands. When he returned a few days later, bees had made a hive in the carcass and gave sweet honey, whence the saying, "Out of the eater came forth food, and out of the strong came forth sweetness." Like a young lion of Judah, Christ attacked the Pharisees, and they killed him, but from his death came new life most sweet. So the cross on the Easter candle is filled with sweet-smelling incense. The wick is like the sacrificing life of Christ; the collected particles of wax in the candle are like His Mystical Body, the Church. By attaching oneself to Christ, the Christian offers himself to a sacrificial life that gives light, life, blessing, and happiness to the world. Still there is really but one flame, one sacrifice — Christ's. Just as the individual's baptismal candle is made in the image of the Easter candle, so too the Christian is made in the image of Christ. Christ's love can burn painfully if one is careless with it, but it is really quite gentle, sending its light and truth into all directions. The baptismal candle should not be stored away in some dresser drawer but set out and burned meaningfully in one's house. . .just as the life of love of the newly baptized is to gently shine forth to all in the house so that people "may see the goodness in your acts and give praise to your heavenly Father." (Mt. 5.16)

11. Signs of Victory. In both ceremonies, a sign of victory is presented. In the **hunkayapi** ceremony, a horse and war bonnet are sometimes given away. These signs recall the great traditions of the warriors and chiefs of the past. These are still alive in the memories and hearts of the people. Their spirit calls forth the pursuit of Lakota honor and dignity. These were great men who sought the best life possible for their people. Their wisdom, bravery, generosity and fortitude, the four great Lakota virtues, now belong to the **hunka**. As lofty and far-seeing as the eagle, as strong and as bold as the horse, the **hunka**s are to find within themselves the calling of the chiefs and warriors of the past. They now have a personal identity and calling with the heroes of Lakota history.

In baptism the individual is anointed with sacred chrism on the crown of the head. This is the sacred oil used to anoint bishops and priests to their sacred offices. By this anointing, the newly baptized shares in the priestly, prophetic, and kingly offices of Christ. It is a sign that the person is now one of God's priestly people. The newly baptized is no mere outside observer at Mass. Through baptism, each Christian is united to Christ in the sacrifice of the Mass. They are united with all the martyrs in the Communion of Saints. Their prayers "through Christ our Lord" come to the Father, not as from people who are distant, but from those who are children of God and members of His Kingdom. The Christian is also anointed to fill a prophetic role: to proclaim to everyone in word and deed the will and plan of the Father. While this message is often received well, disappointment and persecution will inevitably come. In union with Christ, one should offer this suffering for the salvation of sinners in the world. When one does this, he/she merits to be lifted up as Jesus was, to share in Christ's kingship.

12. Prayers. At both ceremonies, prayers are said to God in the traditional way for everyone. When the Pipe is used, this brings into play all the spiritual powers of the material universe, especially the Four Winds and Grandmother Earth. They are asked to give the **hunka** the virtues needed to fulfill the duties as **hunka** within the Indian community. The Christian prayers are made through Christ whose greatest gift to his followers is the Holy Spirit. The Christian's body becomes the dwelling place of the Holy Spirit, who gives the theological virtues of faith, hope, and charity by which the Christian receives a special intimacy with God.

A more perfect and personal coming of the Holy Spirit is associated with the imposition of hands in the sacrament of confirmation. Although some receive this sacrament at their baptism, scripture and tradition have recognized the appropriateness of separating baptism and confirmation. In a similar way, while it is possible for a medicine man to give a spirit to a **hunka,** often through the wearing of a spirit bundle or talisman around the neck, the more common way of receiving a spirit is through a vision quest.

13. Spiritual Food. At both ceremonies there may be an exchange of spiritual food. At the **hunkayapi** ceremony, the **hunka** and the sponsor may serve each other sacred food: **wasna** and chokecherry juice. These foods give strength, health, and life in a sacred way to the participants. This sacred food is also given to any sick person attending the ceremony.

At some Catholic baptisms, adult newly-baptized persons receive not only Confirmation but also First Communion. Receiving the Body and Blood of Christ under the forms of bread and wine, the newly baptized are strengthened unto eternal life in Christ, are spiritually joined to the first Mass with Christ and His disciples, and are prophetically linked to the great eternal banquet on the Last Day. The exchange of the **wakan** and spiritual food is a symbol of many other exchanges to take place in the life of the **hunka** and the Christian within the Lakota and Christian communities, respectively. The **Yuwipi** ceremony and the Mass are two major ceremonies where the religious communities regularly gather, and the making-a-relative ceremony and baptism are often linked to these.

14. The Give-Away. The greatest expression of pride and joy of the day is found in the huge give-away and feast at the end of the **hunkayapi** ceremony. By this the sponsor honors the **hunka** and gains support and approval of the **hunka** within the community. In the early Church, when a person joined the Christian community, all personal property was turned over to the community leaders to be shared as needs arose. But that aspect of Christian community has been followed only by those in the church who make a vow of poverty within a "religious community." Today, rather, Christian sharing is normally spiritualized, and materialized only as real physical needs are encountered. While there is a realization that one is to show pity and mercy to strangers and outsiders, the Lakota and the Christian are to have a special generosity toward "their own," namely one's Lakota people and one's Christian community, respectively.

15. Name-Giving. A name is a mysterious and powerful thing. It establishes identification, control, and security within a difficult situation. People sense the strength derived from a name when they see a young man proclaim his dignity by beating his fist against his chest and saying, **"MaLakota!"** (I am Lakota!). Often I, as a priest, have heard people in the most pitiful condition on the reservation sit upright and say with pride and confidence, "I am a Catholic. I am a **strong** Catholic!" These names contain a great people, a strong heritage, lofty ideals, and lasting security. There is a great affinity between a name and what the name points towards. In a spiritual way, the name carries the power and influence of the one named. It is fitting that the giving of a name is usually associated with **hunkayapi** and baptismal adoption ceremonies.

THE GIVING OF A NAME

In the **hunkayapi,** the **hunka** receives, at least by affiliation, the name of the sponsor. But sometimes an Indian name is given to a person at a Name Giving Ceremony apart from the **hunkayapi.**

When a stranger meets full-bloods and asks their names, they will answer immediately with their surname, their family name. But if one asks specifically for their first name, they will suspiciously eye the inquirer and answer only guardedly. This points to the pride and strength they feel within the extended family and how cautious and humble they feel when alone. Sometimes a Lakota receives a personal **wakan** name that is to be told to no one.

The baptismal name is usually a person's **first** name. Today in White society the social trend is toward using a person's first name predominately. Even if one's first name, say John, is more common than one's last name, say Bleeker, the first name has the connotation of uniqueness, intimacy, openness, and individua love. The last name speaks of class, business, formality, legality, and corporateness. The giving of a first name in baptism emphasizes the special love God has for each individual, whom He calls individually by name. While the strengthening of the individual in baptism primarily takes place through the internalized action of Christ's Spirit, the strengthening of the individual in the **hunkayapi** ceremony is external to the **hunka** through the material and physical actions of the new relatives.

Names are chosen in the Lakota and Christian cultures in nearly the same way. Nicknames are popular in every culture. They usually refer to some small incident that happened, or to some personality trait notable at a particular time of a person's life. Their use is generally limited to a small group with whom it is often an "inside joke," with or against that person.

At other times a name may be chosen simply because it is different, popular, or sounds just right. More often a name is chosen for more significant reasons. For example, the name may have been carried previously by some noteworthy deceased member of one's family or clan. Perhaps the name was carried by some hero, saint, or famous person. Carrying the name thus vicariously carries the life, virtue and dreams of the ancestor who bore it. The name may also point to a special virtue or quality one wishes to convey to the individual; for example, Rose. Perhaps it indicates some special, spiritual event that happened or that one dreamed. The spiritual name often establishes a spiritual bond with some spiritual reality, like an eagle, that is called upon to be an amiable, influential, spiritual "companion."

The Lakota people find it appropriate to publicly and formally give an Indian name to relatives, other Indians, and non-Indians from time to time, thus expressing and establishing a close relationship between that individual and the Lakota people. Name-giving ceremonies may take many forms. They usually follow the format of a brief **hunkayapi** ceremony. When the people gather, some announcer informs the people that a member of the Lakota community wishes to give someone an Indian name. The importance and meaning of giving this particular Indian name is explained. The people are told how it establishes a special identity and association with the Lakota people, culture, and heritage. The person to be named and the sponsor are called to the center. The announcer or a prayer man prays for the individual, often with his hand on or over the individual's head. There is usually a special Indian medallion necklace placed over the bowed head, to rest on the neck and over the heart of the person newly named. Whatever is given has a special meaning. Then a honoring song is sung, and the one named and the sponsor lead the honoring dance. Everyone joins in behind them or stands as they pass. This is followed by a feast and a give-away in honor of the one named. Finally all the people shake hands with the one named, the sponsor, the family who put on the feast and give-away, expressing union with their decision and their action.

There are many interesting stories of how Indians received different names. One Lakota man had several Indian names. This is what he said. "My parents had great respect for a certain White man who used to work with my uncles in the big round-up. I was only three or four days old when they came back one time. My parents said they wanted to honor him by giving his name to me. He accepted the privilege and named me. Then he took the reins of his horse and put them in my hand. Later, when I was five years old, my grandfather gave me the name of my great-great-grandfather in a Pipe Ceremony, so I am honored to carry that name. He was a great and holy man. Later I was also adopted by a family from Pine Ridge. They had lost their son, and I must have borne some resemblance at a distance since they thought I was him. They came and hugged me, crying, 'It's you, my son. You've come back. Let's go home.' So they took me and gave me the name of that son. That is the way I'm known in that district. Then a traditional man prayed for me with the Pipe, so I have another name from him." One young man complained that he had so many names, he thought people would forget who he was. The medicine man told him not to worry. As long as he knew his last name (his family name) he knew who he was.

In Scripture a person often received a new name whenever that individual received a new spiritual vocation from God. Today Catholics usually take on a new name whenever they make a major step in spiritual advancement at baptism, confirmation, entrance into religious life, or when taking on a higher ecclesiastical position, like Pope.

To a large extent the Name-Giving Ceremony has replaced the **hunkayapi** ceremony. The two are different in that the first establishes a bond of respect and a variously appreciated **kola** relationship toward the individual before the Lakota (Le kola/the friends) people. The second bonds the person more closely to a particular extended family.

As a person looks closely at the **hunkayapi** and baptismal ceremonies, one can see how similar they are in general structure and particular aspects. However, it must also be noted that in regard to each aspect, the ceremonies are spiritually and socially very different.

Chapter 2
Lakota and Christian Religious Identity

The personal, ancestral, national, and religious identity of individuals and groups is very important to everyone, especially to religious leaders like the participants of the Rosebud Medicine Men and Pastors' Meeting. Each of us regularly makes identity statements without realizing it, or without realizing the full implication of what is said. Identification with or apart from the Lakota and Christian religions means many things to many people.

The following questions are quite controversial and have been discussed by many. Certainly the following discussion will not be the last word, but hopefully these various, accumulated thoughts will advance understanding. Because of the strong presence and influence of the medicine men in the meetings, these questions will be answered according to the Lakota four-fold way — as the Lakota medicine men repeatedly said, "All things are in fours." As the readers progress through the book, they will increasingly understand the consistency, truth, and theological foundation for this four-fold cosmology. In many ways this Lakota world view applies the Aristotlean, essentialistic categories of material causality, efficient causality, formal causality, and final causality into existential time-space extended reality. But rather than try to epistomologically establish the truth of this method of analysis, let us simply enter into the method through a few illustrations. The first question concerns one's attitude toward pluralistic, four-fold answers.

1) If an answer is four-fold, where does one find the **right** answer? It would appear that the fourth level is the most advanced. Therefore, is not the fourth level the right answer, the most perfect answer?

First of all, the questions above are dualistic and "second level." Such questions cannot adequately appreciate truths found in a "quantized," organic scheme. The four-fold truth of something can best be realized through analogy in parables.

To what in the White people's world would I liken the Kingdom of God? I would liken it to a four-part chorus. Each individual part of the musical chord is sung with its own intensity and local variations. Everything is fine as long as each voice remains attuned to its own proper key. Everything is fine as long as one voice does not override the others in a way unfitting to the whole musical score. Does it make any difference which section one is in? Yes and no. One should sing in the range of talent God has given. Usually a person finds oneself naturally in one range, which he then develops as best he can. With practice, one's range might grow into a second or even a third range. Care must be exercised, for working in another range may result in weakening both. In building a chord, one starts from the base notes in which all of the higher resonances, even the melody are found. Still before any chord is sounded, it is the melody in the mind of the orchestrator which defines the whole piece and every chord in it. Found usually in the higher register, the melody penetrates the soul deeply, while the base notes make the body tremble. The higher notes make the spirit surge beyond the musical scale into ecstasy; the lower ones make one feel strong and firm. To say there is but one answer to the key questions of life is to say it is wrong for someone to sing harmony or to play second fiddle.

From Lakota culture, a different picture can be painted. In the evening when the Lakota gather to celebrate and thank God and the spirits for their blessings or ask them for their help, they sing. First comes the beat of the drum, then the lead singer, then the other men. Finally the women join in, and their shrill trill pierces the night. With each part right and strong, all are happy. That is the way it is. **Hecetu welo.**

2) Can a White person be made **hunka** in a **hunkayapi** ceremony? Can a White person become an Indian relative? There are some Indians who feel that it is wrong for a White person to participate in any Indian ceremony. This leads to further questions: Who can be called an "Indian"? Who is really "Lakota"? There are four levels on which a person can be called "Indian" or "Lakota."

a) First, one's Indian-ness is determined by one's family ancestry. The Indians prefer, however, to refer to this type of association as being "by blood." The Full-Bloods call themselves **"Lakotahci"** (real Indians). The "Mixed-Bloods" have ancestry that is divided about equally between Indians and Whites. Mixed-Bloods are considered Indians because the United States government has **defined** that any person with at least one-quarter Indian blood is an "Indian" legally. On the reservation, there is

-34-

some animosity between Full-Bloods and Mixed-Bloods. The Full-Bloods consider the Mixed-Bloods to be too pushy and fast-talking, **Iyeska,** like the Whites. The Mixed-Bloods consider the Full-Bloods to be non-aggressive and old-fashioned. Still people value very much the degree of Indian blood they have, even if it is only a small part. Very often visitors will speak proudly that their great-great-grandmother was an Indian. That one has **some** Indian blood is important; that one has **much** Indian blood is better. Even if Indians leave the reservation and disappear completely into White society, it is said that their roots are in their Indian ancestry, history, and culture as long as they have one drop of Indian blood in their veins. Through this material ancestry, they always have a right to claim association with the Indian community.

From this perspective, it would seem that a White person could never be called an Indian "by blood." Physically this is true; however, it is possible ritualistically. When an outsider has been through thick and thin with an Indian, the bonds of friendship become so close that a simple, meaningful ceremony seems natural. This ceremony is done not only with Whites but also with Indians of other tribes and reservations. First, the Indian cuts his own wrist; then he cuts the wrist of the other. Putting their wrists together, their bloods intermingle, and they become "blood-brothers." People with strong ethnic background appreciate the tremendous meaning and significance of this act. This Indian blood-brother may go wherever his Indian brother goes. To exclude one is to exclude the other. They are "buddies to the death." And the blood brother's participation in the Indian world continues as long as his Indian brother lives.

b) Another way that a person comes to be respected as an Indian is through an Indian name. The Indian who gives the name establishes a lasting Indian-style relationship with the one named. There are different grades of association here depending upon the quality of the ceremony at which the name is given. Different values are placed on an Indian name, depending on whether one is carrying an Indian family name, whether one receives it because of one's Indian interactivity, whether one receives it because of one's political association with the Indian people, or whether one obtains it through a sacred **hunkayapi** ceremony.

c) The term "sociological Indian" is related to the way a person acts, much like the terms "sociological Full-Blood", "sociological Mixed-Blood", and "sociological White." Such terms are applied according to the way a person thinks of, talks to, and deals with the people on the reservation. Some White people are highly respected because they are able to think and act like a typical

Full-Blood. When Indians act like Whites, they are sometimes called an "Apple"; that is, "red" on the outside but "white" on the inside. While stereotyping is wrong, some individuals simply act very Full-Blood and are readily accepted into the inner circle of Indian life.

On the other side, a situation occurs often enough to be spoken about here. Indians open their houses to many needy individuals. Sometimes an outsider starts helping around the house and is allowed to stay indefinitely. He/she becomes like one of the family. Soon the non-family member starts addressing the members of the family with the traditional titles of respect: "grandfather," "grandmother," "mom," and "dad." One young man stayed with a medicine man for several years. The young man kept calling the medicine man "dad." The old man wanted to call him "son," but he could not. The medicine man said, "He may have a wife or children somewhere; I don't know. What if his parents became needy? If I start to call him "son," I would be obliged to not only help him but also his entire family. And I am not able to do that these days."

d) The fourth way a person grows in Indian identity is through religious ceremonies. Be that person Indian or White, the more a person takes part in Indian ceremonies, the more that one is considered and treated as an Indian. Still, occasionally, one hears, "The Pipe is only for Full-Bloods," or "Only Full-Bloods can become medicine men," or "Only Indians should be allowed on the Sundance ground, to be in the sacred area, to hold the Pipe, or to be pierced," or "Whites should not be allowed in the sweatbath." Still, on the other side, a well-recognized Full-Blood voiced the opinion of a good number when he said, "Look at our children. See how they are intermarrying. Soon there will be no Full-Bloods. It is the sincerity of heart that is important. If a person does it right, it will happen. If they don't do it right, nothing will happen. For the longest time I held that in the future there would be a blond-haired, blue-eyed person sitting in the center of a ceremony because there is one drop of Indian blood in him. Now I know I was wrong. More and more White people are fasting, fasting the real way, the hard way. They are having visions and receiving spirits. I know. I have talked with them. It is true. Oh, some people complain, 'They are stealing the Pipe, just as they stole our land.' Oahh! They are going after it, while we are giving it up. If we lose it, it is our own fault. It's a matter of how sincere you are."

It is my opinion that many Indians think that it is Indians who make Indian religion. But Indian religion did not really originate from the Lakota people but from God and the spirits. Some say that Indian spirits speak only in the Sioux language. Does that mean they are less smart than most Full-Bloods who today speak well in two languages? No, visions are being received in both languages from the spirits, and it is they who tell what they want to whomever they want — usually sincere seekers of the Red Path. Whether a person should attend an Indian Sundance or an Indian ceremony depends upon the spirit of the medicine man leading it. Some Indian spirits, especially Indian ghosts from the past, do not want Whites attending, and that should be respected. Some Indian spirits, who have traditionally associated themselves with the Indian people, however, are allowing Whites to come to their ceremonies. From numerous, apparently authentic accounts, some Indian spirits do come to Whites as guardian spirits. To the best of my knowledge, through the help of a well-known medicine man, there is one White person who has received Lakota spirits for ceremonies, and he quietly ministers to those in physical and spiritual need who come to him. Whether any more Lakota spirits come to more Whites and teach them how to make an altar or lead Lakota ceremonies is totally up to God and the Lakota spirits. No Lakota man can tell a Lakota spirit what he can or cannot do. Every religious person respects the spirits and should be open to the coming of the spirits to anyone they wish to. In general, the Lakota spirits have shown preference toward Full-Bloods, but they also show preference to those who are respectful, sincere, and humble in the Lakota way. Any person whom an Indian spirit would make his **kola** (friend) should be shown the respect and recognition proper to that spiritual relationship. This is my opinion.

3) Who is a Christian? This is another emotional question. The term "Christian" is properly a post-Pentecostal, historical term, first applied in Antioch to the followers of Jesus of Nazareth many years after he had manifested himself as Christ and ascended into heaven (Act 11.26). Usually the term "Christian" is applied to baptized members of the historic Church of Christ.

But a person can ask, "Are not all people who are saved, saved by Christ? And are not all who obtain salvation, then, somehow of Christ, of his Church, and therefore Christian?" If a person wishes to expand the term "Christian" to apply to anyone who is saved, then one must specify four different ways of being a Christian.

a) There are "Natural Christians." Here one must speak of several categories, related to four major aspects of humanity.

First, there is the body or the physical aspect. According to Christian faith, all things were created through the divine Logos, the Word of God. In God's plan, the divine Logos became the man, Jesus of Nazareth. Because of the Father's expressed will and action of the Holy Spirit, Jesus was anointed to be Christ, through whom the salvation of a sinful world would be wrought. By his incarnation and resurrection to glory, Christ's ascending glory effects the eternal destiny of the entire world and each person in it, whether an individual is conscious of that fact or not. Seeking what is good and avoiding what is evil, these individuals are unconsciously bringing the divine Logos' plan for the world toward fulfillment. Even though they may be somewhat confused, their actions show that they are sympathetic to God's Spirit. Insofar as Christ's Spirit and God's Spirit are one, then these individuals are unknowingly sympathetic to Christ's Spirit and therefore are spiritually Christian. For want of a term these might be called "Good-seeking Natural Christians."

Secondly, there is the mind. Through the gift of reason, humans become aware of the presence of universally pervasive, ordering principles in the universe. Those universal ordering principles are greater than any of the particular members and are therefore trans-individual and spiritual. Generalized statements, philosophic principles, and scientific formulae describe the order seen. Following wisdom and science, they are unconsciously following the ways of Christ, "The Way, the Truth, and the Life." Pursuing a full life in association with the trans-individual, universal principle(s) of the ordered cosmos, they are seeking to live according to and know the divine Logos, the Christ, despite their lack of sure and total knowledge. They are pursuing union with Christ in a questioning way. For want of a term, one might call these "Intellectually Natural Christians."

Thirdly, there is the heart. Humans are by nature social. The heart of a person is concerned about overcoming the evils of the world. There is also a dream about a perfect life, a happy society, and lasting love, harmony, and peace. Love of one's own and care for the poor are universally one in spirit and goal. Because of Christ's association with mankind and his concern for the poor, people who care for them are regarded by Christ as caring for His own and Himself. Regardless whether the doer is conscious of that association or not, that spiritual association with Christ's and with Christ is real and recognized by Christ. Such as these might be called "Loving Natural Christians."

Fourth, there is the spirit, which consciously unites humans with a distant God. From the beginning of remembered and recorded history, there have been occasional personal communications between God and mankind. Because the natures of God and man are so different, God must communicate himself in various disguised or intermediary ways in order to be intelligible to people. Recipients of these communications usually become the religious leaders of the people. As in Christianity and all other religions, we are tempted to manipulate, elaborate, and distort these revelations. Nonetheless, more often than not, the leaders of religions constantly seek to retain religious traditions in their most primitive forms. Dominated by a spirit of obedience, they make sacrifices to give glory to the true God and bring His blessings upon the people. Thus Christ's sacrifice does not stand alone. By taking upon himself the title of Son of Man, he united himself with all who are sacrificing themselves for the sake of righteousness and divine blessing. Their sacrifices of love in response to God's expressed will to believers are spiritually one with the sacrifice of Christ, who associated his sacrifice with the purest of sacrifices of his historic predecessors. Of course, religious sacrifices are molded according to the way in which God's revelation has been received and are imperfect insofar as mankind in history is imperfect. . .which is always the case. Nonetheless, Christ's sacrifice did not render such actions valueless, for he came to bring all things of God to perfection and fulfillment. It can be said that the ancient Lakota belonged to this group. If one is looking for a term here, one might call this group the "Religiously Natural Christians."

b) Can the Jewish people in any sense be called Christian? Jesus was a descendant of David and fulfilled many sayings of the prophets. Christians consider themselves spiritual children of Abraham and heirs of the promise made to him. But what about the reverse? It must be remembered that within the mind of God the fulfillment of his promises are eschatologically realized when the promises and prophecies are made; in their original statement, they already somewhat participate in the fullness of their truth. Certainly the promises to the patriarchs and the prophets had their historical understanding and conscious meaning. Certain of these promises later came to have new messianic meanings among the people. In faith it must be realized that the providence of God monitored the process and guided it. No Christian can say that Christ was a liar when he said that he came "to fulfill the Law and the Prophets." Whatever the exact meaning of that expression, it points to a proclamation of the Messiah and his Kingdom from the beginning of the Hebraic covenant. To say that God's word in the Old Testament is not Christian is to say that it was not designed to lead the Jewish people toward the Messiah and the eschatological fulfillment of God's Kingdom. Even today the Jewish religion is explicitly directed toward the coming of the Messiah in glory and the establishment of Israel in perfect peace (shalom). The Jewish failure is their inability to recognize that in Jesus of Nazareth is the historic coming of the Suffering Servant and the son of David they seek. They have great difficulty spiritualizing their world view to see that the Kingdom of God is not ultimately a kingdom of this material earth but a transformed Kingdom of heaven on earth in Christ Jesus. Nonetheless, by his blood and birth, Jesus has a special, personal association with all the Jewish people, who to this day are bearers of the promise. One might call them "Invited Christians."

c) The term "Christian" is usually applied to "Public Christians," who not only hear the Gospel of Christ and believe him but who also publicly proclaim that Gospel in their rituals, their teachings and their lives. There is both a clear, public anointing by Word and Spirit and a public response through baptism within the Christian community.

"What was hidden is now revealed." Some might say that the previous levels should not be called "Christian." Rather, speaking legally, I would say that the previous groups should not be **publicly** called "Christian". . .although one can speak non-publicly so. This is similar to an official in a reservation office who cannot publicly state that a person is an "Indian" until the documentation of the person's blood-line has been formally presented to the officer. Before the presentation of external evidence, people can talk about a person's Indian-ness, but not officially.

There are definite rights, responsibilities, and privileges associated with being a "Public Christian," but that does not deprive the others of the rights, responsibilities, privileges, and benefits they need for a full, happy, and holy life according to the historic, social, and religious situation God has located them in.

d) On the fourth level, which is the transcendentalizing level, there is currently no one who is a "Perfect Christian," not even Christ himself. Even though he is now sitting in glory at the right hand of the Father, he still has not accomplished the final tasks assigned by his Father; namely, to judge the world on the Last Day. He has been anointed for this task as King of the Universe by his heavenly Father, who will tell his Son when the Final Time has come. Thus there are no perfect Christians in the transcendental sense of that term. Christ still prays, "Thy Kingdom come."

4) Why are there so many Christian denominations? They all say that the other groups are wrong and no good. Rather than confusing the Indians, why don't they go back to where they came from and fight it out over there and leave us alone and at peace?

Many Indians are confused by the term "Christian" because of the plurality of Christian denominations. Much of the talk about denominational fighting and antagonism, however, comes from a time that is fortunately now past. Nonetheless, denominational differences do exist. How is a person to understand these Christian differences? There are actually different levels of being a "Public Christian." Similarly, there are comparative levels within the Indian religion.

On the first level, there are Lakota who say that they only believe in the Pipe. As one man said, "Whatever others do is their own affair. As far as I am concerned, they are going overboard and not doing it right. They are making it up. I learned all there is, as far as I am concerned. I take my Pipe and go into the back room and pray with it and smoke it. I pray to God above, the Four Directions, and Grandmother Earth below. That's the way it is. To me everything else the others do is phony." So spoke one middle-aged Full-Blood. In a comparable way, there are Christians who are called Fundamentalists. They only believe in Christ and what is literally stated in the Bible. They pray and sing with their Bibles in hand. If a preacher says something they don't feel is part of the Christian tradition as interpreted by them or their forefathers, they will go off on their own and do it privately or in a small group the way that they believe is right. Everything else to them is the creation of humans and is wrong and phony.

On the second level of the Lakota religion, there are different people whose involvement in religion centers around their own personal **vision**. They pray with the Pipe in the sweatbath and on a vision quest, but they shy away from larger ceremonies. They tend to be very exclusive and loyally follow the teachings and traditions of one particular medicine man. Among the Christian religions, there are a large number of Protestant Churches. Each has its own individual interpretation of Scripture. Each has a few more rituals and sacraments than the Fundamentalists. They reject the ceremonialism, authoritarianism, and traditions of the Catholic Church as being excessive. These denominations are usually founded by one person or a few persons who broke away from another denomination because of some particular beliefs or disciplines, and the followers continue to refer back to the teachings of this founder for its particular direction and identity as a Christian denomination. This is similar to a Lakota medicine man who for a time is very close to an older medicine man, but when the younger man receives his vision to be a medicine man, he usually breaks away, often making negative remarks deriding his predecessor, and gathers a small group of followers around and after himself. So in many ways, the different ways of each Christian denomination is similar to the different ways of each

Lakota medicine man. And just as there are wranglings between Christian denominations at times, so too there are wranglings between Lakota medicine men at times. While people tend to think that it is always best to be peaceful and accommodating, both Christian and Lakota religious history point out that competition and confrontation can have a positive renewal quality, if the disagreements are not allowed to become violent and destructive.

The third level of involvement in the Lakota religions is found among those who are involved in all of the traditional rites of the Sacred Pipe. They are especially involved in the Sundance, the most elaborate and publicly religious ceremony of the Lakota people. They recognize the integration of religion and politics to which the Sundance directs them. They are concerned about the public image of the people and all the Indian traditions. They celebrate especially their Lakota heroes, history, and ancestry. Similarly, that Christian Church which seeks most to be public, historic, traditional, and saint-celebrating is the Catholic Church. It includes all of the seven sacraments and insists upon strong traditions and clear apostolic succession. The public character of the Catholic Church emphasizes universal unity under the descendent of Peter, whom Christ appointed as the rock on which he would build his Church and to whom he gave the "keys" to the Kingdom.

The fourth level of involvement in the Lakota religion goes beyond the traditional seven rites of the Pipe. The **Yuwipi** ceremony is a recently introduced, spirit-filled ceremony among the Lakota people. In various ways, some outsiders are wary of the ceremony, for it is possible that the spirits contacted could bring evil. Those inside the ceremony recognize that the ceremony is really directed to the good of the people. Good will happen if certain precautions are taken to insure that things are done right, especially as it is in association with the traditions and presence of the Pipe. One of the great things about this ceremony is the fact that it brings a person to a very close encounter with the Indian spirit world, which is spiritually very encouraging and supportive of the Lakota people during this time of spiritual and religious confusion.

In a similar way, the charismatic movement is of recent origin in the Church. It invites the Christian to a close encounter with the Holy Spirit. This close-encounter results in a strong, active faith-life in this unbelieving age. Many Christians shy away from the charismatic movement out of disbelief in the experiences reported or out of a fear of being possibly involved with evil spirits. While traditionalists frown on the pursuit of spiritual experiences, the charismatic person, like those who attend **Yuwipi** services, know how much one's personal experience of the Lakota spirits and/or the Holy Spirit helps to bring fullness of life to oneself and vivid blessings to believers.

There are many levels of being a Lakota and practicing the Lakota religion. There are similar ways of dividing up the way a person is identified as a Christian. By comparing and contrasting these elements, a person can better appreciate the uniqueness, values, and religious pursuits and behaviors of different people and different groups.

Chapter 3

Sweatbath and Penance Ceremonies

Purification ceremonies are very old. They have many aspects: correction, healing, strengthening, surrender, sacrifice, petition, faith, union, and many more. So it is understandable that dedicated Lakota and Christians regularly take part in these ceremonies. The members of the Medicine Men and Pastors' Meeting are regularly called to lead and take part in these ceremonies. In this chapter are summarized some of the comparative elements realized through the dialogue.

By comparing oral tradition concerning the coming of the Pipe with archaeological evidence, it is clear that the Indian sweatbath pre-dates the coming of the Buffalo Calf Woman and the coming of Christ by many centuries. The Old Testament specifies that the priests were to determine how much sacrifice a person was to make in atonement for his offenses. Therefore, a confession of sins took place in Israel centuries before the coming of Christ. So the Pipe and Christ did not begin these rituals. Rather, the association of the Pipe and Christ with these sacred actions brought them greater meaning and spiritual effect through the **wakan** power of the Buffalo Calf Pipe and the saving grace of Christ, respectively.

The Lakota word for "sweatbath" is **inipi.** The word is related to the root word **ni** (to live) and the causative form **niya** (to breathe). The two most common reasons for taking a sweatbath are for **wicozanni** (health) and for **wiconi** (life). Thus, a literal translation of **inipi** is "for their life." While sweating and being purified are integral parts of the ritual, the primary focus is upon the "life" of the people. In the sweatlodge the prayers are usually directed toward the healing of sickness, protection of the young and old, and material help and strength for some personal or family goal. In English the Indians often refer to this ceremony as a "sweat."

Different words are used to describe the Christian ritual.

Sometimes it is called the "rite of reconciliation," and the place where it occurs is called a "reconciliation room"; these words point to the fact that this ceremony reunites the repentant sinner with God and the Church. The term "penance ceremony" or simply "penance" refers to the reparation the penitent makes for sins. "Confession," which takes place in a "confessional," refers to the penitent's admission of sins to the priest. Often these terms are used interchangeably. Today the name "rite of reconciliation" is preferred because it expresses the highest spiritual value found in the sacrament, namely, a familial re-union of the sinner with God the Father and His People in Christ.

Some purifications through steam take place apart from the sweatbath. Rocks can be heated, put into a bucket, and brought to people who have not been able to take part in a regular sweatbath. Pouring a little water on the rocks with a dipper, the participants ritualistically wipe their hands in the rising steam and wipe their head, arms, body, and legs with waves of their hands. Sometimes smoldering sweetgrass or sage are brought around, and those attending similarly wipe their hands in the smoke or wave it toward themselves and over their bodies. Confessions can also take place in a very informal way whenever a person meets a priest and confesses his/her sins. These ways, however, are not the ideal and should be considered the exception rather than the rule.

Lakota purification normally takes place in an outdoor sweatlodge. Different Lakota see four things in these simple, small, hemispheric, willow lodges. First, the simple willow lodge is similar to the ones made by warriors long ago. They were places of rest, strength, and protection. To some the sweatlodge is like a womb. Here the participants regain, in a spiritual way, a new life and strength. Third, the sweatlodge is shaped like the ribbed back of a mud turtle. Through the ceremony the participants become like those who live both underwater and above ground. Turtles are slow, patient, and strong-hearted. Even after they are dismembered, the turtle's heart beats strongly. Fourth, the sweatlodge surrounds the participants with the universe in miniature: the rocks, the earth, the grasses, the trees, the clouds, and the sky. All of these are close to the participants and are supportive in a **wakan** manner.

All but one medicine man on the Rosebud Reservation have a shallow pit in the center of the sweatlodge for the hot rocks. One medicine man, according to his vision, puts the rocks on flat ground. The Dakota of the east sometimes have very deep pits. The dirt from the hole is used to make a mound of dirt between the sweatlodge and the firepit. The mound reminds the participants of the hill of the vision quest where one is close to God and the spirits above. The pit inside reminds the participants of the depths of the mysteries they are about to take part in.

The sweatlodge is usually built away from other, ordinary buildings. It is not **ikceya** (ordinary and profane) but **wakan** (extraordinary and sacred). It is often nestled part way down some valley, amidst the trees, in a beautiful spot on Grandmother Earth, under the great, open sky above. The sweatbath is close to the earth and humble. The Pipe is placed against the small ''hill of vision'' or a small pipe rank made of twigs or a skull of a buffalo, who gave his life for the people so that they will not starve. The Pipe's chin touches the ground. In the sweatbath the participants humbly sit close to the Earth. All sit in a circle facing the center and each other. Even while the person to the right of the door leads the ceremony, the leader nonetheless is a full participant in the sweatbath.

Christian churches are normally built in the center of towns, among the people. They are built like many other human structures and are crafted in many human ways. Roman churches look like large meeting halls, where the people gather to hear the leaders of the Christian community proclaim publicly the character and worship of the community. Churches are tall, high structures which publicly proclaim the Christian faith professed there. Gothic churches are like upright swords, piercing the heavens and bringing a burst of heavenly color upon the people far below. In various ways the sacred things of heaven are recognized as being not without but within the structure — not ''out there'' but **within** the assembly and within the person. The confessional is built near the entrance, near the baptismal font or the holy water fonts. The confessional is built of hewn stone or sawed wood. The manufactured crucifix is a repeated theme above the church, on the altar, and in the confessions. The confessional is built in a special way so that it is possible for a person to choose whether one wants to confess face-to-face or unseen behind a screen. The priest is seated so that after hearing the confession he, in his authority, is able to extend his hand over the repentant sinner's head in forgiveness and blessing. The leader cannot use the ceremony to forgive his own sins, for he sits as the sinless Christ to forgive the sins and bring back to the fold those who had gone astray.

In the sweatlodge, sage is used to wipe off bodily sweat. In the process, sage leaves a sweet odor over the body. The sweat is, and is a sign of, what is not right for the participants. This could be a physical weakness ranging from body fatigue to physical or mental disease. The participant may wish to remove ritual impurity, as after a menstrual flow, or establish a **wakan** worthiness, as before a Sundance. Or the participants may be giving sacrifice that they and their people may have a better life. Sage is a medicine. Breathing through it brings refreshment and strength in a hot sweatbath. Chewed or taken in a broth, sage has a number of good medicinal qualities. The sage in the sweatbath is a spiritual contact with all the sacred medicines growing on Grandmother Earth. It is repugnant to evil spirits.

The holy water fonts, found at the entrances of Catholic churches, contain Easter water and unite the Christian to the death and resurrection of Christ. It reminds people of their baptisms, their renunciation of sin, and their faith in the new, divine life received in Christ.

Two important things to compare are the rocks and the priest. It is from these that the powers of the ceremonies immediately derive their action. The rocks come from Earth; the priest from among men. Through the fire, the Great Spirit, as the Lord of the material universe, gives the rocks power to purify the Lakota in this ceremony of the Pipe. Through Christ and the local bishop, the priest receives the power and the right to forgive Christians their sins. In the Lakota religion the Earth is founded on rock. Rock is the enduring foundation of the material universe. The rocks have always been here and give all relationships substance and eternal meaning. They give stability to things. Sweatbath rocks, **tunkan,** have great power, **tun.** They are related to the grandfathers, **tunkašilapi.** In the Christian religion the term ''rock'' is first applied to God and his Christ, upon whom the Church is founded and is secure. Christ changed Simon's name to Peter, which means ''rock.'' Peter is the leading member among the Apostles and is the ancestor from whom all the popes receive their authority. The rocks in the sweatbath establish the spiritual foundation for the Lakota's purification. Many Lakota have a great appreciation for Moses, who went up on Mount Sinai, fasted forty days and nights, had a vision of God, and brought the people the word of God carved on tablets of rock.

The Lakota variously find much meaning in the fire. When care is taken to make the sweatbath fire by laying the stones on criss-crossed layers of wood surrounded by a teepee of wood, the fire becomes a symbol of **Wakan Tanka,** whose power comes and dwells in the teepee of the universe, whose efficient strength comes from the Four Directions — for the first stones are usually put in the four directions first — and whose power gives the rocks of Earth a share of His energy and life.

''In the old days there were just certain men that could tend the fire.'' Stepping aside for others, they were humble, patient, silent, and prayerful men. Many firekeepers today are sloppy and wasteful, and their rocks are not "strong." A good firekeeper brings spiritual power to the rocks, the sweatbath, the men, and the people. Even though he does not go into the sweatlodge, this person shares in the purifications and blessings. Four times the doorkeeper is bathed in the purifying steam at the opening of the flap for his relatives. Doorkeepers drink of the life-giving water. They share in the spirit-filled Pipe. They know the right rocks, the right wood, the right way to build a fire, and know how to interpret the signs found in the fire and the firepit. When they rake through the ashes, they may find different colors, which point to special needs and prayers. Sometimes they will color the stones a certain way. Black is used as a sign of a soul that is recently departed. Red is for a personal, special need. Yellow is for family protection. White is for thanksgiving.

A few medicine men mark the crest of their firepits with four horns, usually scratched in the earth or laid out in rocks. These are symbolic of the four generations prayed for in the sweatbath: the grandchildren, the children, the parents, and the grandparents. It also refers to the spirit named "Four Horns," who is active in sweatbath ministry. It also refers to the four races of men: black, red, yellow, and white, and the Four Winds. After the fire is out, a face is sometimes marked in the firepit with seven rocks: two eyes, two ears, two nose holes, and one mouth. These are symbolic of the sweatbath spirits who perceive much but say little.

The rocks have different meanings. It is commonly said, "They have no eyes or ears; yet they see and hear everything." The rocks were here first and will be here last, so they hold knowledge of all things. Small round rocks, often with special markings, are considered to be **wakan** by many Indians, who will wear these talismans in a little leather pouch with a few herbs from a leather thong around the neck. In the sweatlodge, all historic wrongs are brought out and wiped away, and a person is made strong by what is eternal and sacred. It is said that if people look at the faces of a rock, they may see and read history. Heated, the rocks are the presence of **Wakan Tanka** within the sweatlodge. When water is poured on them, the spirits come and are "Fast Talkers" called **Wašicu.**

As the Lakota know that fire and the sun are effective symbols of the **wakan** action of **Wakan Tanka,** the Christian finds "light" to be a symbol of Christ and the Christian. The light of Christ and of the Christian is described as a thing to be put on a lampstand or on a hill for the guidance and life of all who are near. The Lakota recognize that spirits can come and show their presence by small lights, especially at night. Christian's actions are their "lights" marking the presence of God, the love of Christ and the guidance of the Spirit in the world. Both the Lakota and the Christian recognize light to be a sign of joy, confidence, security, openness, lack of fear, and knowledge.

In the Christian tradition, darkness is associated with sin, evil spirits, Satan, and the Kingdom of Darkness. Christ as the light of the world not only fills the darkness but also attacks every evil thing which is associated with darkness. Rather than wage war with evil spirits, the Lakota respectfully pray that these evil ones will be kept away by one's spiritual grandfather(s). In the Lakota tradition, physical darkness is associated with all spirits, both good and evil, for they come in hidden and mysterious ways. The darkness in the Christian tradition is not a physical darkness but a spiritual and eschatological darkness. In both traditions physical darkness is as day to spiritual beings. There is also a special association between beneficial spirits and lights.

When a person enters a Catholic church, at least one candle is found burning by the tabernacle to indicate the Eucharistic presence of Christ. At communal services, more candles are lit, indicating the presence of Christ within the congregation gathered in Christ's name and within the sacrament itself. These days in the confessional also there is usually a light. Dark confessionals are things of recent origin and are contrary to the tradition of the Church in reference to Christ as the Light of the World.

Those people who have special prayers to be offered in the sweatbath may make strings of tobacco ties, which some Lakota call, "Indian rosaries." Usually six tobacco ties are offered for an ordinary sweatbath. The tobacco ties, ribbon offerings, tobacco offerings, or flag offerings are stuck between the willows and covering toward the middle of the ceiling of the sweatlodge. Different colors may be offered in association with the medicine man's vision or the individual's need as indicated above. Different spirits are attracted to their favorite colors although for rock spirits all colors are of equal value.

In communal penance services, the leaders choose a penitential theme that will be meaningful to the people there, or is relevant to a particular situation in the world. Various people offer suggestions regarding petitions and concerns. These are drawn together with the readings, songs, and responses. In particular, various individual needs are usually incorporated into a long litany of sorrows, petitions, and concerns. For all of these things the participants will pray during the course of the communal penance service.

Not only those with special needs and contributions but

everyone should spiritually prepare themselves before entering into the sweatlodge or confessional. While the leader is filling the pipe, everyone becomes silent, listening, affirming, and praying. One's thoughts turn to the special needs that have already been expressed. One's mind turns from ordinary things to sacred things. The Lakota's eyes and senses widen to sacred things, becoming more sensitive and believing. Christians pray to the Holy Spirit so that they may be contrite and sorrowful for their sins. They ask for an awareness of the evil of sin and the meaning and consequences of the wrong things they have done. The participants reflect on the questions: Why am I here? Why do I need purification and strengthening?

This is not a doing-time but an opening-time as the Lakota waits for the fire to burn down and the Pipe to be filled. Similarly, the Christian usually must wait for the people to gather and all the people involved in the liturgy to move into place. This is a time of silence, thinking, listening, and faith. There is a realization that things have not been as good as they could or should have been. This is the time for building a confident desire to start anew — to recover one's innocence and goodness before God and all things holy.

As the time for the ceremony approaches and the people gather, the leader enters into the immediate preparation. The sweatbath leader fills the Pipe, which is placed in a central, sacred place. The priest places a confessional stole over his neck as a sign of the special priestly office he has received through Christ. As the participants see the Pipe in front of the lodge and the stole on the priest, they are assured of the traditional authenticity and power of these ceremonies, each in its own way.

The Pipe has rules, so has Christ given many. One should reflect on the oral traditions of the Lakota religions and the written traditions of the Christian religion to determine how one needs to be purified in the respective ceremonies. While the Lakota reflects upon the teaching of holy men and grandfathers, Christians examine their consciences through the use of the Ten Commandments, the Precepts of the Church, the Works of Mercy, the Beatitudes, etc. The Lakota examine their respect for God and things holy, for their families and relatives, and for all of their people and leaders. Christians investigate the quality of their worship of God, their involvement in the Church, their dealings with their neighbor, the presence of faith, hope, and charity in their hearts, as well as the presence of anger and unforgiveness. Positively, the Lakota recognizes that this ceremony prepares a person to help all of the people through powers received through the sweatbath. Christians also have a forward gaze as they seek spiritual growth in virtue — especially sacrificial love. The Lakota carry not only their own problems but also the problems of their relatives into the sweatlodge. While the Christian Church is gradually moving toward an awareness of "social sin," the emphasis is still upon the sins of one's deepest heart. The Lakota sweatbath usually takes place with several and only occasionally with one; for Christian confessions, the reverse is usually true. But in communal penance ceremonies, the emphasis is moving away from the forgiveness of **my** sins toward the forgiveness of **our** sins, for we in corporate groups make decisions and carry out actions which hurt others. In the sweatbath the corporate sense of **mitakuye oyas' in** (all my relatives) also focuses upon **my** shortcomings and need for change. The Christian concentrates upon the presence of guilt and its effect within the heart of the individual. The Lakota have a great sense of shame when facing the other members of their close **tiyośpaye** after doing a publicly known wrong. Christians fear eternal damnation on themselves by Christ when he acts as judge on the Last Day for any mortal sins they have committed. The Lakota fear physical retribution by the **Wakinyan** and other Lakota spirits upon one's relatives for any serious violation of the rules of the Pipe. Through these and similar thoughts, the participants become recollected and increasingly intent as the spiritual ceremony begins.

In both ceremonies, the participants perform an act of humility as they approach the place of purification. The Lakota do this physically. The men strip off their clothing, thereby removing all artificial coverings that make them look good. Showing oneself to others as one really is, is an act which produces involuntary shame. This act reminds the person that, before God a man's material possessions are as nothing. A person should not depend upon such things for one's dignity or strength. In the sweatbath, nothing is hidden from the spirits. A person, however, may wish to cover one's private parts with sage, a loin cloth, or a towel as a sign of modesty. When a sweatbath is made with women, the men wear some type of shorts. When women take sweatbaths, they sometimes wear bathing suits, but it is preferred in some sweatlodges that they wear long dresses or cover themselves completely with large towels as a sign of respectful modesty.

Entering the sweatlodge, the participants humble themselves by bending low and crawling into the sweatlodge on their hands and knees, like little children. The participants are led by the leader, who goes around the pit in a sunwise order. Sitting crosslegged, a person keeps one's eyes respectfully downcast, thinking good thoughts, pushing out any bad, angry, or hateful thoughts. Everyone thinks and prays about why they are there and what this purification ceremony will do for them and their relatives.

The Christians' acts of humility are more vocal and interior. Before the actual confession, Christians usually kneel and say an act of contrition. They pray to the Holy Spirit to help them have contrition and sorrow for their sins. They promise to change their lives, but they recognize how weak they are and how change only comes with great difficulty. They humbly recognize their absolute and immediate need of Christ's help. They want to avoid these mistakes in the future. They know they need Christ's help to regain their baptism innocence and start anew. They enter the confessional weak, sinful, and alone with humility and hope. Unworthy though they are, they seek God's personal forgiveness and divine life.

The Pipe Ceremony begins with a recall of the six Directions through the first six rocks. The confession rite begins with a recall of the Trinity and the cross. Each of these recalls the presence and action of the major spiritual powers in each religion. There are three major types of sweatbaths: for vision questing, for purification, and for health. Each has its own length, number of stones, and songs. There are three major types of penance ceremonies: for an individual penitent, for several penitents with individual confession and absolution, and for several penitents with general confession and absolution. Each has its own number of readings and types of priestly counsel. The various Lakota elements, like sage, sweetgrass, cedar, and water, are used to bring the spirits to the lodge and to the healing of the people. The various man-made elements in the confessional are designed to bring penitents out of themselves and to turn themselves to Christ and the priest from whom forgiveness will come.

The bucket of cool water is brought into the lodge and touched to the rocks, indicating union and fellowship. Water is a sign and a means of a full, happy life; hence, the word **wiconi** (life) is usually spoken as the water makes this entrance. Water appears to have no strength, but it can wear down the hardest rock and cut the deepest gorge through quiet persistence. Water makes people happy, especially when it is used to make soup. Water comes from heaven as rain. It is a sign of God's blessing and care for all growing things on earth. The participants raise their hands in affirmation and greeting. This water recalls that the rain clouds come especially from the West and that the **Wakinyan** (Thunderbird) associated with thunder clouds and lightning is the protector of the sweatbath. This water and its consequent steam mark his power and presence in the sweatbath. Uncomfortable at first, his ways have a deep, penetrating, and lasting effect.

With everything in place, the flap is closed. Except for the temporary glow of the red-hot rocks, darkness covers all. Darkness in the sweatbath and other ceremonies of the Pipe has different meaning to the Lakota. Darkness is a place of helplessness, blindness, confinement, and pitifulness. The darkness eliminates material distractions and helps a person focus on the spiritual aspects of reality. Better than closing one's eyes, the darkness is an environment of intense, sincere prayer. To enter into darkness is a physical statement expressing one's awareness of his ignorance, confusions, disorientation, and lack of vision. In the darkness, one also finds hope, for plant-life begins in the darkness of the earth. A child is conceived in the darkness of the mother's womb. The greatest ideas emerge from aloneness, dreaming, and an awareness of darkness in one's understanding of things. Lastly, and most important to the Lakota, when one is plunged into darkness, it is easier to be open and receive spiritual things. Prophetic dreams come at night. Experience shows that the largest number of spirit-appearances occur at night, especially just before dawn, when we are the weakest and most vulnerable. Experienced medicine men say that the spirits are here all the time. The appearance of the spirits is associated with one's spiritual disposition. An intelligent being is more likely to come to a person who is disposed to receive a communication from beyond. The Lakota know that it is to those who sit, pray, and wait in darkness, with faith and anticipation in their hearts, that blessings, life, and light come from spiritual sources.

Each ceremony has a greeting and an explanation of the service by the person leading it. Often this is very brief and done in a rather traditional way. The joy of the leader and confidence in the success of the activity re-enforce the participants' faith and help them settle into the ceremony peacefully. The opening prayer is directed toward God and summarizes the purpose of the ceremony. The leader prays that the forgiveness, purification, healing, help, sorrow, light, conversion, change, and mercy sought for in the ceremony will be truly realized.

Now a period of inspiration comes. The medicine man hails different spirits through his calls, prayers, and songs. He calls to the spirits in the Four Directions, to his own spirits, to spirits needed to accomplish the purpose of the ritual. As he prays, he pours some water on the rocks. Steam fills the sweatlodge, purifying everyone for the coming of the spirits. If anything is done or said wrongly, or if one shows a disrespectful attitude, the spirits may direct the pourer to put an especially heavy amount of water on the rocks in atonement for the violation of sacred things.

It is said that in the old days, when people were stronger and had greater knowledge of spiritual things, the heat was so hot that sometimes an individual fainted. Fainting was approved because a person might have a dream or vision. With crossed legs, the person would merely roll to the side and not burn himself. Still, such a person might be suffering from heat stroke, and one could have shouted **Mitakuye oyas'in** so that the door would be opened. Considerable experience and self-knowledge about visions should be achieved before pursuing the harder course. Older, wise men have frequently said that some beginners use too deep a pit and too many stones. The sweatbath is not meant to be a torture chamber but a place of religious purification and spiritual blessing. The purpose of the steam is to sweat out from the participants what is repugnant to the spirits and to fill the sweatbath with the smell of sage and to purify with steam in order that the spirits may "doctor" those who need it. Pain of itself is of no value, if it does not bring one closer to the spirits.

In a private confession, the priest or the penitent may quote a brief passage from Scripture in which God sends his Word of the consolation and the healing of sinners. Different writers are chosen according to one's needs and devotion. In a communal penance ceremony, the hearing of the Word of God and other spiritual words plays a dominant part in the service. Sacred instruction purges the soul of negative thoughts and feelings and fills the heart with positive, healing, and uplifting ones. Some priests want to give extensive instruction and counselling at this time. There can be too much and too little personal input from the leader. It must be remembered that as a sacrament, the primary teacher and sanctifier is Christ.

Appropriate songs are sung in the sweat and in the communal penance service. In the sweatbath these call the spirits and indicate to them the participants' beliefs and desires. Similarly, Christians recite responsorial psalms and sing songs which match the readings. Received not from visions but written by holy men and women, these assist the people to open themselves and to express their needs to God, Jesus, the Holy Spirit, and the Church. In a sweatbath before a vision quest, there is only one round of pourings. Similarly, in an individual confession, the readings are limited to one. For a regular sweatbath with several people, there are usually four sets of pourings and four openings. Similarly, in a communal penance service, there are usually three readings with associated responses, songs, and litanies. The three main readings in a communal penance ceremony are taken from the Old Testament, the writings of the New Testament, and the Gospels of the New Testament. These readings unite the participants with the major events of Salvation History and the Church's ancient traditions.

The Lakota songs fall into four general groups, which are related to the four openings of the sweatbath ceremony. First, there are the "calling songs," which cry out to the Great Spirit, the Four Winds, the medicine man's spirit friends, and other spirits related to the ceremony. In addition, there are "answering" songs and "doctoring" songs, which ask the spirit to help and answer the people in their material needs. Also, the leader or medicine man may receive a message or instruction, or a blessing from a spirit at that time. Thirdly, a "Pipe" song may be sung before the Pipe is smoked. Finally, a "thanksgiving" and/or a "spirit-sending" song may be sung as the ceremony comes to a close. While it is more traditional to sing several songs during the course of the sweatbath, they are not an essential part of the sweatbath ceremony and are sometimes omitted by beginners.

In the sweatbath after the pouring of water and the singing of the "calling" songs, the medicine man tells the participants which spirits are present. If there are new people or special needs, more explanation about the ceremony, the spirits, and their powers are given. In a penance service, the priest speaks about the readings. He indicates how they apply to the lives of the people taking part in the service. He recalls their association with the Father, the Son, the Holy Spirit, and all the saints of the Church. Even in an individual confession the priest might briefly comment on the passage of Scripture.

In the sweatbath ceremony, each person prays to God and the spirits, starting with the person to the left of the door. Each indicates one's needs, problems, and desires. Frequently a person will describe in a general way the material sickness and needs he/she or a family member may have. Each prays especially for the health and welfare of oneself and one's relatives. When that person is finished he/she says, **Mitakuye oyas'in,** and the person to the left similarly speaks to **Tunkasila** and all who are present. In the penance service, individuals, one at a time, move to the confessional to confess their sins and failings and spiritual needs to the priest. They explain what problems they have in leading a good spiritual life and the sorrow and contrition they feel toward their failings and sins, asking the priest's assistance in seeking God's forgiveness and help.

After the round of prayers, some pourings, and perhaps a song, the medicine man tells each one in a sunwise order what the spirits have said will happen — how their prayers will be answered. If there is no medicine man, the leader reminds the participants about the Way of the Pipe, and the purification and help that comes to the people through the sweatbath. In the penance service, the priest listens to the confession of sins and expression of contrition by the penitent. The confessor then expresses the advice which the Spirit within him indicated him to say. He gives a penance appropriate to the sins committed; he gives counsel to uplift the spiritual state of the penitent. And finally by the Spirit of Christ, he gives his absolution and blessing to the penitent, removing by God's grace all guilt which may have kept the person from a full Christian life. In addition, the priest prays for the special needs and concerns, invoking Christ's healing blessing upon them also.

Sometimes, at this point, the medicine man may give a person some medicine he brought in a container, which the spirits have blessed. Sometimes healings take place through spiritual touches, through blowing hot air on an infected spot, or by sucking on an unhealthy spot. The people wipe themselves with sage or may be wiped by a medicine man. A medicine may be rubbed or chewed. In appreciation for any sign of care or healing, a person says, **"Pilamaya, Tunkasila,"** (Thank you, Grandfather.). In private confessions where there are special, spiritual problems, the penitent may receive special spiritual guidance and counselling. A few words from one's confessor often can be very helpful to the one who is searching to grow in Christian virtue.

Some people think that **everything** can be handled in the sweatbath or confessional. That is not true. The sweatbath and confession are for ordinary purifications and forgiveness. Some unusual things can be taken care of there, but some illnesses and moral problems require extensive healing and counselling — like cancer and annulment cases. These ceremonies are a good beginning to more extensive, long-lasting healings and sanctification.

When the flap is closed the fourth time, the medicine man says, "This is the last." The water is poured, songs of thanksgiving are sung, and prayers of appreciation and perseverance are said. Several songs may be sung, honoring the spiritual things most actively involved in the ceremony: the Pipe, the cloth, the spirits, and the sponsor. Last of all, a "spirit-going" song is sung, dismissing the spirits who were there. Then, all the remaining water in the bucket is usually poured out. Often there is a period of silent reflection. Then the leader cries out, **Mitakuye oyas'in,** and the flap is open. All leave in a sunwise order, following the leader and saying that prayer also. Especially here, everyone loudly responds **"Hau!"** When the confession and absolution are completed, there is a short acclamation of praise to God, urging the fervent soul to continue to give thanks to God for his forgiveness and blessing, "for his mercy endures forever." Thus both ceremonies end with a sign and prayer for peace and unity between oneself, God, and all who are close to us in the invisible and visible world. The acclamation before the Pipe extends this peace to all one's relatives. The priest ends the confession with a prayer for Christ's peace.

After the sweatbath, everyone feels refreshed, not only externally but also internally. After confession, one's spiritual healing and joy come from within to extend even to one's feelings and activities. After group sweatbaths and communal penance services, there are often refreshments and fellowship. One is not alone. One's union with the spirits and with God are complemented by one's union with one's fellow participants. Refreshed and strong, one can now live a new life the Lakota Way or the Christian Way. By doing what the spirits or the priest has said, the participants are confident of a fuller and happier life. The participants know that their relationship with the Pipe and Christ is now wholesome and uplifted.

As seen from the discussion above, there are many similarities and many differences between these two ceremonies. By examining both sides, one should feel less fearful and more understanding of how each ceremony has its own particular power, effect, and purpose. On this level of analysis, the contrary qualities of these two ceremonies are not contradictory. The sweatbath heals within the worldview, beliefs, and concerns of the traditional Lakota; it is primarily directed toward physical needs, health, and life. This purification makes one spiritually in union with the Pipe and the Lakota relatives, and it makes one fit for participation in other Lakota ceremonies. On the other hand, the penance service is primarily directed toward salvation and growth in sanctifying grace. That is, it is directed toward healing any spiritual separation an individual may have with God, Christ or the Church because of some wandering from his heavenly Father's will, and it provides the graces or spiritual helps needed to live a God-like, Christian life in this world. Its purification makes one spiritually united to the Father and the Christian Church and fit to participate in other Catholic sacraments.

Chapter 4

Questions on the Sweatbath and Confession

Since the sweatbath and confession are two ceremonies which have a long history in both the Lakota and Catholic traditions, many different facets and many different attitudes have arisen around them. Young people frequently have many fears and misunderstandings concerning them. It is easy for some people to quickly equate these two ceremonies. The participants of the Rosebud Medicine Men and Pastors' Meeting spent considerable time trying to correct these misunderstandings by answering a number of questions concerning these ceremonies.

1) Are there different attitudes toward taking a sweatbath?

There is a common pattern in the different Lakota attitudes and approaches to the sweatbath. Beginners frequently come because of family associations, friendship, or curiosity, rather than deep faith. They don't know the hard way or the easy way. Rather they are most willing to follow along. After they have been through it a few times and have seen the same actions and heard similar words a few times, they lose interest and become involved in something else. Secondly, adolescents usually are searching for an Indian identity through their participation in a sweatbath. They want to become strong and important. It is important to them that others of their peer group be there; they watch, encourage, challenge, and follow each other closely. They want to become strong and important. After breaking through an initial shyness, they burst onto the scene suddenly, and they are zealous — for a short time. They fluctuate between extremes. At times they are very shy, insecure, and withdrawn; then suddenly they want sweatbaths every day, and they want them hotter and more exactly traditional than ever before. After pushing very hard for a time, something discourages them and they drop out with bad feelings for a while — until they become active again. Thirdly, more mature individuals are steadier. They see this ceremony in the context of all the other ceremonies. They understand the role these ceremonies have in reference to the life of one's family and relatives. Wanting to do things right so they will do good things in the long run, they move more slowly, sincerely, carefully, and consistently. They stay close to the traditional prayer man, rather than thinking that they know everything. They even begin to take responsibility and show gentle leadership within the ceremonies. But after a few years, when something important occurs in one's personal life (like a vision) or family (like a disagreement), one may turn away for a few years — to return later as a more secure supporter than ever. Finally there are prayerful old people. They avoid noisy group sweatbaths, preferring them alone. The welfare and the health of the people are definitely in their prayers, and they spend hours in the sweatbath close to God and the spirits. They are frequently tempted to despair for their people and for themselves, but they continue in patience and perseverance, developing a more personal relationship with the spirits.

2) Why is it wrong for menstruating women to be at or near Lakota ceremonies?

Traditionally a Lakota woman's menstrual period was considered a natural and publicly known event, much like pregnancy and delivery. People schooled in the attitudes of Western Christian sexuality suppress such matters and are embarassed when they are mentioned. The difference in attitude was very obvious at an Indian school workshop where a medicine man was addressing a mixed audience of teachers. The medicine man had been speaking about the Pipe and wanted to fill it, but it was pointed out that since there were young women present, some of them may currently be having their period. Catching himself, he lifted his head to the audience and asked matter-of-factly, "Are there any young women here having your period?" There was shocked silence in the room. "Raise your hands. Which of you young ladies are having your period now? I could tell you a few things?" Well, the girls wanted to crawl under the tables, while the boys loudly hooted! Tell me. Why is it that modern society covers up, perfumes, and tries to deny this fundamental aspect of womanhood? At one time the primary reason probably was the hiding of all sexual things. But today a major reason is female liberation; it is a common desire to want women to do everything that men do. Today there is a push to let women into sweatbaths with men. But that is the subject of the next question. Here we will examine the taboo which places the **menstruating** woman away from traditional Lakota ceremonies.

Taboos surrounding menstruating women are common throughout the folk world. Orthodox Jewish women still go to their community's baths during this period. It is a time of rest away from the demands of the husband and the family. The Lakota word for "menses" is **isnati** (She lives alone.). Traditionally during this time she lived away from others at the edge of the camp in a small, hemispheric lodge. A male relative stayed nearby to protect her from danger. Older women brought her food and things to sew, quill or make. If during this period she stepped over anything, that thing was to be burned.

When a woman is having her menstrual period, it is said by Lakota that she is having "woman's sickness." During this time of blood flow, people recognized that she was weakened physically and believed that those who came in contact with her would be weakened also, physically and spiritually. I found that it was Lakota **women** who were most strict about maintaining this separation. One woman recalled the words of a highly respected medicine man of the past named Chips. As she and some other women were taking their tobacco ties to the sweatlodge, he cried out, "Don't come near. You women are not allowed. You lead men to a downfall." Another reported him as saying at a public meeting, "These women are no good. They jinx me and take my power away." Today the medicine men remain concerned about women at their ceremonies, especially since some young women deliberately reject this separation. They say that a woman in her period drives the spirits away and can make Indian medicine and ceremonies ineffective. Some Lakota make a point to keep their Pipes upwind, away from the house, so that they will not be contaminated by women in their period. If they did contaminate the Pipe, the man would have to pay a price and get the Pipe blessed again. One medicine man talked about the old days when the **eyapaha** (announcer) would warn menstruating women to stay away from the Sundance grounds. When I asked the medicine man what would happen if she did come to the ceremonial area, he said that it would be bad for everyone, especially her. Her menstrual flow would probably increase, her sickness would be longer and more severe, and she probably would not be able to have any more children.

Because of the strength of this belief, I asked many people the reasons why the menstrual flow had such significance. Four basic responses were given: 1) The Lakota spirits have made it known in visions that menstruating women are to be set apart. In respect for the spirits and Lakota religious traditions, they should withdraw. 2) Medicine men and Lakota people have experienced the negative effects of menstruating women on those things that are sacred or **wakan.** Why is this? "We don't know. This is the way it is. It is **wakan,** and we should not think about it or talk about it." 3) Warm congealed blood gives off a rank odor that can only be masked over but not eliminated by perfume. Various evidence indicates that spirits are attracted to sweet odors and repelled by sour ones. 4) Indian medicine is for "health." A woman in her period is bleeding because of something torn and decomposing. In the menstrual flow there is not life but death. The natural activity within the menstrual flow in dispelling a dead ovum goes against the **wakan** activity of the Pipe promoting life.

The primary reason for maintaining this restriction is spiritual. The spirits are negatively affected by this. This disposition of the spirits could change. One medicine man tells the story of a young girl who was very sick and came for healing. Just as they were about to take her into the sweatbath, she began to have her period. The medicine man was at a loss for what to do. He prayed, and his spirits told him to take the girl into the sweatlodge and doctor her even though she had her period. He did, and the cure worked. There were no bad consequences elsewhere. So the medicine man was convinced that the powers of the spirits are greater than the spiritual influences of the menstrual flow and that the spirits can change this tradition if they want to.

3) May a woman take part in a sweatbath when she is not having her period?

In the old days, the men would heat the rocks and sweat together. When the men were gone, the women would then often come down, pull back the covers, and stand over the rocks as they poured water to receive the "leavings." Often for special times, such as after a girl's first menstrual period, the girl would be taken into the sweatlodge to be wiped with sage as part of the Making-a-Woman ceremony. Some medicine men will set up separate sweatlodges for men and for women. Unlike other tribes, the Sioux do not commonly have sweats with the whole family, although some tend in that direction. Medicine men who are younger and mixed blood will regularly open their sweats to whomever comes — men or women.

So there are a variety of positions on this question on the reservation, and at the Medicine Men and Pastors' Meeting, this question was discussed at length. A related question is: What is the role of women in Lakota religion? In some ways their roles are similar to men's; in other ways their roles are different.

Historically there was equality in reference to herbal medicines. There were **pejuta wicaśa** (herbal men) and **pejuta winyan** (herbal women). They knew herbs very well and administered them with prayer. But the use of herbs with prayer has been relegated to the ceremonial medicine man these days. There are stories of powerful women **Heyoka** (Clowns or Contraries) who stopped fires, healed the sick, and helped people by acting in a

"Contrary" way. Even today women are receiving **heyoka** dreams, but they very often go to a medicine man and ask him to "wipe it off." Still a few are beginning to follow these visions and do what the visions direct them to do. I have yet to hear of a woman who has received a vision to lead Indian spirit ceremonies.

In recognizing the **wakan** character of women, it was pointed out that everyone is born of a woman, who feeds us and watches over us. To shut her out is like turning one's back on the person who sacrificed the most for us. It was also pointed out that it was through the Buffalo Calf Maiden that the Lakota's sweatbath was renewed. "Would one bar **her** from coming in?" After the first menstrual period, when it is seen that a girl is now a woman and can have greater life through the bearing of children, the girl is traditionally taken to the sweatlodge for wiping, thereby making her especially **wakan.** In the **yuwipi** and other Lakota ceremonies, it is the woman who holds the Pipe. She represents the Buffalo Calf Woman through whom the Lakota have all the ceremonies of the Pipe. Even if it does have a negative influence, it is recognized that a woman having her period is very powerful and **wakan.**

But one older medicine man said, "I have had sweatbaths in which women participated. They were wrapped in big towels or wore full swimming suits or dresses. Knowing how much protection a small towel can give a person in a sweatbath, I wonder how much effect they receive from the heat. To me it would be like washing my hands with gloves on." There appears to be no real religious barrier to a woman leading a sweatbath ceremony herself, provided she knows what she is doing and does it right. Women pray with the Pipe regularly. The wives of some medicine men give sweatbaths for women, while their husbands give sweatbaths only for men. But women usually consider a medicine man spiritually higher than his wife and want to have their sweatbath led by him. So some medicine men will lead both but keep them separated. Some medicine men say their vision does not allow them to take part in or have mixed sweatbaths.

In the end, it was agreed the women having their menstrual period should not take part in sweatbaths unless such a sweatbath is indicated as allowable by the spirits for healing purposes. It also was agreed that it is really up to a person's vision and sacred tradition whether one takes part or leads mixed sweatbaths with men and non-menstruating women.

4) What is the Making-A-Woman Ceremony like?

The Lakota have a special purification ritual for a girl after her first period. Iva Black Bear told how this ceremony was performed for her. Most other accounts given agreed substantially with this one. Because of its thoroughness the account is recorded here precisely as it was given, even though the events are explained not in the exact order they occurred.

"At the Rosebud Fair Grounds when I was thirteen, my grandfather named Laid On The Ground, a medicine man, told my parents to hold a ceremony for me. In those days, there was a law that forbade it, so they didn't want to do it. My father said, 'They may put me in jail!' I have a grandfather named Walks Fast and another named Never Misses A Shot, and they said **they** were going to do it.

"They built a teepee and put me in the center. Everything I wore was beaded. They gave me a wooden bowl with cherry juice and two kinds of **wasna.** Each of them sang. When they were finished, they each gave me words of wisdom. Prior to this, when I first got my period and after I was over it, there was an old woman who was pretty good at bead and quill work. So my mother paid this woman. She wiped me with sweet grass. During this ceremony, the same woman wiped me again, and I was given special clothes to wear. They told me to have respect and regard for people. They said, 'If you are eating meat and you see that someone is hungry, take it out of your mouth and give it to them. Whoever you see in pitiful shape and in need of clothes, clothe them. If someone needs a place to sleep, let them sleep in your house.' There are seven of these rules, but I don't remember all of them right now.

"When they were through, they smoked; they passed the Pipe around. Afterward, they passed the cherry juice around, and everyone took a drink. The same way with the **wasna;** each one ate some. I came out with the Pipe. There were mourners there from Oglala, so I took this Pipe and I made them smoke it. I made them drink some of the cherry juice and eat some of the **wasna.** When I was through with this, I took off everything I was wearing and gave it to them, all the beaded things I wore. They had an older man sing for me, and they gave him a horse with beaded clothes. These things they taught me I have tried to do."

In the above account, the purification took place through two wipings with sweetgrass. In some accounts the wiping takes place in a sweatlodge, with or without a regular sweatbath ceremony The seven things taught to her by her grandfather probably were the seven corporal works of mercy — a common theme of Lakota-Christian catechists in those days. This list of material responsibilities clearly expressed traditional Lakota rules of generosity. Just as in the sweatbath ceremony the emphasis is upon the **life** of the people rather than purification, so too in the Making-A-Woman Ceremony the purification aspect is handled silently while the emphasis of the ceremony was upon the Lakota woman's responsibility to be generous among her people.

Others have said, "At certains times of life, it is good to take someone to the sweatbath to talk to them. For example, when a girl becomes a woman or a boy becomes a man or when someone drinks a lot or when there are family problems. They should talk to them in a nice way. They should go to the sweatbath from ten years on." Here again, the sweatbath is used to handle problems in the hope of a new, better beginning. The sweatbath becomes a sacred opportunity to "talk to them" so that they and the people may live better, happier lives. As they say. . .**Mitakuye oyas'in.**

5) Is it fitting to take a crucifix into a sweatbath?

A few Catholics always want to bring a crucifix to the Lakota ceremonies they attend. A few medicine men question that practice. One said, "How about the sweatbath? If I asked you to bring your cross in there with that body on it, where would it fit?" In this question he restates that the sweatbath is for health and life. Therefore how unfitting it is to bring in an image of Christ which shows him as one who is dead. Protestants and some Catholics too have protested about the corpus of Christ on traditional Catholic crucifixes. They place a bare cross in their churches. "Christ is no longer on the cross," they say. "Christ is not dead. He is risen. He is alive." Some modern crosses show the figure of the risen Christ. For many Catholics, the crucifix highlights Christ's suffering and their current suffering with him. Unfortunately, the crucifix does not depict Christ as dying but Christ as dead. The crucifix shows the corpse of Christ after his Spirit left the body. Therefore the crucifix technically does not really show how the eternally living Christ **ever** was. Thus the corpus on the cross is **totally** symbolic of Christ's sacrifice and one's total commitment to the Father's will in him. Nonetheless, the symbolic use of a corpse is repugnant, disrespectful, and irreverent to some people. Should a dead body be waved about like a banner? The Gospels, which had so much to say about Christ's approach to death, had little to say about what happened after his death except that everyone wanted him down from the cross in a hurry because of the approaching Sabbath. The witnesses of Christ's sacrifice did not want him left on the cross. Why should we?

Some Catholics take a crucifix to a Lakota ceremony, however, out of fear — fear that an evil spirit might come. There is here an assumption that Lakota prayer will not dispel an evil spirit but a crucifix will. This displays a disbelief in the medicine man's powers to avert a Lakota spirit that will do evil. Such an attitude seriously erodes one's faith in the medicine man's ability to do any spiritual good. Such persons seem to think that at the sight of a crucifix an evil spirit will flee. But if the crucifix displays Christ as he never was, and if Satan found no trouble approaching Jesus himself in the desert, then a blessed symbol will do little to deter an evil spirit. An evil spirit is not a Count Dracula. The popular story of Count Dracula's fear of the cross is pure fiction, and similar uses of the crucifix are superstitious. The real deterrent of an evil spirit is found in the Christian's faith in Christ's victory over sin and Satan. Because of Christ's Spirit within him, the Christian should not fear those who would attack him. Christ watches over his own, and those who believe in him will be protected. A crucifix seems to be useful to some individuals because it helps them express a lively enough faith to establish a victorious peace in the face of what **may be** evil. Many medicine men silently tolerate a person bringing the crucifix and other talismans into the sweatbath or vision quest. But it does not demonstrate the total humility that the ceremonies expect. Besides, any metal or stone object worn in the sweatbath will burn the individual severely because of its heat conductivity. With mature faith, one leaves all such man-made things outside and uses one's fears and general pitifulness to call forth the faith necessary for the sacrificial ceremony to be undertaken.

Still the Christian fears a detachment from Christ, especially as one enters into something so spiritually powerful and religiously different as a sweatbath. It is true that Christ is not present historically in the sweatbath ceremony, but Christ is present in two ways: 1) The Spirit of Christ is found at the spiritual root of the sweatbath ceremony itself in its purification intent, in its revelational basis, in its concern for the welfare of the people, and in its search for union with that which is holy. 2) The Spirit of Christ is found in the faithful, believing, historic Christian wherever one goes, especially when in a ''dying'' situation. Christ is very much in the Christian's sweatbath, both in the heart of the ceremony and in the heart of the participants. But this is not an explicit presence but an interior and spiritual one.

6) How can a Christian take part in a Lakota sweatbath?

The Lakota know that different people have different relationships with God and other spiritual realities. From a Lakota point of view, the Christian's silence is not a denial of one's Christian faith or Spirit, but a respectful holding close to oneself that which is personally most spiritually meaningful. There is, however, a Christian tendency to want to make a profession of faith in Christ. But from the life of Christ, the Christian should know there is a time to be silent, before there is a time to speak. Christ lived a ''silent life'' as a carpenter before his baptism, after which he went to pray in the desert forty days before beginning his public ministry. Christ's proclamation of the Kingdom was made not with clear statements but in parables. Only gradually did he let the "Messianic secret" be known. It was only at the end of his life that he boldy proclaimed his divine messiahship before the High Priest. His divine Sonship was manifested at the resurrection only after being three days in the tomb. The Holy Spirit gave the apostles the courage to proclaim the Gospel of Jesus and baptize people not at the Ascension when Jesus gave his apostles their commission but only after ten days of prayer and fasting. The Christian's commission, like Paul's commission to evangelize, is not to be immediately implemented but always after a time of prayerful silence and inspiration. One must receive before one can give. Like Jesus who asked questions of the teachers in the temple, like the apostles whose hope for the Davidic kingdom was a part of their search until Christ's departure, like Paul whose zeal was grounded on the instruction of Gamaliel, Christians are, in God's providential plan, to first silently learn from and be blessed by those sacred revelations that preceded the coming of the Gospel, so as to adequately appreciate it and subsequently promulgate it in a Christ-like inculturational manner. The Christian should pause and reflect deeply on the previous sentence. It is a key notion in the art of being a fully authentic Lakota-Christian.

When Christians go to Lakota ceremonies they should give themselves totally in a completely orthodox Lakota way. Note, that I did not say they should totally give themselves in a completely orthodox Lakota way. For the Christian, Lakota religion only affects **some** of one's spiritual relationships and **parts** of one's religious existence. There is no deception of hypocrisy here. Even in Lakota life, there are **ikceya** (secular) aspects that are outside of the normal concerns of those things which are **wakan** (sacred). In this way many Christian values can remain silently and respectfully within, until that time when it is appropriate in God's plan for them to be expressed in the world. It is like the man who is capable of saying both "yes" and "no." Sometimes the situation is such that "yes" should be said aloud and the interiorly potential "no" should wait for another time. Both "yes" and "no" have their time in truth and virtue. So too the Lakota sweatbath and Christian confession have their time in the realm of **public** truth and virtue.

There is legitimacy in Christian participation in the sweatbath if they experience within themselves that the sweatbath spiritually touches, helps, and matures them. This is the primary reason why Christians should study the **Old** Testament in a deep authentic way. Pre-Christian revelations still have unique spiritual powers to sanctify our religious reality on the most fundamental levels. It is like the person who studying calculus realizes that one must study and understand more deeply the fundamentals of arithmetic. It is commonly recognized that the study of comparative religions deepens an appreciation for one's own religion, and fosters a great respect and theological acceptance of others. But what we are is not mind only but flesh and will as well. So then, participation in compatible religions can deepen people's grasp of their own religion and foster an intimate spiritual relationship with the others, thus making them spiritually more catholic, that is more, universal spiritually.

6) But there is a more important question. Why is a Christian **sinner** in a Lakota sweatbath in the first place?

Some go because it is family tradition. That is how one was taught. That is what our grandfathers did. For these people it would be almost disrespectful not to go, at least once in a while. Others go out of a desire for friendship or identification with Indianness. Still others go in a desire to revitalize Indian history and culture. All of these reasons are good but they are not religious ones.

Every race that strives to be a holy people needs purification rites that re-establish **that** people as a holy people after some of its members break the God-given covenant and the spirit-given visions which make them a sacred people. The revelation of the Buffalo Calf Woman made the Lakota a specific, holy people through the Buffalo Calf Pipe. Thus the sweatbath is first of all for the correction of those wrongs which removed those members of the Lakota people from the holiness associated with **this** covenant and revelation. The purification aspect of the sweatbath is constantly but implicitly present. While the leader constantly emphasizes the positive side so as not to embarrass or put down any of the participants, the participants will talk about how they have been drinking too much and need this sweatbath or how this sweatbath is a "hard" one so they know they needed it, or the others may kid another participant who is having a hard time by saying, "You can tell someone in here has been fooling around."

Within the sweatbath the prayer **Mitakuye oyas' in** (All my relatives) is properly understood in terms of the Lakota people. In the sweatbath and in other Lakota ceremonies one often hears, **Wakan Tanka, onsimala ye. Wani kta ca lecamon welo.** (God, have pity on me. I do this so that I may live.) At other times they pray, **Tunkasila, onsiunlapi ye, ho ca lena oyate kin nipi kte lo,** (Grandfather, pity us, so these people will live.). When people enter a Lakota sweatbath, they are saying, "I recognize that we as a people are called by God and the spirits to live a specific, sacred way. I recognize that I (we) have done things to violate that sacred trust and relationship established through the Pipe. I also know that God gave this sweatbath through the Pipe to the Lakota people that they may be made right and strong. By this action the sacred relationship or covenant between that which is Sacred and we people will be renewed and strengthened. In this way we will again be a blessed, holy, virtuous, and single Lakota people again, and the sacred hoop will be made one again.''

Christians go to confession to be purified for their unfaithfulness to the universal covenant and eternal salvation effected by the sacrifice of Christ Jesus. Confession establishes them as sanctified members of the historic Christian Church. For both the Lakota and Catholic wrongdoer, the essential spiritual attitude is one of humble repentance from one's violation of God's will as historically expressed to the Lakota and Christian people, respectively. Spiritual meanings are known, and religious violations are forgiven only within specific historic contexts. In their repentence, the Lakota in the sweatbath and the Christian in confession are spiritually one — one is seeking union with God through the means given them by God in their respective covenants. Being both spirit and matter, they are not truthful in their commitment to union with God unless they express that union in the ways materially specified by the revelations of God in history. Thus if a Lakota-Christian does something that is unrighteous in both the Lakota and the Christian ways, one is to seek purifications in both the Lakota sweatbath and the Christian sacraments of penance, for one has violated two covenants, two historically and culturally different relationships with that which is Sacred. This is similar to the situation of a professed religious person who has taken the vow of chastity. If one commits a sin of unchastity, one must confess two sins: the sin of unchastity and the sin against one's vow. Some may not wish to bear this double burden, but then they do not participate in the double benefits.

By going to both the sweatbath and confession, the participants receive life, strength, and help from the Lakota spirits and Christ's Spirit. They are assisted not only by the Four Winds [**Tatiye topa**] but also the persons of the Blessed Trinity. They are supported not only by all the Lakota spirits of Earth but also the Christian saints in heaven. Some may ask, ''Why should I go to the Lakota spirits when all I spiritually need I find in Christ?'' My response to Catholics is, ''Why pray to Mary and the saints when you have Christ?'' And to Protestants I say, ''Why go to any minister or even the Bible if faith in Christ is sufficient?'' The fact is that God made us social beings and that loving, and being related to, and drawing assistance from one another is a divine calling. As Vatican II and Chief Sitting Bull have said: We are to draw that which is good from whatever source presents it, and reject the bad wherever it appears — even among our own. The Lakota religion and the Christian religion relate us differently to everything in heaven and on earth. The sweatbath and penance are to rectify and strengthen each person's and the whole people's life as specified respectively in the Lakota and the Christian Ways.

7) If the Lakota religion and the Christian religion specify a different relationship with all things, then does the Lakota understanding of "wrongdoing" differ from the Christian notion of "sin?"

This is a very significant question. Only a few preliminary thoughts can be given here.

The medicine men and pastors showed very different responses to the discussion of "evil." The Christian pastors were very aggressive to expose and deal with every aspect of evil from both a theological and pastoral point of view. Lakota medicine men were very guarded and cautious to talk about such matters. As with the topic of evil spirits, they said, "When you name it, it comes, and something bad will happen." They closely associated material evil with sin and had a hard time talking about and living with both. The pastors on the other hand said, "When the evil is brought out in the open, one can look at it, learn something from it, and correct the wrong elements so that it won't appear again." In ordinary conversations, however, Christians tended to avoid talking about various evil things because it was thought to be unloving and unChristian. Among the Lakota, gossip about misconduct is constantly present.

Many times I have heard, "We Indians never sinned." "Before you Whites came over here, the Lakota didn't know 'sin'." These and other similar statements appear in a variety of settings and have several layers of meaning. Sometimes these statements were made by Indian romantics, who looked longingly and honorably at the Indians of the pre-reservation period and could not see any wrong doing despite the fact that the legend of the coming of the Pipe, winter counts, **ohunkaka** stories, and oral and written history would indicate otherwise.

Another reason for statements like the above is found in the word for "sin" in Lakota, **wowahtani.** Most Christian words were translated well into Lakota, but "sin" was not. **Wowahtani** is the absolute form of the Santee word **ahtani** (to labor for one), which is from the root **htani,** which means "slowly, carefully." While "to labor for one" and to be "careful" point to suppressive, unpleasant, and dangerous activities, the roots of **wowahtani** provoke an understanding nowhere near the meaning of "sin." Besides, **wowahtani** was a derived Santee word, which was not found in the Lakota vocabulary before the coming of the missionaries from the east. So the Lakota did not know the word "sin" before the coming of the White man, and knowing not even the related words, it was difficult for them to appreciate the theological concept.

Today the Lakota use **wowahtani** only in Christian prayers. It is not applied to ordinary wrongdoing. The Lakota will say that something is not right or fitting [**Hecetu śni**]. They will come close to the Hebraic root when they say, "Forgive me, father, I made a mistake." But they see the "mistake" as a simple human failure to which there is public embarrassment and need for public apology, but these are viewed as not having any real consequences before God. They also say, **Taku śicaya econ,** (He did something hurtful or bad.). Looking at the context of these expressions, they cannot be properly understood or translated as "sin" — as usually thought of by Christians. Although Christians regularly speak about sin as a lack of personal love of the Father and all men in his Son, sin is still normally conceived of as violations of the Father's will as specified in positive, **universal** statements (or laws) found in Scripture.

Lakota directives are very relational. Different actions have different effects upon different people. Particular actions are normally not bad in themselves but bad insofar as they have a negative impact on other people and the relationship the doer has with other people. Certain relatives and people deserve greater respect than others; certain enemies and outsiders deserve greater contempt than others. A person is to be very respectful to one's grandparents and very ridiculing of one's in-laws, for example. Thus what may be recognized as "good" in front of one person may be considered "bad" in front of another. The notion of sin is associated with a standard that God has applied equally to all. The notion of "sin" normally concentrates upon the **action** of the doer to the receiver rather than the **relationship** of the doer to the receiver.

Christ regularly concentrated upon one's actions — one's fruits — rather than one's relationships. He healed those who came to him, and then sent them on their way. Their following of him made his ministry difficult. Consider the story of the Good Samaritan. Who was a neighbor to the beaten traveler? The person who helped him by binding his wounds and taking him to an inn. The story in no way speaks of an interpersonal relationship being established between the traveler and the victim. In contemporary times Christians are emphasizing the virtue of "love" in terms of interpersonal relationships. In the Gospel of John, Christ says, "If you love me, keep my commandments." The obedience and imitation of the disciple to his teacher and master is recognized as virtue. Disobedience and a lack of imitation is seen as unfaithfulness and sinful. The Christian's doing of deeds specifies one's relationships. The Lakota's relationships specify the doing of deeds. Christian directives are general and universal; we are to treat every human very much alike — but a person may treat a horse very differently from a human. The Lakota would show greater respect for one's horse than for an enemy. The Lakota do not have a sense of an absolute, divine command **in the ordinary [ikceya] parts of Indian culture.**

A full-blood described how his grandfather always talked to him. "Grandson, show me respect and do not interrupt me. Listen to what I say, then do what you want." The grandfather first told the boy that he had to show respect for him by keeping silent while he spoke. Then the grandfather told the boy he would respect him by not interfering with the course of action the boy might choose. It was more important that the grandson listen to his grandfather properly than to do something wrong somewhere else. Then it would probably be out of respect for the grandfather that the grandson would follow the wisdom of the grandfather, not because the acting had any inherent moral value. Christian morality has tended toward absolutizing "right" from "wrong" and dividing the insider from the outsider by specific actions. The performance of wrong action, regardless of the real consequences, always was accrued to a person as guilt, which had to be formally removed by reception of the sacrament of penance.

One medicine man said, "They didn't preach about sin because that word is bad. We didn't have it. Our parents preached about shame, **wiśteca.**" The greatest punishment in a familial setting is disassociation, being a social outcast. If a person's deed caused difficulty between family members or between one's family and some outsiders, then the family members would pull away from the trouble-maker. They normally did not perform an action against that person; rather they removed themselves **from** that person. In a closed and close family society, the sanction of shame works well, but in a modern, mixed society where interfamily communications do not prevail, this sanction has little effect.

Within Lakota culture, however, they did have a concept of sin **within the domain of the Sacred.** The Lakota say, "The Pipe has its rules." There are spiritual punishments that come from breaking the Pipe rules concerning spiritual things. These are **wakan** matters and are considered to be outside of the ordinary affairs of life. The notion of sin can be found in terms of the

Lakota's dealing with God and the spirits, **taku wakan kin** and not in terms of one's ordinary dealings with others. In the Old Testament God identified Israel as "his son," and the commandments related offenses against other Israelites with offenses against God. In the New Testament the Son of God is identified with the Son of Man; the incarnation unites the divine and the human orders of things and makes violations against other Christians and other humans into violations against Christ and his Father. The concept of "sin" is intimately related to the unique relationship between God and man in Christ. The "sins" of the Christian primarily pertain to the domain of ordinary life. That which is purified in the sweatlodge is primarily from the extraordinary, **wakan** domain of the rules and ceremonies of the Pipe.

8) What happens if a Lakota or Christian are not purified for their wrongdoing?

Among the Lakota whenever a person wants something from the spirits, one is expected to "pay the price." A Full-Blood said, "The problem today is that everyone wants something for nothing. They want the medicine man to get something from the spirits for them, but they are not willing to put anything back." As one medicine man said, "You have to come half way." As more material gifts and helps are wanted, more material sacrifices, like tobacco ties or food offerings, are required. Similarly, the notion of "penalty" is closely associated with the notion of "price." There is a certain sacrifice if one is to ask the spirits to "wipe out" something bad that is coming. If a person does something wrong, bad luck or something bad is going to come either to yourself **or to one of your relatives.** One often hears younger people say, "I am having a string of bad luck, so I must have done something wrong." Or "I knew doing that certain thing would bring me bad luck." By "bad luck" they mean that the spirits are letting or are guiding bad things to happen to them for a mistake. There is a doubling up of "price" or sacrifice here: first, for not doing the right deed in the first place and second, for correcting the retributional bad that is coming because of the wrong deed. Consequently sacrifice for wrongdoing always hurts more. Of significance is the belief that if something is *"done wrong,"* the spirits will demand restitution from one's family or oneself at most in a few years. Because of the closeness of family relationships and their emphasis upon material restitution, Lakota relatives may sacrifice and make restitution for another Lakota who has done some sacred wrong.

While the Christian believes that material restitution for sin is carried out in union with Christ's sacrifice on the cross, the primary emphasis is upon the spiritual aspect of sin, which can only be altered by the conversion of the sinner and the forgiveness of Christ. The consequences of sin are not found primarily in the material sphere but in the spiritual sphere. Grace, the presence of the Holy Spirit, and divine assistance in one's religious activities is variously withdrawn. The real consequence of sin is realized not in this life, for Christ constantly seeks the conversion of the sinner, but in eternity where Christ must act as "judge of the living and the dead."

So in many ways the Lakota and the Christian ceremonies of forgiveness are similar, but in very clear ways they are different. They both respectively serve as means of bringing the wrongdoer back into the sacred relationship that the Pipe and Christ seek to establish among God's special people. It should be more clear to the reader that in many ways the religious worldviews of the two religions are complementary.

9) Why do the doors of sweatlodges on the reservation face West; didn't Black Elk say they face East? Many people have read **The Sacred Pipe: The Seven Rites of the Oglala Sioux.** This is an excellent book written by Joseph Epes Brown from his interviews with Nicholas Black Elk. A few local people have pointed out that most people do not recognize Black Elk's association with the **Wakinyan** (Thunder Spirits) as a sign that he was in some respects an **Heyoka** (Contrary). On the reservation, a sweatlodge which faces the East is called an **Heyoka** sweatbath.

Walker and Black Elk also have different sequences of colors for the cardinal directions. As far back as they can remember, today's medicine men told me the traditional sequence is: West — black; North — red; East — yellow; South — white. A few medicine men and people fear a full confrontation with the spirits of the West and use another color for that direction, like purple.

It is important to remember that, especially in regard to ceremonial details, what one medicine man says is the right way, is truly **his** right way, but to discover the **Lakota** traditional way one must observe and listen to many Lakota spiritual leaders.

Chapter 5

Vision Quest and Comparable Rituals

The Lakota spirits and the Christian Holy Spirit are the immediate, dynamic, spiritual elements within the Lakota and Christian religions. These spirits call and empower medicine men and priests. Consequently, spirit-empowering ceremonies have long been close to the hearts of the participants of the Medicine Men and Pastors' Meeting.

The expression "vision quest" is a translation of the Lakota word **hanbleciya,** which literally means "crying for a dream." It refers to the intensity of the crying or prayer, **wocekiye,** which takes place on the hill as a person seeks a vision or an experience of a Lakota spirit.

A person breathes in and out almost all of the time, and usually is not conscious of it. So too every individual gives and receives spiritually many times each day, usually unconscious of the love exchange. Both the Lakota and Christian religions maintain that there is continual contact with the spirit world, at least in a materially supportive way, even though ordinary people are little conscious of it.

At various times, most individuals have fragile, child-like, globular faith-experiences, which expose to the perceptive observer some of the great spiritual realities operative behind the external facade of the material world. Some people have a talent for making lively human friendships, and others seem to have a natural disposition for making relationships with spirits. As some individuals are more interested in developing closer associations with spirits, likewise, spirits also appear to want particular relationships with certain people. The freedom of love is neither inherently egalitarian or "fair." While these interpersonal, spiritual relationships are in some aspects exclusively personal, still from both the spirit and human sides, these spiritual interrelationships seem inevitably linked to communal religious traditions. Thus it is understandable that special religious rituals publicly recognize, support, and disburse the effects of these human-spirit relationships.

Frequently, a private calling precedes involvement in public ritual. Most medicine men who started practicing twenty, thirty, and forty years ago indicate that it was a shocking, private calling which led them to perform the ceremonies which brought them to their full medicine man powers. Most of the medicine men who started within the last ten or twenty years have received their visions, however, as a consequence of conscientious participation in Lakota rituals. It might be said that, in a negative environment toward religion, private callings seem to be necessary to jar the individual from his negative religious prejudices. In a positive religious environment, less shocking but more demanding ways are necessary. While the first group must struggle against the un-belief found within their environment, the latter must struggle against the unbelief associated with the discouragements of ceremonial perseverence.

There are actually a variety of ways that a medicine man may receive spiritual power: 1) From a medicine bundle received from another medicine man. A Lakota spirit will attach itself to a medicine bundle out of loyalty to the original medicine man. If the original medicine man dies or takes back his medicine bundle, the spirit may withdraw or return to the original medicine man, but not necessarily so. There are some complaints about the people who do not receive a medicine man's spirit the traditional, hard way. Since they obtain their power frequently by buying a medicine bundle from another medicine man, they are not seasoned spiritually and tend to be less true to traditional at-titudes and rituals. Trained too quickly they often have difficulty managing their responsibilities. Still, with a medicine bundle, some medicine men have been able to get a quick start. They ex-perience what it means to have a spirit companion. Then, knowing what to look for, they are able to find more quickly spirit friends of their own.

2) Because of the care and interest that medicine men have with certain grandchildren and dedicated helpers, the prayers, direc-tions, and spiritual assistance of the grandfather can sometimes trigger a human-spirit relationship. Ultimately the individuals must make their own contacts and friendships with the spirits, but a loving grandfather can act like a ''match-maker,'' arranging various meetings of his human and spiritual relatives in an-ticipation of a fruitful friendship.

3) Through prolonged years of making vision quests, a dedicated person gradually learns the spirit ways. Such an individual must be zealous to persevere, and the spirits respond to the pitifulness

realized in that lonely perseverence. That perseverence can get in the way, however, for there may be proud, selfish, and controlling motives at the heart of that perseverence. If so, spirits usually do not come.

4) A person may receive a sudden, shocking, vivid vocation from the spirits, calling the person to a life of service to the community through the traditional religion of the Lakota. One young medicine man told how one evening he began to see small sparks, and with each spark there came a word. He went to get advice from some experienced medicine men, who put on a ceremony and put medicine on his eyes, ears, lips, and hands. After this he was able to hear and understand more, slowly developing spirit friends and began to minister to his people.

In the Catholic religion, the empowerment of a priest only takes place in one way: through the laying on of hands by a bishop in union with Christ through apostolic succession by the power of the Holy Spirit. Still there are conditions leading up to this culminating event: 1) A vocation from God, a sudden or gradual awareness that God wishes the individual to be a priest or religious. 2) The demonstration of understanding and a willingness to make this commitment. 3) A public recognition of worthiness from the people of God. 4) Approval and consecration by a bishop, the authorized and sanctified agent of Christ, His Spirit, and His Church.

In the pursuit of a special spiritual relationship, the notion of "death" appears in various guises in both the Lakota and Christian religions. In the **hanbleciya** (vision quest), a person is usually taken to a distant place, usually a hill, to fast absolutely and alone, exposed to all the elements. This ritual is also sometimes called simply a "fast" or a Pipe-fast, because this is one of the ceremonies of the Pipe, which is usually held throughout the vision quest. Locations which provoke fear are favored because they expose one's pitifulness quickly. "The place I usually go to is a graveyard, so it is scary." Some have been dropped down the side of a cliff by means of a rope to spend several days on a small ledge jutting out over a deep canyon. One person was dropped into an eight foot pit and left there for four days. Another was buried alive with only the stem of a pipe to breathe through. Others have been "staked out": cords are attached to four skewers pierced through the flesh of the chest and back, and the ends of these cords are tied to the limbs of nearby trees so that the person could not lie down or sit down through several days of the vision quest. Following a dream, one man was staked out several days on his horse. These examples are the exception rather than the rule, but they show the severe dedication and sacrifice some will show during their vision quests. Nonetheless, simply standing on top of a hill under the blazing August sun or in the middle of a thunderstorm is a great challenge to one's very life. Each year when I was preparing to go up on the hill for my visions quests, Moses would always remind me, saying slowly, "Remember, when you go up on that hill, you go there to die. . ., and some have!"

The Christian speaks of death primarily from a spiritual perspective where the emphasis is upon a "death to oneself." In the course of salvation history, God moved the Judeo-Christian people away from physical sacrifices of animals and flesh to the sacrifice of one's spirit. Christ's prayer in the Garden of Olives was, "Father, let not my will but yours be done." Because of man's great regard and respect for individual freedom, everyone has real difficulty with this kind of dying. As Jesus said, "If anyone wishes to come after me, let him deny himself and take his cross daily and follow me." The dying of a Christian in ritual and religious activities is not all that different from dying in the performance of one's duties in everyday life. In a Christian retreat or spiritual renewal, individuals rededicate themselves to the Word of the Lord as He comes in the Christian assembly, in Scripture, in the Eucharist, and in His graceful Spirit. By seeking out God's Word as it comes to them at various points of their lives, Christians become totally obedient to it out of love and self-surrender. In everyday life, this inner death comes to express itself in various material sacrifices ranging from generosity in one's family, through giving alms to the poor, to surrendering one's total body in martyrdom. The Lakota seek spirit-associations in physical ways primarily for temporal and physical ends. The Christian seeks spirit-associations in spiritual ways, primarily for eternal and virtuous ends. Nonetheless, Lakota value spirit-relationships in themselves; many medicine men speak fondly of the regular conversations they have with their spirit friends. Christians value the charismatic gifts they receive because of the blessings they give here and now in healings, exorcisms, and infused virtues.

Some Lakota call **hanbleciya** an "Indian retreat." Vision quests are in some ways similar and in some ways different from Christian retreats. When a person prayerfully and reflectively decides to make a vision quest, that person fills a pipe according to the pipe ceremony and presents it to a person knowledgeable and practiced in the Lakota religion, asking him to put the seeker on a hill on a particular date for a certain number of nights and days, up to four. If the person agrees, he will take and smoke the pipe, binding himself spiritually to do it.

The vision quest seeker then prepares the spiritual offerings.

Usually 405 or 600 tobacco ties are made in one long string to surround the sacred area. Six yard-long flags are made of the six colors: black, red, yellow, white, blue, and green. One flag is made of red felt with an eagle feather and a shell attached to a tobacco tie in the center. All flags have tobacco ties in one or two corners. These are attached to cedar poles, cherry branches, and/or fruit trees. . .according to the leader's vision. The flags will be put in the four corners and across the front of the sacred area. Sometimes the medicine man requests other offerings like a bucket, dipper, knife, and cutting board to be put in the sacred area. The male seeker usually covers himself only with a star quilt, while the female seeker usually wears an Indian style dress.

When all the material preparations are made, the medicine man fills the pipe the seeker will hold throughout the vision quest at the sweat lodge. Then the seeker is purified in a sweatbath using seven rocks. Then the offerings and the seeker are taken to the vision quest area and enclosed in a circle of tobacco ties. After the medicine man prays and sings, everyone leaves, and the seeker fasts, prays, and cries for a vision alone until the medicine man returns at the appointed time to cut open the circle and take the seeker to the sweatlodge where the seeker tells the leader and the others in the lodge the things he heard and saw during the vision quest. The medicine man may give an interpretation then or at a **wopila Iowanpi** (thanksgiving ceremony) in the evening following the vision quest.

A Christian retreat is a period of intense prayer and spiritual reflection, usually at a separated place. For a retreat, a Christian is usually together with at least one other person, usually with a retreat director, in a withdrawn place where the food they eat and the clothes they wear are quite ordinary. Fasting or eating, speaking or silent, Christians choose whatever way the Spirit prompts them as having the greatest spiritual effect. While the Lakota focus on one ritual, Christians usually take part in Mass also and often other religious ceremonies as well. On the hill, Lakotas sing and cry out their prayer. Except for group liturgies, Christians retire to their rooms or secluded places to pray inwardly in silence. The Lakota look for an external coming of spirits in signs, songs, or messages from birds, animals, apparitions, etc. The Christian looks for movements of the Spirit within, especially in insights and understandings. Each fills the environment with various signs of the spiritual individuals that one wishes to be close to. The Lakota surround themselves with flags of different colors, reminding them of the major spirits of the Pipe. Christians surround themselves with the cross, the Bible, statues of saints, etc. Still the Lakota are very much alone and pray as best as they can out of their own experience and the oral traditions that have come to them. Christians use the Bible, the writings of others, the advice of a retreat director, or the sharings of fellow retreatants to help them with their prayer. The Lakota prays for long periods, usually repeating very short prayers or songs. The Christian tends to pray with little repetition and for only short intervals, with much reflection, reading, and rest in between. The Lakota seek a graphic vision, which usually comes in a highly symbolic and personal form; the Christian seeks understanding and insight, which usually come in the form of self-knowledge or theological knowledge.

Many Whites do not appreciate the material/monetary side of a vision quest. College students have difficulty understanding why it is fitting to spend around $250 for quilt, cloth, and offerings to make a vision quest. Similarly many Lakota do not recognize their responsibility to help pay for the cost of food, lodging, transportation and spiritual direction at a retreat house. While these expenses are simply a fact of life on the Christian side, such offerings are an essential, sacrificial part of the vision quest on the part of the vision seeker and/or one's family.

While the prototype of a retreat today is a withdrawal to a house of prayer for several days to pray, do spiritual reading, and quietly reflect on various personal, spiritual matters under the direction of a retreat director, there are many alternate forms of retreats: parish days of recollection, monthly days of renewal, teenage ''Search'' for Christ, faith-encounters where different individuals share their faith experiences with others, or a private retreat where one goes to an isolated place alone to pray and be with God. Similarly, there are many ways that Lakota make a **hanbleciya** other than the traditional way indicated earlier. One Indian lad said that he regularly just walked out into the hills and the draws to pray and be with the spirits a few days. A Full-blood elder talked about his annual **hanbleciya** in an empty church near his home. One man set up his flags in the dirt floor of an old log cabin. Some Indians simply stay in a sweatlodge and pray for several days at a time.

The **hanbleciya** is comparable to several Christian religious ceremonies and activities. When it is made annually by dedicated individuals as an intense form of prayer for their own spiritual development and for the welfare of the people, it is similar to the Christian retreat. The vision quest is also a means by which ordinary individuals may receive a personal vision and a relationship with personal guardian-spirits for assistance in one's everyday life; this is similar to Christian confirmation. When this Lakota ritual is an essential part of a program of spirit empowerment and enlightenment for a medicine man, it is akin to the Christian sacrament of Holy Orders, in which deacons, priests, and bishops are ordained.

Many people have the idea that only religious professionals, like medicine men, priests, and sisters, ever receive visions or spiritual callings. Contrariwise, when a Lakota or Christian receives any kind of vision or calling, they expect that person to become a medicine man, priest, or religious. Both of these opinions are wrong. Increasingly these days, young Lakota are going on the hill and receiving visions that are strengthening and directing them to a fuller, more religious **personal** life within the Lakota community. It is difficult for people to hear of an ordinary person receiving a **wakan** calling without becoming a public **wakan** person. Today one of the effects of the reservation's poverty culture is that Lakota leaders are expected to do everything; rather each person should be doing their share. In the old days, many warriors had their own special visions and guardian spirits to help and protect them in their daily lives. People soon look up to these and follow them as a leader in the community; they didn't have to become a professional medicine man unless their visions specifically directed them to those kinds of activities. Similarly, the charismatic movement is exposing ordinary Christians to intense spiritual experiences and into various services within the community and the Church — but as lay people rather than professional clerics. These blessed Christians and Lakota are meant to be **very** religious and be personally **very** close to the Spirit(s). They are usually directed toward being very active in religious ceremonies — but as helpers rather than as leaders. It is wrong to assume that the office of religious helper is meant to automatically grow into a ritualistic leadership role. It sometimes happens, but the spiritual character of that step indicates it to be the exception rather than the rule. Knowledge and experience are valuable, but the special blessing by the Spirit(s) is essential for a religious headship role in both traditions. A large variety of religious stewardship roles are open through spiritual callings to ordinary individuals in both traditions.

Examination of different types of spiritual experiences demonstrates differences between the visions of medicine men and the visions of ordinary persons. The medicine man's visions are usually very clear and precise. In particular, the altar, offerings, medicines, songs, and prayers that he will use in his ceremonies are shown to him. A special feature of medicine men's visions is the revelation of the spirit's sign, which will be etched in the earth altar at ceremonies. One of the ways that a Lakota herb man, **pejuta wicaśa**, is distinguished from medicine man, **wapiya**

wicaśa, is this marking of the sacred circle. In the medicine man's vision, the spirits establish a special relationship with him in reference to these ceremonies. One medicine man said publicly at the meeting that when he received his vision, his spirit showed him the altar that he was to use in calling the spirit. Then the spirit said to him, "Whenever you call, I will come." On the other hand, an ordinary man's vision usually involves a particular animal or spirit that will be there to help him in times of personal need. An ordinary person may hear, "Whenever you call, I will come," but the personal, rather than the communal aspect of the vision limits the assistance of the spirit to his ordinary, personal life with his relatives and his people. In this vision the words have a totally different level of meaning and efficacy. This personal friendship and support from a spirit are not for leading public religious ceremonies like the **Yuwipi** or the Sundance even though they are **wakan.** Different levels of visions give different domains of empowerment: the ordinary vision and guardian spirit for personal needs; the medicine man's vision and healing spirits for the needs of others in the community. Still both types of visions and vocations come from basically the same Pipe ceremony, the **hanbleciya.**

The laying on of hands by the bishop is the same central ritual act at confirmation and at the ordinations of deacons, priests, and other bishops. The physical signs, like the priestly vestments, the sacred vessels, the readings, and the words of the blessings all set the ritual act of laying on of the bishop's hands within a definite context and give a special sacramental character and meaning to each. The power, authority, responsibilities, and privileges of confirmation and various ordinations are linked to the special spiritual relationships that are established through each level of ceremony. Sacred chrism is used to anoint those who are baptized, those who are confirmed, and those who are ordained deacon, priest, or bishop. Depending upon the duties as specified within the consecration formulas, the priesthood of Christ is shared by the newly-baptized, is manifested by the newly-confirmed, and gradually expressed in liturgical fullness by the deacons in their direct assistance of Mass, by priests in their officiating at Mass, and by the bishop who manifests the fullness of the powers of Christ's priesthood by his ability to ordain others at Mass. And surrounding the altar are other people with a variety of God-given gifts for the service of God's People both within and without the sacred assembly.

Within the Lakota religion a person not only receives a vision, but he is to share that vision with others -- at least with the medicine man and his friends in the sweatbath. The sharing of that vision is a **wakan** action. Thus great wrong is done in sharing it wrongly. Within the Catholic tradition, there is also an official, negative attitude toward the public sharing of spiritual experiences. Only a very few visions by Christians are meant to be public. Experienced religious recognize that most religious experiences are meant to be private, where they are a sign of and an incentive toward further religious dedication. Unfortunately, many ordinary people tend to be obsessed with unusual spiritual experiences, both in the Lakota and the Christian religion. They crave for anything unusual. They get excessively excited over spiritual events and cannot wait to tell everyone and everybody about them. This produces mass excitement that is often misplaced and can take a person away from the more important and more basic concerns of the leaders in the Lakota and Christian religion. Looking for strange signs moves the person's focus from sacrificial giving to sensational receiving. If a person has a **wakan** or unusual spirit experience, it is very important that a person discuss these matters with a balanced, sympathetic, experienced person who can help the individual evaluate personal spiritual experiences more objectively. In such **wakan** matters, one is easily led astray by confusion, emotion, and even evil spirits. The whole object is to draw out the spiritual fruit that was meant to be drawn from the spiritual experience. Beginners are often blinded by many prejudices that they have grown up with. Beginners are so over-zealous concerning unusual spiritual experiences. Many elders, like the medicine men and pastors, are much more experienced, careful, and composed when speaking about them. There is a check-and-balance here. It is also very important that a person either write down the experience or tell the experience to another, understanding person soon after it happens — as in the sweatlodge immediately after the visions quest. It is very easy for the mind to begin to add on things that one would like to have happened in the experience or to forget things that do not have an immediate meaning. One must prayerfully and repeatedly return to such experiences in their original form in order to draw forth the fruit that the spirits (and not the self) want to be known.

Public testimony about visions and miracles does have a place. It is to be remembered that the original Pipe ceremonies were derived from the public accounts of Lakota visions. The Early Church spread through the public witness of miracles seen by the apostles. Today Lakota **Yuwipi** ceremonies begin with the medicine man's account of his visions. Priests touch their congregations more meaningfully by giving accounts of the various spiritual struggles, triumphs, and experience they personally have had. If these experiences have helped him, they may help another in a similar situation. Of course, the time and place for these sharings should be ritually appropriate.

The medicine men pointed out an important difference between the medicine men of the past and those of the present. In the past, the medicine men were specialists. Each had a vision to work with only certain diseases. Today the medicine men are "all-arounds," as they say, medicine men whose spirits deal with every type of problem. In the past when someone was sick, family members would load that person on a horse or in a wagon, together with some gifts, and go to the house of a medicine man. He would come out and look at the sick person in various ways and then tell the relatives whether he could heal the sickness or not. If he couldn't, the specialist would indicate another medicine man who was able to take care of that particular sickness. In those days, medicine men supported one another. Today each medicine man tries to heal **every** kind of disease and solve every kind of problem through his spirits. This has resulted in a certain degree of competition and jealousy over clients and a number of negative statements from one medicine man and his followers against another. One frequently hears that medicine men are not strong and powerful as in the "old days." It is said that they don't spend enough time "out back" with their spirits; it also may be that they are expected to do, or are trying to do, too much.

One significant but confusing aspect of both the Lakota and Catholic religions is the regular disparity between spiritual experiences and their associated rituals. For example, some medicine men received their spiritual calling to be medicine men at home, and only after they received their visions did they make the appropriate Pipe-fast. This is similar to the case of Cornelius (Acts 10.1-23), upon whom the Spirit first came and indicated that baptism was appropriate and called for. Human beings and human history are multi-layered realities, and these layers fit somewhat loosely upon one another. They are related and influence each other, but not in absolute, immediate, mechanical ways. The normal sequence of activities is from the more material aspects to the more spiritual aspects. One prepares himself and then enters into the ritual, and some action of the Spirit(s) soon follows. Occasionally, especially when some radical change is to occur, the Spirit(s) will jar a person loose from some religious reticence through a significant spiritual experience prior to the corresponding religious ritual. That does not mean that the religious ritual is not necessary, but that for some reason, the religious ritual had been unnecessarily delayed or repressed. People regularly seek the ideal in which the material ritual and the corresponding spiritual experience climax together. This is difficult to achieve, but it is possible. The Lakota prepare themselves for a long time so that they might receive their visions during the vision quest. Religion teachers also try to bring Christian students to a lively experience of the Holy Spirit through spiritual exercises near the time of the confirmation liturgy. The temporal disparity of the experience of the religious ceremony and the spiritual experience is confusing and humiliating to many in both the Lakota and Christian religions. If individuals do not receive a spiritual experience by the time they go through the ritual, they are very prone to give up and remain spiritually disappointed and lethargic for a long time. It should be remembered that this disparity is not unique but very common, and that one simply must continue on with prayer and dedication until that time when the Spirit(s), for reasons known best to them, judge the time right to have some meaningful experience of the Lakota and/or Christian Spirit(s).

One must clearly distinguish between spiritual experience and spiritual presence. To be conscious of spiritual activity is different from and usually consequent to, the fact of a Spirit's activities. Both the Lakota and Catholic religions recognize the presence of the Spirit(s) at all ceremonies rightly done, even though the Spirit(s) are not experienced distinctly. The Lakota insist that at least the medicine man experiences the spirits personally at a ceremony, but at sweats and other ceremonies led by simply virtuous Lakota men, the spirits may not be experienced personally. Both religions recognize personal experience of the Spirits to be a special grace to those called to do something special in their lives or in the community.

In many ways the Spirit-giving ceremonies of the Lakota and Catholic religion have similar aspects. But as one more closely examines those particular characteristics and activities of Lakota and Christian spirits, the dissimilarities become more apparent. These differences are not to be taken as reasons for ignoring one while respecting the other. Rather the differences should be taken as pointing to reasons why each has its own special place in the world.

Chapter 6
Ghosts

Full-bloods shared with me a good number of their personal experiences of ghosts and spirits (1). Mixed-bloods and Whites in general had fewer experiences of ghosts and were tight-lipped about such matters. Whites tend to be over-critical toward spiritual experiences. Culturally they have been raised to consider ghosts to be "child's play" or "something out of the Middle Ages." On the other hand, most Lakota know that ghost and spirit encounters do happen. Culturally they tend to be over-accepting about such matters because they consider them **wakan** and are fearful of them. They consider it disrespectful to critically examine such experiences, for an objective attitude toward the data implies a pervasive disbelief in spiritual beings.

Many things can be said about the proper discernment and examination of these things. There are problems of auto-suggestion as well as spiritual blindness. But these matters would get too complicated and involved for this book. In this chapter I will include: a) a number of reported contacts with ghosts, including a description of a personal experience of a ghost, b) a comparison of the Jewish, Christian, and Lakota descriptions of the after-life, c) a discussion of the Lakota belief in reincarnation.

Factual ghost stories are usually not about ghosts at all but about how a person met and reacted to a ghost. When one follows the ghost's actions, they are usually very minimal. Frequently, persons who experience a ghost do not know they are dealing with a ghost until they finally recognize that that person is one known to be dead, or they witness that person doing something without the usual related physical phenomena following.

A Full-blood long experienced in spiritual matters tells this story. He was driving his team and wagon to town through freshly fallen snow one moon-lit night. He came upon a man walking

(1) A ghost [**wanagi**] is a spirit form of someone who previously lived in a particular material form. Spirits [**taku wakan kin**] start life in a spirit form and then may take on a material form.

down the road. He asked him if he wanted a ride to town. The man didn't say anything but simply climbed in and sat on the seat beside him. The driver knew the face of the man but couldn't place him. He liked to ride silently to town, but it bothered him that he couldn't remember the man's name; his face was so familiar. Suddenly it dawned on him. He had helped bury this man about a week before in the cemetery that he had just passed. Cold sweat began to break out all over him, but he didn't panic and slowly regained control of himself. He then looked over and checked it out. It really was the man. When he got to the middle of town, he stopped his team. No one was in the street. The man got off and walked toward the seed store. He opened the door and went in. The driver looked down. There were no marks in the two inches of freshly fallen snow. He got off the wagon and went to check the seed store the man entered. He was right. The front door was still chained closed. No one had gone into that store through the front door for years. He was sure he had seen the man open the door normally and go in. He peered inside and saw no one. He decided it was time to get home.

Ghosts most frequently appear in conjunction with an unwillingness to leave this world. It seems that they do not accept death for a variety of reasons. They are not at rest and are still wandering. They linger and are sometimes seen. One medicine man tells this story of a ghost who had some "unfinished business." "My grandfather was married. He buried some money in a can under the head of the bed where they sleep. (He lived in a log cabin with a dirt floor.) After he died, he appeared to his brother-in-law, who fainted when he saw him. He said to him, 'I forgot something. You are going to go back and tell my wife something. At the head of the bed where we sleep — underground — is buried some money.' So he did. When he got there, he dug into the ground and at the head of the bed, and they found the money in a can just as he'd said." The ghost never appeared after that, as far as he knew.

A Lakota might joke and say this was a sign of how much he loved to give his in-laws a hard time. But beyond the joke, some people seem to be more receptive to such appearances than others. The story first says the ghost was recognized consciously; then, without any recognized break, the ghost continued to present itself to the person even though he was in a faint, dream-like state. The change of modality of the appearance made no apparent difference to the message and purpose of the visit. The Lakota show equal credibility to encounters with ghosts in ordinary sight, in a vision, or in a dream. The important thing to the Lakota is the interpersonal experience and communications. They recognize the real presence of the ghost but are not concerned with questions of modality, they recognize that the ghost is other-than the person seeing it and are not interested in determining **how** the ghost-cause makes a person see or dream this encounter. The fainting seems to have been caused by the viewer and not the ghost. The author knows of only two cases where a ghost is reported to have caused any physical violence. Contrary to the opinion of many people, when the author listened to the stories the people told, not only were ghosts non-violent but they were frequently helpful.

So many Lakota erroneously react violently to the appearance of a ghost. An old man came to my office one day. He was obviously anxious and worried about something. I invited him in. With jerking glances, he checked the room out. I waited as he quieted down. He relaxed a bit, bowed his head, and buried his eyes into the floor. I greeted him pleasantly and asked him if I could help him in any way. He paused, and then finally blurted out, "Do you exorcise people?" Caught off-guard, I fumbled, "Well, I. . .if there is a need, I can exorcise a person. But I have to know what you are dealing with, though, so I can know how to pray." The old man was resistive. He simply wanted me to exorcise him, and I kept insisting that I had to know what I was dealing with. Finally he gave in, and he told this story.

They had buried his grandson just the day before. He had been very close to his grandson and was very sad over the death. In his great grief, he couldn't climb the hill of the country cemetery to see his grandson's body return to the earth. He stayed at the bottom of the hill to cry alone. Then he felt a hand on his shoulder. He lifted his head, and as he turned he looked right into the face of his grandson! The grandson said, "Don't cry, grandpa. I am at peace." "Then immediately I looked back up to the cemetery. The people were just lowering the casket into the ground. Then I looked back immediately to the person standing beside me, and there was no one there. He was gone. I looked all around, and there was nobody around where I was standing. There were no people, no bushes, no cars, nothing. So will you exorcise me?"

This old man knew he had seen a ghost, and he was afraid that this meant something bad was going to happen to him. It took a long time before the author's talking slowly began to break through his cultural prejudice against ghosts. Slowly the old man began to see that the appearance and the message from his grandson's ghost were beautiful things. He began to be at least partially convinced that the appearance should be taken not as a curse but as a blessing. Such prejudices were built up over many years, and could not be completely broken in a couple of hours. I prayed in thanksgiving, for healing, for protection, and for good times for the old man, his grandson, and all the relatives. He was more at peace when he left, and I hope he was a little wiser.

Lakota prejudices concerning ghosts are very negative. There is a stretch of road where many sightings of a ghost are rumored. One winter a group of men walked far around that area rather than travel that stretch of road on foot. All of them were severely frostbitten; one became very sick. This fear reminds the author of the fear of God that is recorded in the Old Testament. While the Jews thought one sight of God meant certain death, the Lakota think one sight of a ghost means great physical harm.

Wanagi kte (Ghost kills) is the name given to a stroke in which a person becomes paralyzed on one side. In particular, the face becomes distorted on one side. It is a common belief that if someone sees a ghost, that person will get a stroke, **wanagi kte.** Conversely, if a person gets a stroke, it is commonly assumed that it happened because that person saw a ghost. One day a Lakota Full-blood woman, who was active in the Lakota religion, had a stroke. Everyone said that she had seen a ghost; some even named the ghost of a certain relative. When I visited her in the hospital, she drew me aside and told me privately — avoiding an argument or disapproval from her relatives in her weakened condition, "Everyone is saying I saw a ghost. I know where I was and what happened when I had this stroke. I was there; they weren't. I know what I saw. I know that I didn't see no ghost (Lakota double-negative), regardless what all these other people say."

A Full-blood man tells a story that happened in his youth. "A bunch of us kids were going down into the draws to play. Then one of the fellows decided to be funny and he cried out, 'There's a ghost!! A ghost!!!' Everyone bolted and started scrambling up this steep hill. Everyone acted scared, screaming, and panting from running up the hill. Then one of the kids came up behind another and suddenly grabbed him by the shoulder. The boy turned his head around to look back. When he saw someone behind him, the whole side of his face became paralyzed. He had seen a boy! Not a ghost!! But still he got **wanagi kte.**" Through this incident, the story teller was able to see that different bad things are attributed to ghosts that really are not true. Then he gave this classical advice, "When a person meets a ghost, they shouldn't run away or want it driven out. They should respect it and pray."

Some cases involve several people experiencing the same ghost sightings. At the Rosebud Hospital, the ghost of a former nurse, who died an unseemly death, was seen by many of her professional peers. It seemed as if she was still going around, trying to do her nurse's duties. Here the ghost was also seen opening, entering and closing doors that were locked. The Catholic and Episcopal priests came and prayed for the soul of the departed nurse and blessed the hospital. The ghost did not appear again.

Religious people put forward this general rule: If you see a ghost, pray! — either the ghost or someone else is in need. It is the observation of a good number of people that the number of ghost appearances has gone down greatly since the coming of Christianity. It is noteworthy that the ghosts contacted in Lakota spiritual meetings are almost all from pre-Christian times. A ghost medicine man did not want to be involved with the dialogue because he said that a medicine man's association with Christ in such matters would result in a dilution of his powers. From the very first meeting medicine men said, "The Pipe is for health; Christ saves souls." It is the priests and not the medicine men whom the people call to have their houses blessed and protected from ghosts. Christian Lakota have very elaborate and intense wake services. A repeated Christian prayer is: "Eternal rest grant onto them, O Lord. And let perpetual light shine upon them. May they rest in peace. Amen." It is the author's experience that prayers through Christ have a peace-giving power on departed souls. They help ghosts accept their death-status and help them go to where ghosts are to go until the Last Day.

A number of ghosts of relatives were sighted at the bedsides of people who were seriously ill. Patients who were fighting death or wanted to die did not report any sightings. Rather the sightings that were reported to me were from people who preferred to live but were indifferent to death. Most reports were given to me only after the person was well and out of the hospital. Seeing ghosts at one's bedside, then, is not a sign of imminent death, for all these got well. There seemed to be a variety of reasons for suppressing these sightings until they got out of the hospital. In these sightings the actions of the ghosts were minimal. They were usually standing or sitting at the far side of the room, out of the way. They said nothing; their quiet presence said everything.

Some ghosts appear in a pitiful condition. The religious persons dismiss their own shock or curiosity to pray for these individuals, speaking soothing words, and offering gifts of food and drink as expressions of love and relationship. Sometimes it is helpful to tell wandering ghosts gently but firmly that their time has passed and that they are hurting themselves and others by not trusting in Jesus' mercy and going to where the souls of the dead go. I have personally experienced a ghost in such a situation. This is the story.

One day I was driving a friend around the reservation. I had been a pastor in Rosebud a number of years and wanted to show him a few things. As I slowed down for the stop sign at the end of a street near the parish CYO building, I saw a young Indian fellow whom I had been very close to when I was in the parish. He was walking catty-corner across the lot and intersection in front of me. I pointed him out to my friend and tried to get his attention by waving and hollering. My happiness at seeing him was unusually great, it seemed to me. Deep in my soul I heard, "Yes, rejoice greatly, for this is the last time you will see him." There was a note of finality and death in the words "last time". Inside I protested. I said to myself, "Oh, there might be an accident soon, a month from now, no six months from now, no, a year. . .I'll make it a point to see him before that happens." Despite my waving and hollering, he just kept walking. His head was bent very low, and he seemed absorbed in his thoughts. I thought it would not be right to press myself on him when he didn't want to talk. But strange, he was walking a way that was unusual for him, past the agent's house. He probably wanted to be alone for a while. The expression on his face was so sad. My heart went out to him, and I said a sincere prayer for him. Then I turned and drove past the CYO where there were a number of cars. I peered in but couldn't see any people. I said to my friend, "There must be a meeting or something." We drove on without stopping because it was getting near supper time.

About a week later, I was speaking with another friend, who asked me why I had not come to the wake and funeral. Who died? It was the young Indian fellow that I had seen. I said to myself, "When are you going to accept these things that are given you — the way they are given you, Stolzman?" As it turned out, everyone seemed to have assumed that someone else had called me; things are often confused at a time like that. At least I was missed. Inquiring about the details of his death, wake, and burial, things gradually began to fit together. He had died Thursday morning, and they had brought the body to the CYO around 5 p.m. on Friday. It was about 5:30 p.m. on that Friday that I had driven into town. I had wanted to get home by 6 p.m. and was running late. I had seen this young man's ghost. He was walking from the CYO to the sidewalk that runs beside the community college office, which seemed at that time an unusual path for this fellow to take. On hearing the tragic circumstances of his death, the path he was taking made sense because it was the shortest path from the CYO to the place of his tragic death, a few miles out of town on a back road where he had frozen to death, surrounded by a field of burnt grass which he apparently lit trying to keep warm and/or to signal help. I went there to pray for him. The evidence still remained that showed his desperate attempts to stay alive. I talked to his ghost, as if it were still there, with comforting words. Offering sacrifices and prayers, I asked God to be merciful, and I asked my friend to trust in God and go where He wants souls to go after death, for both Christ and I would cover any sins he may have, since we both knew the goodness and sincerity of his heart. What a sublime gift God had given me in allowing me to see my friend one last time before he ''passed on.'' There seems such great providence in the fact that I had missed the funeral but saw **him.** What a bitter-sweet memory.

The after-life of separated souls is a theological topic of great interest to many. The Lakota, Jewish, and Christian traditions hold many statements concerning the after-life. Since these statements speak of highly spiritual states it would be wrong to take the following descriptions too literally. Similarly it would be wrong to say that because of their haziness there is nothing that can be said at all. Each term has many shades of meaning even within one tradition. There are historical as well as local variations to the meanings and uses of these terms. A chapter could be written about each term used here. My intention here is only to lay out a general, comparative outline of the major after-life concepts found in the Lakota and Judeo-Christian traditions.

Each term in this section is highly symbolic and there are multiple understandings of each term. For example, ''heaven'' can refer to: 1) The physical sky above the earth, 2) God's dwelling place ''above'' the physical heavens ''outside'' the material world, 3) The place where the separated souls of good people variously go to be near God, his angels and his saints, 4) The final place of glory where God and His holy people will dwell in a trans-material paradise that is associated with a new Earth, 5) Figuratively, the term ''heaven'' may be applied to any place on earth that is now happy, good, and beautiful.

Similarly ''hell'' can refer to: 1) The physical depths from which boiling volcanoes erupt, 2) Sheol or Hades where relatives go to live in a rather inert, inactive state in the shadows, 3) Gehenna — where the separated souls of the wicked are tormented and afflicted by the evil demons of the deep, 4) Hell — the eschatological place of suffering where sinners suffer both in body and soul in eternal fire, 5) Figuratively, the term ''hell'' may be applied to any place on earth today that is evil, hurtful, and terrible. These are very graphic, apocalyptic images. It is important for every person to get beyond the sense level of the images and seek their spiritual meanings.

There are some people in and near the Christian tradition who do not believe in hell for a variety of reasons. For example, some Christians say a loving God would not punish a person, much less than forever, even for the worst, hard-hearted sins. In the end there can only be a peaceful, loving, harmonious eternal state for everyone after death. Similarly, there are some people in and near the Lakota tradition who do not admit to a state of suffering for any Lakota soul after death. All relatives are believed to be destined toward a happy union with their loved ones after death. Still the older, more full traditions recognize different states after death, one of which is a state of suffering.

The following scheme displays soul-states from the more traditional Lakota, Jewish, and Christian traditions. Each of these soul-states will then be described.

Lakota	Jewish	Christian
1) "Here" — Keep-A-Soul	"Sleep" — Sheol	"Rest" — Grave
2) Ghosts wander on earth.	Souls in Gehenna.	Souls in hell.
3) Lakota heroes and medicine men go to Rawhide Butte in the West.	Heaven where Elijah, Enoch and martyrs go.	Heaven where Jesus, martyrs, and canonized saints go.
4) Righteous Lakota souls go to Ghost country in the South.	Heavenly paradise and bosom of Abraham for worthy Jews.	Heaven where the souls of the purified Faithful go.
5) When the Great Buffalo falls, the world will come to an end.	Earthly kingdom of Israel established in peace among the nations by God.	Kingdom of heaven comes to earth by Christ on the Last Day when all shall rise.

These three traditions divide these different soul-states in this way: 1) immediate state, 2) state of the wrongdoer, 3) state of the hero, 4) state of the ordinary good person, 5) the final state at the end of current history.

A number of people asked me if the Lakota believed that an individual has several souls. At no time in the dialogue did the medicine men indicate that an individual has multiple souls. Direct inquiry of several men brought flat rejection. I believe that some of the difficulty in the older ethnographic literature came from a linguistic problem. The Lakota easily slip from saying **yamnica** (three types of) into saying **yamni** (three). In **Fools Crow** by Thomas E. Mails (Doubleday, p. 47), the medicine man is translated as saying, "There are three spirits that are involved when a person dies, and each person will enter one or the other." Further in the quotation, Fools Crow makes another distinction between the good and bad in a final judgment. In the Appendix of the same book, a 1904 article by Charles Eastman is quoted in which he first distinguishes a state for the wicked and then tells of the three souls (or soul-states) of deceased good men and women. The following descriptions are composites of thoughts shared by a number of the Rosebud medicine men and associates.

1) "The souls are here." This Lakota statement was heard from a number of sources, and it has different levels of meaning. Some traditional Lakota hold that after a person dies, the soul of the dead person stays near the body three days and then leaves on the fourth. Sometimes food and material things are placed at the grave and are believed to be used in a spirit form by the separated soul who stays near its grave. At other times, feasts are held at gravesites, especially on Memorial Day. Portions of food are set aside for the deceased who are believed to come and spiritually partake of the food presented. Sometimes the soul of a recently dead person is kept through a religious custom called Keep-A-Soul. In this custom, a lock of hair is cut from the head of the deceased, put into a special container, and put into a special place. One person is responsible every day for praying for, talking to, feeding, and protecting the soul from argument and spiritual contamination for one year. The guardian is to avoid drinking, arguing, fighting, and bad thoughts while performing sacrifices and gathering things so that in a year the soul may be spiritually well-prepared for its spirit journey. At the end of a year, the soul is ceremonially released with a feast, speeches, prayers and a request that the departed soul look back occasionally upon the loving relatives.

Unfortunately, the **nagi** (soul), **ton** (spiritual power), and **wakan** (sacredness) of the Keep-A-Soul ritual are rarely referred to today. This ritual has been recast into a Memorial Feast that takes place near the anniversary of a person's death. The words are seldom directed toward the departed soul or the gifts are only sparingly distributed to the poorest and oldest in the community. Rather the words are directed to the living friends and relatives and the gifts are given in appreciation to the pallbearers, ministers, all-night wakers, and supporters in the period of grieving. The emphasis is upon thanking the friends who helped rather than helping the needy and departed.

In the Jewish tradition at the time of Jesus, the Jews believed that the soul stayed with the body for three days and left on the fourth. In the New Testament it is noted that Jesus, who rose on the third day, did not experience corruption but Lazarus, who was in the tomb four days, was said to smell.

Although it is not currently popular in the Western Catholic tradition, the older Eastern Catholic tradition regularly refers to death as a state of "sleep" for the soul after death. This is understood to mean that when an ordinary person dies, the soul lapses into a state of unconsciousness at death so that the next moment of consciousness is the resurrection on the Last Day. People who think of death as sleep often consider the soul of the person remaining near the body in the cemetery. To disturb the remains of a person's body is to disturb the soul of that person. This helps explain why many ghost appearances are said to occur in or near a cemetery. Associated with this belief, the Roman Catholic Church has maintained the prayer, "May the souls of the Faithful departed **rest** in peace."

The Jewish word **Sheol** is associated with the Greek word **Hades** and the Latin word **Limbo.** Sheol was a shadowy place just beneath the ground; the grave was its entrance door. Here there were no activities, praise, or hope. One's relatives were there, but there was no joyful interaction, only stillness and quiet. Christian theology speaks of the limbo of the patriarchs and the limbo of the infants. The word "limbo" refers to the "rim" of hell. The annotated Apostles' Creed adds that Christ "descended into hell." This "hell" was not the fiery pit of "Gehenna" but the limbo of the Patriarchs, who were righteous but who needed to be saved by Christ to enter into God's heavenly Kingdom (I Pet 3:19). In Sheol and Limbo, there is no physical pain from sin but a sense of loss of full life. In the Lakota, Jewish, and Christian traditions, there is an awareness that in some sense the soul of a dead person remains close to the edge of their past life — inactive but near the body of the departed, whether buried, laid on a scaffold, or spiritually held in a hair-lock from the body of the deceased.

2) The Lakota recognize that some individuals, even of their own, do not live respectful lives. If wicked persons fall off the Red Path, traditional Lakota say that they have lost their sense of direction toward the south toward which they are going [**itokagatakiya**]. They say that lost souls wander [**onuniya u**] the earth, hiding in the distant shadows by day and wandering over the countryside, especially around favorite old haunts, by night. These are the pitiful, hungry ones for whom traditional Lakota make and toss outside a food offering before every meal. It is said that at night a person can hear them howling and gnashing their

teeth. One Lakota said, ''I saw a man with blood flowing from the left side of his mouth.'' The religious Lakota shows pity for them by regularly offering them food, sweet drink, and tobacco. The author never heard any prayers that these wandering ghosts might find their way to the ''good land'' where righteous ghosts go; Lakota prefer to avoid any reference to them and simply let them go their own way. There is an implicit association between their fear that ghosts will do some harm to a person and their notion that wandering souls are bad, or are of bad people. Consequently, priests are regularly requested to bless houses and drive them away. They are also asked to say Masses for poor souls who are described as painfully wandering nearby and in great need. The sacrifice and prayers of Christ are recognized as having a corrective effect on the fate of unsettled souls.

The Jews too recognized that there were unrepentant sinners, who had violated God's law and had hurt many people. ''Gehenna'' became a term used of the lowest part of the underworld, **Sheol;** it was the ''bottomless pit'' leading to the abyss where all the evil monsters of the deep were found. The greater the depth, the greater the darkness, the greater the isolation from the people, the more terrible the smell, the more chilling the fear, the more horrible the pain at the hands of the monsters of the deep. Linked with this was the coming of God's punitive and purifying fires from the heavens, as at Sodom and Gomorrah. In many ways this was a dungeon image.

''Hell'' is described as being beneath the earth, and those who ''wander'' from the narrow path of righteousness and become ''lost'' are said to go there. While the Lakota graphically picture the ''wandering'' as horizontally away from them toward the unknown parts of earth. Christians graphically picture the ''wandering'' of a sinner as downward into the depths of the earth. With the Lakota's respect for Grandmother Earth, it is understandable that the offenders are pictured going off into hostile, enemy territory. Since the Jews and Christians generally see the earth as at a distance from God and cursed, it is understandable that they would graphically depict the worst place as the lowest place. As a counter-point to the heavenly Messiah, the Christian hell also has a leader, Satan.

For many years there was a debate over the question: ''When do the damned go to hell; after the final judgment or after the soul's particular judgment?'' Rome finally terminated the debate saying ambiguously that the damned go to hell **mox** (soon) after death. The true Christian hell is different from the Jewish Gehennah insofar as separated evil souls go to Gehennah after death but evil **people** go body and soul to hell only on the Last Day. There, the unrepentant, hard-hearted sinner will be in darkness, outside the heavenly banquet hall looking in, angry, crying, stubborn, hurting, etc.

Many people have great difficulty with the idea that there are places of punishment and pain after death for the unrighteous. The oldest Lakota and Christian traditions recognize that everything is not all sweetness and pleasure after death. But can we say for sure that anyone will go to hell? The Catholic Church has repeatedly made judgments concerning saints whom it recognizes to be in heaven. But the Church has refused repeatedly to make any absolute statements concerning who is in hell. There are scriptural teachings that indicate that **most** go to hell, but these are eschatological warnings and are therefore somewhat exaggerated. As to the question who will go to hell, that decision has been given only to Christ, who both sees our deeds and can read our hearts fairly, since he was one of us and shared in our struggles. (It will be seen later that the Lakota have a similar judging person.) The Church even refrains from saying definitively that Judas is condemned to hell. Still the eschatological warning remains: Beware, change, repent, hell is a definite possibility for you!

The Lakota asked many questions concerning hell. One Lakota-Christian grandmother put her greatest dilemma this way: "Will all my relatives be with me in heaven? If some of them are going to be apart from me in hell, then heaven will not be heaven to me, for I love my relatives very much and am sad whenever I am apart from them." This is a very Lakota question, although Augustine asked a similar one. I will answer it in a Lakota way with a story that has meant a lot to the Indians I have told it to.

What is the Kingdom of heaven like? The Kingdom of heaven is like a great feast put on in honor of one's grandfather. All the relatives are invited. One girl, however, doesn't want to go and show her respect for her grandfather. Rather, she wants to go with her friends to a movie. The mother talks to her and tells her that she cannot give her money for the movie, for then **she** would be a party in the granddaughter's disrespect. When the girl arrives at the grandfather's home with her mother, she stomps in the house, plops down on the couch, folds her arms, bows her head, and sulks. Everyone else is happy to be there and greets each other with laughter and stories. Their happiness makes her all the angrier. Their greetings are answered with "Hunhhhhh's", as she buries herself more and more into the corner of the couch. All the other relatives are happy to see her and each other. She sees none of them — only herself, and she hates herself as she is. All the other relatives are feasting heavenly; she is starving in a hell.

In both the Lakota and Christian religions, it is possible to distinguish **two** "happy" soul-states: one special and the other ordinary. The first tends to be active in relationship to the living; the second tends to be passive. These two states are related to the two aspects of eschatology: one is primarily active now, and the other is primarily active later. In some ways, these are one, but there is value in looking at them as two.

3) A good number of Lakota talked about the souls of Lakota chiefs and medicine men going to the mountains in the West. Rawhide Butte was mentioned a number of times. It is also from that direction that the ghosts of Lakota heroes and great medicine men come to help the current medicine men in their ceremonies for the people. These ghosts come with power, visions, and wisdom. They call individual men forward into leadership positions among the people. Thus these ghosts are associated with the "renewal" of the medicine men and the people. It is fitting that they come from the West, the first direction.

In Judaism, there was a gradual movement from a dark, earthly Sheol state for the ordinary person to a bright, heavenly "Paradise" for religious heroes. Elijah was taken up to heaven in a fiery chariot. Enoch was said to ascend into the heavens. Popular tradition had the body of Moses taken up into heaven after his burial. In the Book of Daniel, the martyrs, corporately under the title "son of man," were presented to the Almighty in heaven before being given God's kingdom on earth. Like the "son of man," Enoch, Elijah, and Moses, the great prophets were to return to earth to share in the establishment of God's kingdom and dominion on the earth.

After the death, resurrection and ascension of Christ, the Church recognized a special place for the apostles and martyrs in heaven (Rev 4). These were recognized to have special influence on the direction of the patriarchal churches and the reparation of sins, respectively. Later the Church expanded its recognition to include those holy people whose entire life was a profession of Faith and sacrifice for the Faith, the confessors. These three groups are said to have a special guiding and intercessory role for the welfare of the Church even today.

4) The Lakota traditionally talked about how the ordinary good person walks the spiritual Red Path from North to South during this life. In death, the soul is said to take the Ghost Path [**Wanagi Canku**]; they say this pointing upward to the Milky Way. The place where ordinary good souls go is called by several names: **Wanagi Makoce** (Ghost Country), **Tahca Makoce** (Deer Country), **Ta[k]te Makoce** (Deer-killing Country). The last name is close to the White's expression "Happy Hunting Ground." Some

say there is an Old Woman who stands near the end of the Ghost Path as it passes over that river in the South which is the boundary to this land. Those who are not fit, she "throws off the cliff." She has been called the "Ghost Woman" and "Owl Woman." Some say judgment is made according to good deeds; others say religious deeds; others say she looks for a tatoo. The South is the gathering place of all of the relatives and all the animals. This is an earth-like paradise, with feasting, hunting, dancing, and family reunions. The Lakota only mention their blood relatives being there. Other races or nations are not mentioned.

After the Jews realized that righteous heroes had a place in heaven, they gradually began to recognize that the ordinary righteous person also had a place in heaven. Gradually, the Jewish heaven opened to all righteous Jews. It was in this context that Jesus spoke of an angel taking Lazarus up to Abraham's bosom, above the firmament of the sky (Lk 16:19-31). Paul speaks of the paradise in the third heaven (2 Cor 12:2-4). It was to this heavenly paradise that Jesus was probably referring when he spoke to the good thief (Lk 23:43). The idea that **ordinary**, virtuous Christian's souls go to heaven sometime between their death and the final resurrection on the Last Day is a rather recent belief in the Christian Church. In the early days, the focus was upon the Last Day, which they thought was very imminent. The idea that the ordinary Christian "sleeps" in the grave until the Last Day was sufficient. Gradually the notion of a particular judgment after death anteceded and supplemented the general judgment on the Last Day. After death, the life history of an individual is said to be brought forth at a particular judgment before Christ. If there were no mortal sins, then the soul of the person would be purified on its journey to heaven. (The Church never said Purgatory was a place but a state or passage or journey of purification between earthly and heavenly life for a venial sinner.) To me it seems proper to say that there may be **some** souls besides the officially canonized saints that the Lord may judge worthy to go to a heavenly state now, still there may be **some** righteous souls whom the Lord may see fit to suspend in a sleep-like state until the Last Day.

5) Just as the Lakota have few origin myths, so too they have few myths concerning the end. The author heard this myth in several places. Some people say that there is a Great Buffalo standing over the earth. He has lifted one leg. He has lifted a second leg. He has lifted a third leg. Now he stands on the fourth leg. It is said that when the Lakota do not live right, he will lift his fourth leg, and the Great Buffalo will fall, and the world will end. It is also said that each year a hair falls from a leg of the Great Buffalo, and that a leg falls off at the end of each age. He is on his last leg now.

When the last leg is gone, he can no longer hold back the flood from the West, which periodically purifies the world of all life.

The Jews hold tightly to the promises that God made to Abraham. When Elijah returns, the Jewish people will possess the land of Israel, and the kingdom of David will be established in peace and prosperity before all the nations. When that happens, all the dead Jews will rise to share in the benefits of the eschatological kingdom.

Christians believe that as Christ went up to heaven, he shall return to the earth. The dead of every nation shall rise to be judged by Christ, and the evil ones will be sent to their perdition. The worthy will witness the coming of the kingdom of heaven on earth where they shall prosper, rejoice, never weep, and see the face of God eternally. Thus the heaven of the saints today is not the Kingdom of Heaven of the End Times. Then those who are worthy will experience God, Christ, and the Holy Spirit, and the Holy People of God not in the spirit only but also in glorified, immortal flesh — humanity totally fulfilled and transcendent.

A summary thought for this section. Several times the Lakota participants asked the priests the question, "Where do ghosts go after death?" In answer the priests were ambiguous for several reasons. They always gave a **type** of place rather than a specific location. Because of their modern, scientific training and study of scriptural exegesis, they knew that the descriptions in scripture were highly symbolic. They spoke of soul-states rather than soul-locations. Christian descriptions of after-life states are ranked vertically according to the soul's relationship to God. The Lakota descriptions of after-life locations are conceived in a horizontal plane marking the soul's relationship to his/her relatives. Therefore, when a person realizes that the priests and the medicine men describe different aspects of the after-life (relationship to God/relationship to relatives), one can see that there is nothing theologically incompatible between the Christian and Lakota descriptions of the after-life.

The Lakota's belief in limited reincarnation caught the pastors by surprise. The fact that the Lakota brought out this suppressed belief in the dialogue indicates the openness that was fostered there. The critical reaction of the priests was taken as a great insult to the trust that the Lakota had extended to the pastors. These Lakota were mostly faithful Christians. How could they believe also in reincarnations?

Most of the priests' understanding of reincarnation originated from the Far East. The Hindu teaching of reincarnation is linked to the law of karma and is applied to all. The law of karma says that one's future life depends entirely on what one did in one's previous life. A sinner would receive a more pitiful state the next time around; the saint would receive a higher state the next time around. Thus a person's ascent toward God (Brahmin-Atman) is a mechanical response to a person's own efforts. Buddha indicated a shorter way to union with God through (nihilistic) meditations in which the material world and its forms are affirmed to be not real but only illusions [maya]. A Christian cannot accept the Eastern teaching on reincarnation for two very solid theological reasons. In its own way, this scheme is Palegianistic; it says that union with God is really the product of a person's own efforts rather than a gift from God through Christ. Secondly, the final state is one of total dematerialization, which is contrary to the Church's teachings on the true incarnation of the Son of God and the resurrectional character of the Kingdom on the Last Day. Theologically, the strongest Christian complaints against the Hindu theory of reincarnation is not the reincarnation aspect, as such, but the principles of karma and maya which give Hindu reincarnation its progressive character.

In inter-testamental times, the centuries closest to Jesus' day, the Jews believed in multiple reappearances in a way that might be called "reincarnational." Heroes of the past were prophesied to appear humanly among the people again; they did not necessarily have to have the same form, but the people expected them to act in the same, great ways. In one of the most popular apocryphal books of the Old Testament, God was represented as saying, "For your help I will send my servants Isaiah and Jeremiah." (2 Esdras 2:18) Not only Elijah (Mal 3:23) but also Jeremiah were regarded as forerunners of the Messiah and champions of the people when they were in need.

What was **Christ's** attitude toward reincarnation? The notion of reincarnation, especially of great men, was popularly accepted in Christ's day. Toward the middle of his public ministry, Christ asked, "Who do people say the Son of Man is?" And they said, "Some say John the Baptist; some, Elias; and others Jeremia or one of the prophets." (Mt 16:13-16). This response indicates that some popularly thought Jesus was a returned figure from the past. (See also (John 1:21).) Rather than reacting against this popular understanding, Christ goes on to a more important question, "But who do you say that I am?" Simon Peter replied, "You are the Christ, the Son of the living God." Notice Christ's response in reference to the popular belief in multiple reincarnations. Jesus never condemned their notion of reincarnation as false, invalid, or pastorally counter-productive. Rather Christ handled this notion of reincarnation as he did other Old Testament ideas. He respectfully accepted it as given within the Old Testament and Jewish tradition, and then after making reference to it, he invited his hearers to go beyond it.

In the New Testament, one statement seems to go against the possibility of reincarnation, namely, "Just as it is appointed that all die once, and after death be judged, so Christ was offered up once to take away their sins." (Heb 9:27) In this quotation, how is the word "appointed" to be understood? Certainly it cannot mean a positive, divine law. Both Elisha and Jesus raised people from the dead, and the implication is that these would die twice. The Greek word for "appointed" is **apokeitai,** which means: laid off, laid aside, reserved, appointed. This is not an absolute juridical term. Throughout the Letter to the Hebrews the method of argumentation is very Jewish. This statement is illustrative and reflective rather than absolute.

The Church, however, a few centuries later did formally condemn **Christian** belief in reincarnation. Examining the notion of reincarnation theologically, one can see how it is inconsistent for a person to believe in Jesus as his Savior and believe in reincarnation **for himself.** When a person believes in the death and resurrection of Jesus, he knows that he is saved and is destined for union with God in heaven. The word "believe," however, is very different from the word "know," especially in the Greek tradition. This difference permits the following distinction. While it is wrong for a Christian to believe in reincarnation as a possibility for oneself or any believing Christian, one can intellectually know of non-karmic reincarnation as a possibility for a non-believer.

After talking to a good number of priests on the subject of reincarnation, the author found that their main objections to reincarnation were not theological but philosophical. Maintaining the Jewish view of humans in which there always remains a uniquely identifiable body-soul unity, they always want to associate **this** soul with **this** body. Yet science tells us that all the cells of our body are regularly replaced. One's current body is materially linked to the code within one's DNA molecular chain, which can be severely altered through various chemical and radiational treatments. These days organs are removed and added. Plastic surgery can radically alter the looks of people. A person can suffer from extreme amnesia and effectively begin a new personal life. A person can suffer a severe personal trauma so that one's psyche is radically altered. The resurrection narratives indicate that the physical appearance of the body of Christ changed radically and unrecognizably in his "reincarnation," yet despite the change of appearance and behavior, his disciples knew it was Jesus. In what ways are the resurrected body of Jesus and the pre-resurrected body of Jesus one? There are many things that we scientifically know today which raise many questions about the long-held Judeo-Christian philosophical understanding of the unity and identity of the human body and soul.

When the pastors asked for evidence for reincarnation, the Lakota tended to be not as precise as the pastors wanted. The Lakota publicly spoke of two different ways. They noted that sometimes, soon after a relative dies prematurely, a child will be born who has the distinctive physical markings, mannerisms, attitudes, and knowledge of things of the one who died. They also noted that sometimes an adult comes up quietly behind a child as he/she is talking like an adult to his/her companions, teaching them and showing them things with the wisdom and ways of an adult. The child is said to stop this as soon as the adult observer is recognized. Privately, different Indians mentioned various **deja vu** experiences, where they knew what was in an area ahead because they "knew" they had been there before. One young man described the inner intricacies of a very old building as it was some sixty years before; old timers later verified that that was the way it was long ago before multiple renovations. But there are multiple different explanations for these phenomena besides reincarnation.

One of the better scientific studies of reincarnation was done by Dr. Ian Stevenson as reported in the **Journal of Nervous and Mental Diseases** (September, 1978). After a 20-year study of 1,600 cases of reported reincarnation, Dr. Stevenson's work indicates a clear pattern in cases involving young children. Here between the ages of 2 and 4 such a child starts telling parents and others that he/she remembers a previous life and begins showing behavior patterns which fit those stories and which are often strikingly different from the child's current upbringing. Often the children indicate who their former parents are, where they live, and their desire to go there. There, the child identifies different people of that area. "The child is then usually found to be accurate in about 90 percent of the statements he has been making." After rising to peak of obsession and detail, the child's "memory" starts to fade between 3 and 5, and the child then returns to develop normally. Still, phobias often remain that are associated with the "remembered" death. In these cases there is a very high incidence of violent death in the previous "life" — sometimes suicide and often murder.

There are various possible explanations for the above phenomena other than reincarnation. For example, certain children at that age may be highly resonant to or easily possessed by the wandering, lost ghost of a dead person. An examination of the data indicates that the traditional Eastern principle of universal karma is not operative in most cases. Likewise, the evidence goes against the common Western notion that reincarnation is a "second chance" for a life "botched up" the first time. These accounts indicate that reincarnation incidents, like many ghost appearances, seem to be regularly the product of psychic confusion associated with a violent and unseemly death. Rather than being glorified or denied, the reincarnation accounts indicate a situation that generally should be pitied and prayed for.

Rather than talking dogmatically like those Christians who theologically and philosophically deny the possibility of reincarnation in every case, or speaking fatalistically like those Hindus who theologically and philosophically assume the inevitability of reincarnation to all but the highest caste, the Lakota treat reincarnation as a thing that is possible, occasional, exceptional, and **wakan.** When a Lakota observer is faced with data that indicates experientially that one is dealing with a reincarnated personality, one tries to keep a respectful distance from that phenomena, and then tries to live as sincerely, generously, and ordinarily as possible around it. In my mind the traditional Lakota position on this matter has a tremendous amount of wisdom and respect to it. Similarly, the author finds a tremendous amount of wisdom and respect in Christ's position. He never rejected the popular understanding of occasional, non-karmic reincarnation as theologically impossible; all things are possible with the Lord. Rather his concern was the lifting of the minds and faith of the people above this, proclaiming the good news that eternal peace, salvation, and fulfillment **will** be realized by all who believe in him as the Son of God and their Savior.

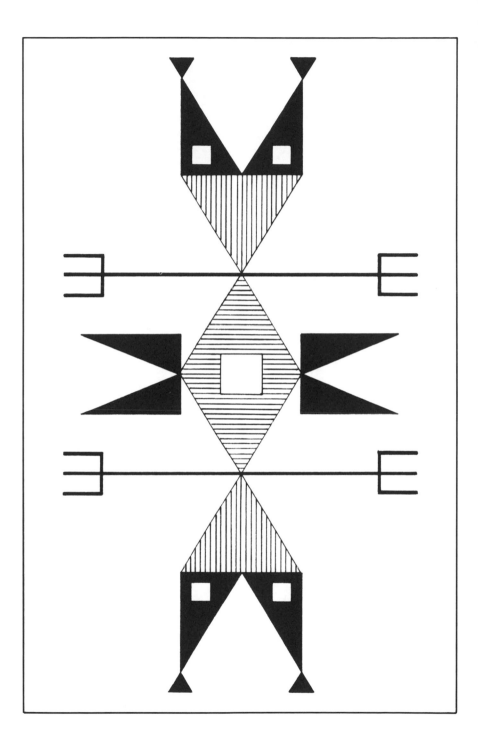

Chapter 7
On Lakota Spirits

Some Lakota people objected to the discussion of Lakota spirits at the Medicine Men and Pastors' Meeting; they said that it would bring misfortune, for people should not be misusing things that are sacred, **taku wakan kin.** The subject of Lakota spirits was not considered until after several years of discussion when an air of mutual religious respect was established. The medicine men made an important distinction. They said that some things are general and should be generally known, like the Buffalo Calf Woman story. These things should be taught to the people so they will have understanding and respect for sacred things. They said that other things are specific visions for a particular person. Many visions, like a medicine man's visions which give him his spiritual power, should either not be shared with anyone or should be shared only within a strict Lakota ceremonial situation. A few personal visions can be shared with many; most are not. So what is presented in this chapter are general statements about Lakota spirits and only specific spiritual experiences that the teller felt were more important to tell for the instruction of others.

Many people have the impression that all spirits think and act alike. That is because of their unfamiliarity with them. . .just as all Orientals, or Blacks, or Mexicans look alike to those who have little dealing with them. But as a person has closer contact with Lakota ceremonies and perhaps even Lakota spirits, different spirits show very different ways of listening and responding. Some spirits take the words spoken in a ceremony very literally; other spirits are able to know what a person is feeling, more than one's words would express; others are able to read thoughts while others cannot. In my experience, some spirits appear to be quite child-like and naive. Some appear to be adolescent and crafty. Some seem to be adult and businesslike. Others appear to be old and spiritually very profound. The personalities of the spirits who come into meetings to a medicine man are frequently quite different from the personality of the medicine man putting on the meeting. It seems quite wrong for someone to make a single judgement about all Lakota spirits, for some are very different from others.

The Lakota generally perceive their spirits to be locational, that is, at only one place at one time. For example, at a ceremony, a woman asked the spirits how a relative of hers was doing in a very distant hospital. The medicine man said that the spirits would go and find out. There was a quick sound of motion and then silence. The medicine man called for a song. About halfway through the song, there was suddenly a flurry of sound about the room as the spirit returned. Through the medicine man, the spirit's report on the condition of the patient was announced. It seems that the lower-leveled spirits show themselves in very localized and recognizable shapes; the higher-leveled spirits are much more omniscient and spontaneous in their effects in distant locations. The Christian Holy Spirit is very pervasive primarily inside of things, although he works on the outside in the material world at times. Christian angels are, however, usually reported as extrinsically located in the universe.

Over the years there has been a shift in the type of spirits used by the medicine men. In the past, most of the medicine men used animal spirits predominantly. Today there is an emphasis upon human-like spirits. The Lakota believe that there are spirits of every type of animal and thing in the universe. Appearing in the form of these animals and obviously closely related to them, these spirits can communicate with different individuals. Animal spirits closely associated with medicine men's ceremonies these days are: blacktail deer, eagle, buffalo, prairie dog, hawk, bear, and spider.

The rattlesnake is called a tester. On the hill during a vision quest, one may hear the sound of a rattlesnake's rattle coming from under the sage one is sitting on. The following story is told about an early **Yuwipi** man named Chips. A certain man wanted to be a medicine man, and he kept nagging Chips to help him become one. Finally Chips told him to follow him. They walked a long distance until Chips stopped in front of a curled up rattle-snake. Chips told the man to grab hold of the snake. Did he have faith enough to pick it up if Chips told him he would not be hurt by it? The man was very scared and didn't want to do it. Chips pointed out that he would have to do very hard things to become a medicine man. If he couldn't do this, he could never become one. Finally the man got himself to the point where he quickly grabbed the snake and immediately turned away. But what did he have in his hand? Only a cow chip! It had only appeared to be a rattle-snake. Chips said, ''To be a medicine man, you have to be ready for things like that." The man no longer wanted to be a medicine man.

Another story is told by another medicine man. As he was sitting on the hill surrounded by tobacco ties with only a Pipe, a rattlesnake slowly came up the hill toward him. He prayed and had faith in the power of the tobacco ties to protect him from harm. But the snake came right toward him, crawling right over those tobacco ties. It came right to his crossed legs and crawled over them into his lap and coiled himself there. Then the snake slowly peaked its head out to the left and pulled it back. Then the snake peaked its head out in front and then to the right. Meanwhile the medicine man was shaking inside with fear and praying his heart out. The snake then bumps his head against his belly and then slid itself up until it looked straight into the eyes of the medicine man. It lowered its head then, turned and slowly crawled deep into his crotch. Then the snake crawled over his legs and headed back toward the tobacco ties around the sacred area. The rattlesnake then stopped, turned toward the medicine man and said, "Brother." It then turned back, crawled over the line of ties, and disappeared in the grass. After this story, the medicine man said cynically, "And who wants to be a brother to a rattlesnake?"

Another medicine man said that he had a dream about finding a particular medicine. In the dream, he was walking in a certain place. Suddenly he heard rattle sounds above. He looked down on the ground and there was a snake coiled around a tall weed. He looked carefully at the weed. It was the medicine he was to use. When he woke up, he went to the place indicated in the dream. Everything happened just as the dream indicated. The snake showed him the medicine to use for healing a particular sick person.

The black-footed ferret, **itopta sapa,** is noted for its ability to foresee the future. It lives in prairie dog holes alongside of rattlesnakes. But they haven't been seen on the reservation for a number of years.

The black-tail deer still commonly appears in visions and ceremonies. Its tail is often attached to the central pole in ceremonies. It is known by its snort. Little is said about the actions of this spirit other than a general healing power, sometimes associated with touches.

Originally, healing ceremonies were performed in daylight rather than in the darkness as now. One Full-blood tells of his grandfather's healing ceremonies. The living room was cleared, and the person was placed on the floor on the other side of the room. Since his grandfather was a bear medicine man, after the sweatbath he put a full bear robe over himself with the bear's head as a cap. Even though he was blind, he put on a blindfold. His hands were fitted into the huge bear claws. (The Pipe was not reported being used in this ceremony.) The grandfather then stood at the door opposite the patient. He always told his vision, even though everyone had heard it many times. Then he sang several of his songs, calling the spirit to him. Then he got on his hands and knees and started to sway back and forth as he growled and crawled toward the sick person. Just before he reached the sick person, the medicine man reared up on his hind legs and gave a huge roar. Suddenly he pounced upon the patient and started sucking at the place of the sickness. After a short time of sucking feverishly, he turned suddenly, and the people said, ''He has it.'' The medicine man then bounded across the room and vomited something into a bucket standing beside the door. After he rested a bit, there were further prayers and songs. After the meeting they dug a hole out back and dumped what was in the bucket into the hole. ''He must have helped the people because they kept coming back for healings.''

Another animal with healing power is the prairie dog. A woman gave the following testimonial. ''I had a stroke, and they were going to take me to Omaha. We got this medicine man to doctor me, but he didn't use gourds. One eye was down and half of my body was paralyzed. But something doctored me that had small hands. They said that this was a prairie dog. I got well the next day. My body returned to normal.''

The ceremony of the hawk medicine man was performed during the day, similar to the Bear Ceremony described above. It was said that whenever the medicine man sang his songs, one could always hear the call of a hawk coming in from outside.

At one time in the past there were a good number of Eagle medicine men. Now there are only a few. In their ceremonies, they usually use a square altar with green flags and tobacco ties. The different parts of a whole eagle are spread out before the altar. When the eagles come into the ceremony, they come from all directions, especially from the West. One can feel the gusts of wind coming from the flapping of their wings. This ceremony is done more for higher insights and solving difficult problems than for healing a sickness.

The fanning of a person with an eagle feather or eagle fan is refreshing in both a physical and spiritual way. Often an eagle fan is used to flutter the purifying and blessing smoke of sweatgrass on a person. Eagle feathers are greatly prized by Indians, and their distribution is monitored by the federal government. In a powwow, the falling of an eagle feather from a costume in the public area is considered spiritually very bad, requiring great sacrifice for the reparation of this wrong. At one dance, when an eagle feather fell from a dancer's roach, everyone felt so bad that the dancer gave his car away in atonement.

The owl is not used in Lakota ceremonies. It is often a forewarner of death. Although many consider such an association superstitious, I have found a surprisingly high correlation between the coming of an owl to a house with an imminent death of a relative of that household, with the departure of the owl thereafter. It is said that the softness of its feathers tells how gentle a person should be with one who is sorrowful.

The following experience happened to me which made me raise my eyebrows. One day I was driving along the interstate not too far from the reservation. I saw an owl laying dead at the side of the road. I thought I might use its parts for something, so I stopped to put it into the trunk. When I got in up front to drive on, my car's engine would turn over but not start. After checking the motor, I still couldn't get it to start. So I tried to reconstruct the situation from the time the car was last running and removed the bird from the trunk. I got in again, and the car started right up. I drove off, but after going a short distance I thought this was ridiculous and superstitious, and I turned around and drove back. This time I kept the car running. I put the bird into the trunk and started to leave. The car sputtered to a stop. I tried to get the car started but couldn't. Again I took the bird out, got in front again, and the car started right up. Keeping the motor running again, I went back and set the bird in the trunk. The moment the bird touched the trunk, the motor stopped! I then took the owl and threw it far into the ditch. I got back in my car, which started immediately, and drove off rapidly, never looking back. I never experienced trouble with my car like that again.

The Rock-spirits, **Inyan Wašicu,** are used by the Lakota not only in the sweatbath but also in vision quests and in other ceremonies. There are said to be 405 of these spirits, which is the number of tobacco ties usually prepared for the circle of offerings around the sacred areas of ceremonies. They are said to come from the stars. They protect the seeker from all harm from other spirits; thus they are very powerful and strong in comparison to other spirits. They speak to the medicine man in the sweatlodge; they speak fast and are called **Inyan Wašicu.** Some medicine men say they put 405 small quartz stones from the rim of ant hills into hardened leather pouches to make ceremonial rattles that are used by the spirits in a **wakan** way in **Yuwipi** ceremonies. Quartz and other unusual stones are used to line and decorate Lakota graves for aesthetic as well as spiritual reasons. Small, smooth, round stones or stones with special marking or spiritual power are put into leather pouches and worn around one's neck as a medicine, that is, a spiritual healer and helper.

The following story was told by a Full-blood who was present as a child at a rock-medicine man's healing of his aunt. She was placed all alone on the floor of their house. Everyone was told not to go in until the ceremony was over. The medicine man made a sweatbath outside. While he prayed inside the lodge, the young nephew ran back and forth between the lodge and the house. When the medicine man opened the sweatlodge, he told the boy that he could go in the house now. The boy dashed in and asked his aunt whether a spirit had come. She said one did and pointed to a small stone lying on the floor beside her. She said it appeared from nowhere and began to hit her all around the place of her sickness. When it was finished, it simply dropped to the ground right where he saw it. She didn't want to touch it. He couldn't believe what his aunt had said. It sounded so fantastic. He just stared at that stone on the ground. The aunt quickly got well.

A number of medicine men have an **Heyoka** (Clown or Contrary) spirit. The clown is associated with the West and lightning. A woman received a clown spirit, and she said she could hear the thunder come long before anyone else could. It scared her, so she got it wiped off by a medicine man.

A story is told of a woman who kept her clown vision. A large prairie fire broke out and was spreading toward a large Rosebud powwow encampment. Everyone was scared. They did what they could but they couldn't put it out and it just kept coming. Then this woman, known to have a clown spirit, ran forward. She unbraided her hair on one side. She tore off the bottom of her dress, her legging, and her sleeve on that side. Then she dashed in and out of the flames with the one side exposed. Suddenly the fire just died, just before it reached the edge of the camp.

The **Heyoka** spirit has a person do things which a person would not normally do, for the welfare of the people. It demands a great willingness to sacrifice oneself for the life of the relatives. A Full-blood woman said, "My father is a clown, and he has participated in the clown ceremony. I have pictures of my father participating in the clown ceremony to prove it. They put three poles together there and hung the kettle there. They boiled the dog. When the fire died down, my father came singing. He put his bare hand into the kettle and fished the dog head out. I have pictures. 1957. The log house at our place, that is where he did the ceremony." The dog head that was fished out of the boiling-hot pot of soup with his bare hand was given to the sickest person there as a medicine.

In preparation for the coming of the **Heyoka** spirit in a meeting, a dog is strangled. The Lakota do not have the same beliefs as the biblical Caananites, who strangled animals to keep the spirit of the animal inside so that they would absorb the life characteristics of the animal within them as they ate it at a meal. Quite to the contrary. The Lakota beliefs are much closer to the Judeo-Christian understanding of things. "The dog was very important to the Indians, for before the horse arrived, the Indians relied on the dogs, who helped them more than any other animal. To sacrifice a dog was to sacrifice the animal closest to you," said a well-educated, traditional Full-blood. The dog is strangled because that is the least violent and the most quiet way of doing it. The Lakota are very careful that the dog does not let out a yelp. The affection accorded a dog by Lakota children is like the love shown a lamb by a nomad family in the Middle East. As in the Jewish sacrificial tradition, it is the offering and the communal feast, and not the death of the animal, that is important. The killing of the dog for the **Heyoka** is a contrariness: the dying of the dog marks the healing of the sick human. As a Full-blood said, "In doctoring a sick person, the dog takes the place of the sick person so that he can become well." The dying of the dog for the healing of the sick person is the Lakota parallel to the Christian belief that Christ died that sinners might live.

Contrariness is the essence of humor. Indian Clowns exercise their visions by doing things backwards, like walking backwards, talking backwards, wearing winter clothes in summer and summer clothes in winter. Their role as corrective mimic can still be seen at some powwows. Here they do not dress in their finest feathers but in the rags and costume seen in their vision, often whitened skin or tights, blue or black lines, and big circles around their eyes and a long nose. At a dance, a clown will come up behind a dancer who is dancing or dressed in an unusual way. The clown will then mock the fault terribly and thus point out to everyone that what the **Heyoka** is mocking is not **"right,"** and the person doing it **"wrong"** will stop doing it and walk away from the clown at whom everyone is laughing. This is but one of several ways that the Lakota people not directly but indirectly tell others of their mistakes.

When the **Heyoka** spirits come in a ceremony, usually near the end, they talk contrariwise. For example, they might say, "The Pipe is not sacred," which means "The Pipe **is** sacred." "This man will die" means "This man will live." "You are all stupid to be here" should be understood to mean "You are all smart to be here." "You are right to say this man will get better" really is a nice way of saying, "You are wrong to say that this man will get better." Through the clown-spirit, a negative message may more easily be said. But there is a problem here. I asked a medicine man, "Do you have a clown?" He answered, "Yes, but I don't use him. He mixes people up. People don't understand him. He comes in and says things backward, and people go out and say my spirits say this and they get it backwards and get me in trouble."

One of the last of the spirits a medicine man becomes familiar with are the **Pehin San** (Grey Hairs). They are the Old Men. They are very quiet. The medicine men use a square altar in calling them. "They are there to see that everything is right. They don't say much, but what they do say is deep. You don't understand what they say for a long time, and then all of a sudden, you understand a part of it. They are there to keep the medicine men in line. If they are there, you must do it right." It is said these spirits are the best healers. The **Pehin San** are spirits and should not be confused with the **ghosts** of medicine men and warriors of the past who come to some spirit ceremonies to help the people. Ghosts are spiritual manifestations of humans who once grew up from childhood in a material form, died, and then subsequently took a spiritual form. Spirits never die, originate in a particular spiritual form, and only occasionally take a material form.

One of the first spirits that the medicine men usually encounter are the **Iktomi** (Spider-spirits). Some **Iktomi** spirits are clearly female. They are sometimes called the trickster, and it is with this spirit that both Lakota and Christians have difficulty — but for different reasons.

Iktomi is the central character in many Lakota stories. Many of these stories are fictional and created for entertainment purposes. However, while some are bawdy, others are educational. **Iktomi** is usually described as a man with a big body and thin arms and legs. In the stories, the **Iktomi** is a semi-hero. They usually get what they want from others through their cleverness and stealth. Still they can get hilariously and painfully caught in their own webbing. Tales from Western Europe make all-good victims and heroes face and overcome all-evil villians in a dualistic struggle in which the evil ones are destroyed and the good ones live happily ever after. Lakota tales show **Iktomi** to be both greedily self-centered at times as well as generously helpful at times. Rather than promoting absolute idealism, **Iktomi** portrays a mixed realism. The real **Iktomi** spirits do not always show a good side, and therefore they are easily identified by some Christians with evil spirits who sometimes show themselves as angels of light. We will have to discuss this matter more later.

In many ways, the **Iktomi** spirits appear to be adolescent. They need strong direction by the medicine man. They are concerned about receiving many material things. They take the words of a person literally. For example, the story is told of a woman who came to a ceremony because a couple of bigger boys were continually beating up her son. She asked the spirit to stop them. The spirit responded, ''Do you know what you are asking?'' The woman said she did and repeated her request. The spirit again said, ''Do you know what you are asking?'' The woman again responded that she did and started to repeat her request as before. Suddenly across the room another person shouted, ''Do you want the spirit to kill them?''•''Oh, no. No. No. I didn't mean that. . .'' Various other accounts point to this type of spirit's literal interpretation of requests. A person may wonder why would a person want to deal with an adolescent, trickster-type of spirit. The common medicine man's attitude is: They have talents that can be used to help the people. Keep them going the right way and don't let people use them for their own selfish purpose or in a wrong way.

The **Iktomi** spirits are especially good in dealing with material and secular problems, although they do some healing. They help a person get a needed car. They assist in getting relatives out of jail or winning a court case. They are sometimes called **wakiye wicaśa,** lawyers. Politicians praying for victory often come to medicine men so that the spider spirits can help them win elections. Of course, spiritual rivalries break out between the backers of the spirits of one medicine man and the spirits of another. As the years progress, more and more medicine men are refusing to let their spirits get into politics. The Lakota from experience are learning that what the spider spirits might do in a secular matter really may result in more harm than good. For example, when things seemed impossible in court for a certain young man who was in jail, the mother came and said she was lonesome for her son and wanted him home again. The spirit protested and asked if that was really what she wanted. She said, ''Yes.'' Through some small matter, the boy was released from jail the next day. He got drunk, went home, tore up the house, and beat the mother. The fellow was returned to jail, and the mother returned and said that the spirits were right in questioning her whether this was really the best thing.

For very difficult tasks, the **Iktomi** demand great prices: offerings in tobacco, large food offerings, sacrifices of various sorts. Many times the spirits say that it will do no good to know something or do something. For example, a person may want to know who stole a wallet with a large amount of money in it. The spirit tells that person that the money is gone, and there is no hope of recovering it. In a desire for revenge, the person wants to know nonetheless. For this knowledge that the spirit does not want to give, **Iktomi** indicates a great price. If a person has been lost in a storm and people cannot find the body, sometimes the spirits are able to tell the people, sometimes not. But if it can be done, **Iktomi** spirits often ask a great price.

What is a great price? A soul!!! This demand of a soul by a spirit brings to mind the story of Dr. Faustus, who sold his soul to the devil for worldly possessions. However, what is meant by "taking a soul" in the Lakota language is different from what it meant in the Faustus story. In the Faustus story, "selling his soul" to the devil meant that after Faustus' death, the devil would take dominion over Faustus' immortal soul and hold him forever in hell. For the Lakota, the soul **nagi** exists only to the point of death, then it leaves the body and becomes a ghost, **wanagi**. What the Lakota mean by the expression, "The spirit will take a soul" is "A human life must be offered in sacrificial payment for the spiritual blessing given." In other words, if persons wish to bring a special blessing to the family this way, they assume that every member of the family individually and corporately agrees that the spirits can take the life of any relative in order to receive this blessing. This is the type of religious thinking behind the sacrifice of Isaac, which God utilized to elicit Abraham's greatest act of faith: a faith that brought a blessing through Abraham's seed to all the nations of the world. At this offering, however, an angel of the Lord stopped Abraham's hand, and thereafter God condemned child sacrifice for the welfare of the people. Still, God did not spare his own Son, who died on the cross for our salvation. Nonetheless, in the course of Salvation History, God has been gradually moving the people away from human sacrifice and from blood sacrifices of all sorts. If one listens to the reticence of the **Iktomi** spirits within the meetings and from reports, one can hear their desire not to do those favors which require such a great price. Really, how great a material benefit is equal to the physical life of a relative?!!!

To a large extent, the **Iktomi** will do what is asked of them. In this way this Lakota spirit is like so many Lakota people, who will do just about anything because they can't say "No" to a request from a relative. Thus it is the morality of the medicine man which tempers and directs the **Iktomi** to do good material favors rather than bad ones. One medicine man said, "They are cooperative, but don't make fun of them, they can turn the tables on you." I asked a medicine man if any spirits were hard to handle. "Yes, the **Iktomi.** You have to control them, or they will lead you wrong." Another medicine man was more negative about them. "Spiders are dangerous and tricky. They are in medicine bundles.

They help get a woman, money, crookedness. They are daring. So you don't have to have money. There is death in it. I don't go too deep. I got too many grand-kids. N. had it. He would help anyone. He didn't live long. It fell on him. Powerful! The spider medicine man warns you. Don't get off the road. They will knock down your doctoring power."

I asked another Full-blood, "Long ago were there **Iktomi** medicine men?" His response indicated a distinction in his mind between **Iktomi** men and medicine men. He answered, "They didn't have anything to do with that spirit, that type of spirit. That's where you border on witchcraft. That was the type of spirit that a person would use if he would do anything for power, and I mean **anything!** The good medicine men never got involved in that kind of stuff. They had their own spirits and their own medicines." Do you know any **Iktomi** medicine men today? "No. I have never been at such a meeting." Besides the **Iktomi** spirits, are there other spirits that are bad? "Yes. Certainly. And you stay away from them."

Another person was asked, "Are there bad spirits?" This man answered, "Certainly. And the good spirits can warn of their coming. When people see one, they get palsy and their face wrinkles up, and they get paralyzed." When the medicine man prays with the Pipe and speaks about the Pipe, he tells the bad spirits not to approach, to stay away. Repeatedly in the medicine man's prayers one will hear them pray that nothing bad will happen. . .that only good will happen. The medicine men and the Lakota people know that they are dealing with something powerful. Unlike the traditional Catholic, they would prefer to avoid the bad and seek the good rather than suppress both.

One medicine man tells of another. "A man had a spider vision. The spirit told him, 'Wherever you live, wherever you are, toward your place there will be dust flying.' (This meant that people would be traveling the dirt roads to reach his place for ceremonies.) He continued practicing his spiderman vision. As he kept on going, there was good and bad. So he goes along, but he keeps the bad underneath." Another said, "If they are going to use this, pray to **Tunkasila.** If they want to do it in an evil spirit way, that could be done. And it could be in a good way too. Pray for it in a good way. There are two ways."

The Lakota are very afraid of the evil way. An old Indian said, "So this good and bad is in the spirit world. This good thing is pretty hard to do. We try to do something good, and this bad spirit comes, and he tries to stop us. Try to keep your senses. If you go into the bad spirit, you will have it. The bad spirit will try to stop you from doing good. It is possible for you to have a bad spirit as a friend, as you have a good spirit. But it would seem that the bad spirit would be easier. But doing this bad, you will pay for it with your loss of manhood." One medicine man said, "I keep that bad behind **nahma yuha**. I keep it out of sight, and just the good appears. So some of the medicine should do good, but they can do bad. I keep the bad part hid and just practice the good. I just want to practice the good and not practice the bad."

A good number of others said, "If they do it the bad way, the wrong way, it will backfire on them." Especially when major spirits are asked to assist an individual to seek revenge, say on an ex-boyfriend who is dating another girl, the spirits and the medicine men say that not only will the other girl get hurt, but for getting the boy back for only a short time, you will have more trouble. In so many domestic squabbles, revenge is sweet and the backlash is worse, but some will willingly suffer great pains tomorrow to have one's wants and pleasures today. In the Lakota way, revenge through the spirits is possible, not recommended, and painfully obtained.

Many priests think that the Lakota are not aware of, or morally responsive to, the dangers associated with evil spirits. In general, the Lakota do not like to talk about these things. They suppress them so strongly that they don't even like to mention them and their names. In the Lakota religion there is a tremendous emphasis upon the positive in approaching spirit matters. Traditionally the Catholic church has been very negative in its approach to spirit phenomena, always on the look-out for evil spirits, Satan, and sin. Professional Lakota medicine men are well aware that some spirits do come into ceremonies in such a way that they can do harm. That does not stop the Lakota medicine man from entering those ceremonies. Rather they pray more intently for protection and strive more intently for the welfare of the people and in the midst of many material and spiritual difficulties.

As a person listens carefully to the descriptions and attitudes of the medicine men, they have a different understanding of "evil spirits" than do Christians. When Christians speak of "evil spirits" they think of spirits who are always associated with Satan, the prince of darkness, and always want the eternal downfall of people. The Lakota, however, think of "evil spirits" as spirits who sometimes do things that are materially hurtful to people. Just as some would say that there are not evil men but only men who do evil, a Lakota would say that there are no evil spirits but only spirits who do evil. The reconciliation of the Lakota and the Christian understanding of spirits, especially "evil spirits" was most important in the medicine men and pastors' dialogue.

Chapter 8

Lakota Spirits and Christian Theology

The topic of Lakota spirits presented a number of theological difficulties to the Catholic pastors at the Medicine Men and Pastors' Meeting. Christian Scriptures and tradition have historically been very much against spiritism. The many negative statements against the **Iktomi** spirit increased the difficulty since the **Iktomi** are the first and most common spirit encountered. This is a most important topic, for just as the Holy Spirit is the primary dynamic force which sanctifies the Church and its members, it is the Lakota spirits which are the dynamic sources which affect the blessings and visions within the Lakota religion. If the Holy Spirit and its associated revelations are not compatible with the Lakota spirits and their visions, then the two religions at their root could not be compatible.

To establish the nature of the compatibility of the Christian Spirit with the Lakota spirits, we first re-examined the Scriptures concerning spirits and found the revelation not as absolute against spiritism as is often presented. Then we examined more closely the described behavior of spirits in relation to doing what is good and bad, finally there emerged an awareness of how the whole body of Lakota spirits can compatibly fit **within** and can complement the Christian theology of spirits.

In the Old Testament, there are various laws against invocation of ghosts and spirits. The following Scriptural passage when quoted in its entirety demonstrates that the censureships given are not absolute but have a definite theological context which gives meaning and purpose to them.

> When you come into the land which the Lord your God gives you, you shall not learn to follow the abominable practices of those nations. There shall not be found among you any one who burns his son or his daughter as an offering, any one who practices divination, a soothsayer, or an augur, or a sorcerer, or a charmer, or a medium, or a wizard, or a

necromancer (one who invokes ghosts). For whoever does these things is an abomination to the God, and because of these abominable practices the Lord your God is driving them out before you. You shall be blameless before the Lord your God. For these nations, which you are about to dispossess, give heed to soothsayers and to diviners; but as for you, the Lord your God has not allowed you so to do.

The Lord your God will raise up for you a prophet like me from among you, from your brethren — him you shall heed — just as you desired of the Lord your God at Horeb on the day of the assembly, when you said, ''Let me not hear again the voice of the Lord my God, or see this great fire any more, lest I die.'' And the Lord said to me, ''They have rightly said all that they have spoken. I will raise up for them a prophet for them, a prophet like you from among their brethren; and I will put my words in his mouth, and he shall speak to them all that I command him. And whoever will not give heed to my words which he shall speak in my name, I myself will require it of him. But the prophet who presumes to speak a word in my name which I have not commanded him to speak, or who speaks in the name of other gods, that same prophet shall die. And if you say in your heart, ''How may we know the word which the Lord has not spoken?'' — when the prophet speaks in the name of the Lord. If the word does not come to pass or come true, that is a word which the Lord has not spoken; the prophet has spoken it presumptuously, you need not be afraid of him. (Deut 18.9-22) (RSV)

Some Christians use the first paragraph of this **Old** Testament commandment literally to condemn **Christian**-Lakota for attending Lakota ceremonies where Lakota spirits and ghosts are called upon for help and advice. They ignore the purpose and setting of this commandment, as clearly specified in the second paragraph.

The jealousy of the God of the Old Testament is a major theme in the above passage. Unlike the Priestly Writer after the exile, the Deuteronomic Writer does not argue the non-existence of urban gods outside of the Jewish tradition. He rather emphasizes the monotheism and faithfulness of Israel. ''The Lord your God has not allowed **you** so to do.'' Israel is His chosen people. The closed, folk character of this passage forces the hearer toward an either/or decision. The open, universal character of Christianity would necessarily modify the Christian use of the passage. With the universal dominion of Christ, what are the relationships between these spirits and Christ and the Christian community? Moving into the non-Jewish, Gentile world, Paul had to come to grips with this problem several times. Is it allowable for a Christian to receive instruction or assistance from any spiritual being other than God himself? The Christian must answer "yes," for Christ, Mary, and all the canonized saints and the heavenly angels are recognized as legitimate helps of Christians. The Jew would say "no," for his monotheism pushes him to even identifying the words and actions of the angels of the Lord as those of the Lord himself.

The second paragraph of the above scriptural passage points to God's "true prophet." After outlawing all spirit-senders of messages except the Spirit of God Himself, the lawgiver outlaws all message-transmitters except the "true prophet" to whom God has spoken. One criterion given to the people for knowing the **true** message-bearer is that what is prophesied does happen. There were many true prophets in the Old Testament times; the Old Testament contains the writings of only a few. Christianity recognized Christ as the fulfillment of the True Prophet, but the early church also recognized other prophets within the Christian community. A question then might be asked by the Christian: To what extent is a medicine man a "true prophet?" Does accuracy of his predictions indicate that he is a prophet of the Lord? Does his bringing of the people to a greater faith in God through his prophesies constitute him a prophet of God? Does his direction of people to a great participation in religion and in the faith community make him a prophet of God?

The Lakota traditionally insist that the medicine man, as a diviner, conveys the message accurately. They say that the spirits tell the medicine man not to say "above it or below it but tell the people exactly what you were given." The accuracy of a prediction stands as a sign of "something sacred," [**taku wakan kin**] and of God, [**Wakan Tanka**]. If the medicine man makes a prophecy that does not come true, he is considered not to be **wakan**. In ceremonies and in public assemblies, one can sense the Lakota medicine men's attempts to be moral teachers and correctors, which are characteristic of later prophets. They invite people to walk the virtuous and traditional Sacred Red Path. They indicate the bad consequences that will come to a person who does not do sacred things rightly or sincerely. They dream of the time when all wrongs will be healed and the Sacred Hoop will again be one.

The Gospels, which portray Jesus' life among monotheistic Jews, describe spirits dualistically. All angels come directly from God and are pictured as beautiful, young, and good. Demons come from hell and are responsible for all man's sicknesses and troubles. Other dualisms permeated the Palestinian scene. The Jews rejected the Gentiles; the "clean" rejected the "unclean;"

one political group rejected every other group, etc. Christ used the virtues of the outsiders and the vices of the insiders to break down these traditional divisions. Jesus regularly broke the rules of uncleanness by touching the leper, the dead, the sinner, the possessed. Christ also tried to break down the Jews' notion of the Messiah, presenting him as a prophet to be persecuted and killed. All revelation did not come directly from God or through his heavenly angels. The incarnation of Christ himself was a revelation "among us." And Christ pointed to the things of this world as living illustration of God's life and will. To Christ, the material things of earth were prophets and teachers of God's kingdom.

Jesus spent most of his time trying to get his followers to open up and accept all people; he made only indirect statements about universal acceptance of all God's creatures. Jesus followed a two-pronged pastoral policy toward men, which fore-shadowed Paul's two-pronged approach toward spirits. When non-disciples of Jesus were using his name to expel demons, Jesus said against the objections of disciples, "Those who are not against me are for me." (Lk. 9.50) But in a conflict with the Pharisees who said that Christ himself was possessed by a demon, Jesus said, "Those who are not with me are against me." (Lk. 11:23) These two general statements indicate a Christian's leeway in a religious judgment not only about humans but also about spirits. One can be tolerant and open when the environment is favorable to Christ, but one is to be hard and negative when the situation becomes critical and difficult for Christ and his followers.

Luke is recognized as the author of both the third Gospel and the Acts of the Apostles. It is interesting to compare his account of Jesus' **immediate** exorcism of the "unclean spirit" in (Lk. 4.33-37) with his account of Paul's **delayed** exorcism of a "python spirit" in Philippi (Acts 16.16-18). Luke's description of Paul's exorcism of the python-spirit is interesting from a missionary point of view.

And it came to pass as we went to pray that a certain maiden, who had a python-spirit, met us. This one brought her master much gain by soothsaying. This one, following after Paul and us, cried out saying, "These men are servants of God the most high, who announce to you a way of salvation. And this she did over many days. But becoming greatly troubled, Paul, turning to the spirit, said, "I charge you in the name of Jesus Christ to come out from her," and it came out in the same hour.

The maiden's spirit was not labeled "unclean" or even a "daemon" but a "python," an animal that was noted in the

Hellenistic world for its healing power, especially in the devotion to Aesculapius at Epidaurus, "the Lourdes of the Ancient World." Snakes are still today used symbolically on the medical caduceus.

Paul did not exorcise it immediately but did so only after it became an irritating nuisance to the apostle. At the subsequent trial, Paul did not reject the spirit of the maiden as unreal, evil, or unholy; he remained usually silent. From this and other instances, the author of the Acts of the Apostles recognized the reality and spiritual power of such spirits. In fact, here as elsewhere in the Acts, Luke used the recognized knowledge and power of these spirits to show the greater power of the Name of Jesus. It is difficult to determine the exact motivations behind Paul's patience with this proclaiming maiden and her python-spirit. It would appear that as long as the proclamation was positive and truthful regarding Christ and not hurting anyone, the Apostle to the Gentiles shows considerable missionary tolerance and restraint. Paul's letters also indicate measured recognition and tolerance toward spirit phenomena, indicating that they have a proper place among Christian priorities.

With the Corinthian community there appears to have been a considerable amount of various types of spiritual phenomena. Behind Paul's words one can hear echoes of the Hellenistic tendency to name a different spirit behind each different type of spiritual phenomena or activity. But Paul argues that there is only **one** God, who has **one** Spirit, who recognizes **one** Lord, Jesus Christ. In discussing the employment of "multiple spirits," Paul compares it with — and in the same process distinguishes it from — the idol worship of their pre-Christian days. Paul does not outright condemn the spiritual phenomena experienced by the Corinthians, although he does associate it with the paganism of their pre-Christian days and most emphatically rejects any spiritual message that says, "Jesus is accursed." One can sense Paul's struggle to recognize the virtuous spiritual phenomena that is part of the Corinthian's pre-Christian tradition. In his letters he struggles to relate these to and bring them under the dominion of the Spirit of God and the Christian virtue of love.

While the earlier writings of Paul tend to be more open toward Hellenistic spirits, his later writings appear to be negative. But a close examination brings out an important distinction.

In the exhortative conclusion of his letter to Ephesians, Paul associates the Principalities and Powers with the devil.

> Put on the armor of God so that you are able to stand against the craftiness of the devil; because our conflict is not against flesh and blood but against Principalities, against

Powers, against the world-rulers of this darkness, against the spiritual host of evil in the heavens. Therefore, take up the whole armour of God in order that you may be able to resist on the day of evil and, having done all things, to stand. (Eph. 6.11-13)

This passage is full of poetic imagery; it speaks about the Last Day. Typical of all Christian writers, Paul reverts to an absolute dualism and apocalyptic when he speaks about the last "day of evil." The Christian is told that he must reject even the spirits in the heavens if those spirits are not absolutely of Christ on the Last Day. Through graphic, poetic imagery, Paul exhorts the Christian to fight mightily, using the powers of God against anything that might hinder him from being totally upright and one with Christ on the Last Day. The strict dualism of the Last Day forces one to be either for Christ or against Him.

But what should the Christian's attitude toward the Principalities and Powers be **now**? The answer that Paul gives for "now" is not the same as for the "Last Day!"

The expression "principalities and powers" can be understood in several ways. They can be understood in an ordinary, secular sense, as in (Jer. 13.18) and (Titus 3.1). Usually, however, these words refer in Paul to spirit beings. "For I have been persuaded that not death nor life nor angels nor principalities nor powers nor things present nor things to come nor heights nor depths nor any other creature will be able to keep us from the love of God in Christ Jesus our Lord." (Rom. 8.38) Paul recognizes the Principalities are of the heavens and not from under the earth. Since the Principalities and Powers were of the heavens and Jesus Christ was from earth, there was a real question as to "Who tops whom?" Christ is recognized as their creator. "He (Christ) is the image of the invisible God, the first born of all creatures. In him, everything in heaven and on earth was created, things visible and invisible, whether thrones or dominions, principalities or powers. All were created through him and for him." (Col. 1:15-16) Thus the Principalities are not inherently or absolutely evil, for they were created **for** Christ. Using imagery associated with the theology of the Mystical Body, Paul speaks not only of a priority but also an inter-dynamic ordering between Christ and the Principalities and Powers. "Beware, lest there be anyone robbing you through philosophy and empty deceit or according to the traditions of men or according to the elements of the world and not according to Christ; because in him dwells all the fullness of the Godhead bodily. And you are in him, having been filled, who is the head of all Principalities and Powers." (Col. 2.8-10)

Paul conceived the Principalities and Powers as spirits who held the sins of the people against them. Paul saw the death of Christ on the cross for the sins of Christians as the means of deflating the dominion that these spirits in justice had over the people who had sinned. "And you, being dead in your sins and in your uncircumcised flesh, he co-quickened you with him, forgiving you all your sins, wiping out the handwriting against us in the ordinances which were contrary to us. And he has taken it out of our midst, nailing it to the cross. Putting off the principalities and powers, he exposed them, openly triumphing over them in it." (Col. 2.13-15)

But Paul spoke not only of humiliating and exposing the Principalities and Powers who held man's sins against him; Paul also spoke of **evangelizing** them.

To me the last of all the saints was given this grace: to preach to the nations the unsearchable riches of Christ, and to bring to light what is the stewardship of the mystery hidden from the ages in God, who created all things, in order that it might now be made known to the Principalities and Powers in the heavens through the Church — the manifold wisdom of God according to the purpose of the ages which he made in Christ Jesus our God. (Eph. 3.8-11)

Here Paul points out not only his stewardship but the Church's stewardship of the Gospel as well. God did not let the Principalities and Powers know everything. Certain things were hidden even from them, even though they are heavenly spirits. Thus the Church is capable of and by God's providence called to evangelize and teach the Principalities and Powers of the mysteries made known to the Church in Jesus Christ.

The Son of God became not a spirit or an angel but a man. It is man who was chosen to be the first fruits of creation in reference to the eschatological kingdom. Salvation was brought to all creation through one man, Jesus Christ, the Son of God. Paul indicates that not only is the Church to be the instrument in bringing salvation to all men but also to every creature — even to spirits, like the Principalities and Powers in the heavens.

Now then — If evangelization of those spirits called Principalities and Powers is to be considered a real possibility, then one's theology of the spirit world must include some spirits that can be converted. In other words, in this age, prior to the Last Day, Paul recognized that there were spirits that had not yet submitted but still could submit to Christ. Although initially not under Christ and prone to pull people to themselves and consequently away from Christ, Paul recognized that these spirits were not absolutely of Satan but could be brought under the dominion of the Son of God. Therefore, these spirits, whom Paul recognized as being convertible, had to be free and not locked into a single negative attitude toward Christ as is found with those spirits irrevocably associated with Satan.

In this context Paul's statement makes much more sense: "Know you not that we shall judge angels?" (I Cor. 6.3) Some angels must be in a pre-judgmental situation. The idea that men are to judge the heavenly spirits is a shocking one, especially to the Lakota who have such reverential fear of spirits. Such a dignity is not something that originates from man's pre-eschatological nature. Such an honor is realized only through Christ, who is both God and man, and whose death is the formal means by which sin in the world is covered and by which the eschatological kingdom in justice will become a reality for all the world — in heaven and on earth.

The important discovery that this examination of scriptural texts from Paul is that he did not hold an absolute dualism in regard to spirits. For Paul there were some spirits of the heavens that were still volitional and free to accept or reject Christ, to help or hinder Christians.

This close examination of Paul's writings helped the Medicine Men and Pastors' Meeting to break out of the traditional dualistic, apocalyptic description of the spirit world. It broke from the scholastic argument which said that since spirits are "simple" beings, they were capable of only one will-act in their whole existence. By examination of Scripture, it became clear that on the **Last Day** there will be only spirits of heaven and spirits of hell, but **now** there are also spirits of earth and sky. These are in a free, convertible situation. Not only can these spirits help man materially; man can also help the spirits salvifically.

It took a long time to come to the above conclusions. The Christian tradition is so strongly dualistic when it speaks about spirits. But I had several articles on poltergeists and other types of spirits from reputable authors for whom the data did not allow them to judge **all** spirits and ghosts as being either of heaven or of hell at this time. As the medicine men continued giving descriptions of their experiences of spirits, it became clear that the standard dualistic categories just did not fit the data. While the spirits generally sought the good and even got after their medicine men friends when they did wrong things, got drunk, or such like, there were times when they would do hurtful things and be justly feared. Sometimes they would ask or suggest things which were not within Christian moral standards, such as leaving this wife to take a woman who is closer to the spirits. The stories pointed to moral ambiguity and even a change of heart at times toward their medicine men and others. So in many ways the

Lakota spirits showed themselves to be as the medicine men called them — "men." They were in some ways powerful, but they were not absolutely good or bad. They generally did good, but occasionally, especially at the request of a human, would do things that were hurtful, that is, **sica.**

There is one first-hand report in which a woman was seeking a healing from the spirits of a particular medicine man. She was told that it was first necessary for her to stop receiving Holy Communion. The woman declined and sought help elsewhere. At a **Lowanpi** ceremony, after a person was doctored, the spirits said that he must continue going to ceremonies if the cure was to stick, and that he was to go to church every Sunday if he wanted blessings on his family. One time a friend of mine was at a **Lowanpi** ceremony, and he decided to pray silently for me, a priest, in the Christian way. The moment he started to pray using the name of Christ, he was violently battered about in his place — even though he was far in back where no one could touch him. He tried twice later. Each time he was jostled as he prayed that way in his heart. This medicine man is known to be antagonistic to priests, and his spirits are also. Others are positive toward priests, as an incident I will soon tell will indicate.

John gave his fellow Christians the following rule for judging and associating with spirits.

Beloved, believe not every spirit but prove the spirits to determine if they are of God, because many false prophets have come forth into the world. By this will you know a spirit of God: Every spirit which professes [**homologei**] Jesus Christ having come in flesh, is of God, and every spirit which does not profess Jesus is not of God. (I Jn. 4.1-2)

The Greek word **homologei** is more than a simple statement of belief; at its root it refers to "an expression that is alike" and indicates a "homily" or an in-depth teaching into the total reality of Christ. More than any other statement in Scripture, this discernment statement disturbed me. As far as I knew, no Lakota spirit had ever made such a profession. I had taken in deeply the attitudes and spirituality of the Lakota people. The thought of approaching this crucial, demanding matter filled me with awe and apprehension. In long silence, I wondered about this deficiency in my own experience of the Lakota spirits. I asked a Full-blood elder if the spirits knew Christ. The man responded immediately, "Of course they do. They know everything that goes on the reservation." This answer, however, was not satisfying because it indicated that the spirits knew the Lakota and **their** profession of Christ. To ask medicine men about this question seemed unsatisfactory. They might give their own opinion on what they thought the spirits probably would say.

One day the words of the medicine men finally sank in. Several times the medicine men in frustration over the many questions of the priests said with obvious faith and humility, "If you've got some questions about the spirits, you should put on a ceremony and ask the spirits themselves." I decided to do just that. Care had to be taken, not only in the preparation of the ceremony, but also in the wording of the questions. For example, it would have been disrespectful to the spirits to ask an obvious question, like "Do you know Jesus Christ?" After a month of prayer and thought, two questions were formulated in Lakota: "What can you tell me about Jesus?" and "What can the pastors do to understand the Lakota religion better?"

The usual preparations were made. A respected Catholic medicine man presided. When the spirits came into the meeting I asked my questions. In typical fashion the answers given by the Lakota spirits were fast and short. (This type of answer was totally untypical of this medicine man, who regularly talks 30-40 minutes around a question at the Medicine Men and Pastors' Meeting and never gives a straight, piercing answer.) The answer to the first question was: **Mahpiya ekta na maka sitomni.** This answer overwhelmed me. Such a succinct expression of the core truth about Christ. Literally these five words translate as "Into heaven and throughout the earth." Both **ekta** and **sitomni** are "traveling" words. **Ekta** means going "to" and "into." The "sitting" expression in **mahpiya ekta nanke cin** translates "who art in heaven" in the Our Father. Coupled with **sitomni** the expression **mahpiya ekta** expresses most perfectly the Ascension of Christ into heaven and his glorification there as God, far above the stars of the Lakota spirits. "Heaven" is the dwelling place of **Tunkasila Wakan Tanka,** God the Father/Grandfather. The statement that Jesus **mahpiya ekta** says much more than Jesus is divine, it speaks of his being transcendentalized into God's glory from the world below. It is most interesting to me that there was no verb, as if there is no Lakota word that can express the nature or character of the moving action.

The expression **maka sitomni** delighted me to the point of humor. **Maka sitomni** is a very common expression applied to the spirits who travel about the world helping the people and seeing the people in various ways. It points to a continued friendship with "the relatives." This statement is spiritually very egalitarian. By this expression, the Lakota spirits point out that the Spirit of Christ is active in this world very much as they are. In this respect, Christ's Spirit is no better than all the other Lakota spirits who know and help the people concretely in this world. The coupling of these two phrases together says, at least to me, ''Jesus is above us in one area, but he's just like us in another.'' Unlike the domineering tone of many of the New Testament texts, the statement of the spirits indicates both **their** respect for the divinity of Jesus and **his** respect for their virtue as well. In effect the spirit's message says that Jesus operates both from above and among equals. I know of no medicine man who could have made such a profound statement.

The answer to the second question, concerning the pastors' learning better about the Lakota religion, was also very short. ''If the fathers come, they will hear something.'' The answer did not mean much to me, but it shocked my Lakota mentor. I knew from his own personal experiences that Lakota spirits would talk to a priest or anyone who was sincere in making a vision quest. The spirit message indicated that priests who attend regular Lakota spirit meetings would **themselves** hear the spirit messages within the **Lowanpi** ceremonies. My Lakota mentor said that the statement implied the possibility that a dedicated father could hear a spirit within a ceremony just like the medicine man does. In effect, that a priest could take the place of a medicine man in the center. I personally think that is going beyond the words of the message. To hear the messages of spirits directly from spirits at a meeting is one thing, to be able to call them and speak to them as friends, **kola,** is an entirely different matter.

After that ceremony, other verifications of the compatibility of Christ's Spirit and the Lakota spirits became clear. The Lakota spirits become **kola** (friends) of the medicine men. In interviews they told how their spirits got after them if they got drunk or did other wrong things. It then occurred to me that if the Lakota spirits found their medicine man's going to a Christian Church service repugnant or unfitting, the Lakota spirits would get after the medicine man, at least in the next sweatbath or ceremony. Quite to the contrary, in various ways, the Lakota spirits indicated to the medicine men and to those who attended the Lakota ceremonies that it was a good thing for them to associate with Christian missionaries and go to church regularly. I heard these types of statements very early in the dialogue. Still these were always only just suggestions from the spirits. Their function was to heal the people, and being a Christian preacher was not their job.

From time to time I heard reports of hexing. This topic will be covered in a later chapter more thoroughly, but here a few observations are relevant. I noticed three trends in the distribution of these hexing reports. First, the larger number of complaints referred to geographic areas that were farther away from the Christian mission center, in areas of lower pastoral service. Second, the larger number of complaints were associated with medicine men and others who were quite withdrawn and negative to the Church. Third, when I asked older people if there were more hexing in the past as compared to now, all said two things: The medicine men now are not as dedicated to their profession as the ones in the past, and the frequency of hexing, say with love-medicine, was much stronger and more frequent in the past. As these different reports began to accumulate, I said to a Full-blood friend that it seems that Christianity on the reservation has been purifying the Lakota religion long before Vatican II indicated that it should be done. To this the Full-blood elder replied, ''Yes that is true. But don't forget. The Lakota religion has been purifying the Catholic Church too, especially since Vatican II. I don't know why it has taken you smart guys so long to get with it.''

The medicine man and his spirits are friends, **kolapi.** This means that there is a two-way communication between them. In many ways they think and work alike, each doing his own part. Sometimes one takes the lead; sometimes, the other. I have heard of disagreements between medicine men and their spirits; sometimes they break up for a while. The Lakota spirits give calling-visions, inviting a man to become a medicine man through the Lakota ceremonies. The Lakota medicine man asks the spirits to help certain people in particular ways. If the Lakota medicine man is Christian, his spirit friends cannot help but be influenced by his beliefs and moral values. The Christian medicine man, on the other hand, is directed by his spirit friends to traditional Lakota beliefs and moral values. In this way it can be said that a Christian medicine man ''evangelizes'' his Lakota spirit friends, who ''traditionalize'' him.

In my opinion, the Lakota spirits have shown greater appreciation and love toward the Church than the Spirit of the Church has shown toward the Lakota spirits. But times are changing. Oh, there are still negative spiritual attitudes on both sides. Nonetheless, so many things are pointing to an increased understanding of the distinction and compatability of the Lakota spirits and the Christian Spirit. The historic record shows that starting back many years, there has been increasing mutual respect and interaction between the spiritual elements of both the Lakota and Catholic religions. Unfortunately, during this time of most intense interaction, many ordinary people have become confused, insecure, and have pulled back. Hopefully the dust will settle soon, and the ordinary person will understand the profound inter-religious things that have been taking place in the last decade.

There is also another side to the discussion of Lakota spiritual beings. The Lakota believe that one's ability to communicate with rock and animal spirits is closely related to their ability, under exceptional **wakan** circumstances, to communicate personally with rocks and animals. Lakota animism is not general and vague but very particular and clear. Lakota animism recognizes that each individual thing in this world is relational, loving and personal. The Lakota maintain not only that spirits are more human-like than Christian theology would currently accept, but that material things are more human-like as well. Christian theology has traditionally maintained that the higher orders of beings — God, immaterial spirits, and man — are free to love others and establish inter-personal relationships, but that all other creatures, which the God who is Love made, do not themselves possess a God-like quality of love in any degree, in any way. The Lakota, and a good number of reflective Christians, do not accept the second part of the previous statement. The thorny, theological discussion of the possibility and character of a Christian animism must wait for another time. Such a discussion cannot focus on proving the existence of free will within any creature by means of external evidence. If external evidence only is used, even the free will of **man** can be put in doubt formally. To handle this question philosophically one must first replace Western essentialism with a Lakota-styled "relation-alism" and then determine what are the commensurate characteristics of rational psychology within that cosmology. Regardless, it is not man's free will but God's Spirit and Christ's grace that establish man's God-likeness. The discussion of Christian animism must focus on **Christ** and the relationship which his divine-materialization and salvation have not only with humans but also with everything in this world — from creation to the establishment of the Father's kingdom at the end of time. This is a complex question and must be discussed elsewhere. Suffice it to say: The Lakota people sometimes experience help, guidance and communication in a personal way from **all** individual creatures of Earth, whom they endearingly call Grandmother, **Unci.** These are not divine but they are sacred and personal and should be given loving respect and an open ear.

Some non-Indians are concerned about nature and the environment, and they assume that the Indians will have the same type of respectful attitudes as they. They become confused when Indians do not. First of all, the Lakota people demonstrate a full spectrum of attitudes toward the ordinary, **ikceya** elements of nature. Secondly, these attitudes are relational and therefore vary from place to place and time to time depending on the **effect** something has had or probably will have upon one's relatives. Many Whites would call the Lakota's position inconsistent, and from a mechanical point of view it is. From the standpoint of relative respect, however, their position is quite consistent. A good example of this is the following:

An Indian man tells how he travels a lot, driving to different parts of the country. For all the beautiful and wonderful things he sees in nature, he does not have a special awareness of **wakan** things. Off the reservation he does not experience any special, **wakan** presence in the trees, mountains, or animals. As he drives closer to his reservation, he begins to recognize familiar landmarks, and he starts to get a sense of things **wakan** and spiritually significant to him. Driving onto the reservation, he recognizes a river and remembers all the fish that his relatives have caught there and the deer that drink there. He feels an awesome respect for the things that are there. From the Lakota concept of respect for one's relatives, one develops a deep sense of awe, recognition, and peace toward others, and this overflows to those things that are special and **wakan.** When he sees an eagle over his home, it is not just an ordinary eagle or **any** eagle. Rather **this** eagle over his place is bringing a message to his family. **This** eagle is **wakan. This eagle** cares and is bringing an extraordinary blessing to his people. He feels God's presence and providence here. The respect he has for **this** eagle does not really alter his desire to capture other eagles — those he is not familiar with — those he is not related to. When he begins to generalize, universalize, or become abstract from this eagle to all eagles, the notion and sense of **wakan** falls flat. The eagle he sees flying over him on his way home tells of something **wakan** for himself and all his relatives. To a Lakota, the "nature" of a creature is not that important. Rather it is the quality of the personal relationship that any creature, spirit, or human has with a Lakota that is of primary value to him.

The ordinary word for "love" among the Lakota is **waśtelake.** Its root is **waśte** (good). For the Lakota something is not good in itself. Something is judged good or bad according to the impact that thing has on someone else. For example, this is a **good** day — because it makes me feel good and want to do things. He is a **bad** man — because he hurts my girlfriend and so hurts me. Whites judge a person good or loving if there is something positive coming from inside a person toward another. For a Lakota "to love" is "to cause something positive and good in the other." Consequently, the Lakota do not get hung up with the question whether an action originates from free will to be a loving act. A mother, who unreflectively picks up a child to comfort it from its crying, may be acting reflexively, but she is still acting lovingly — according to the Lakota. By their deeds and not their reflection will you know them. Consequently, it is easier for a Lakota to say that this morning when my horse took me out to fix fence and I later fed him, we loved each other and felt a lot closer to each other than I do with many of the people down the road. Certainly one's horse has its own nature or way and relationships are closest with one's family and relatives. Nonetheless, for a Lakota, love can bridge differences of nature — both ways. . .for are we not all relatives, **mitakuye oyas'in?**

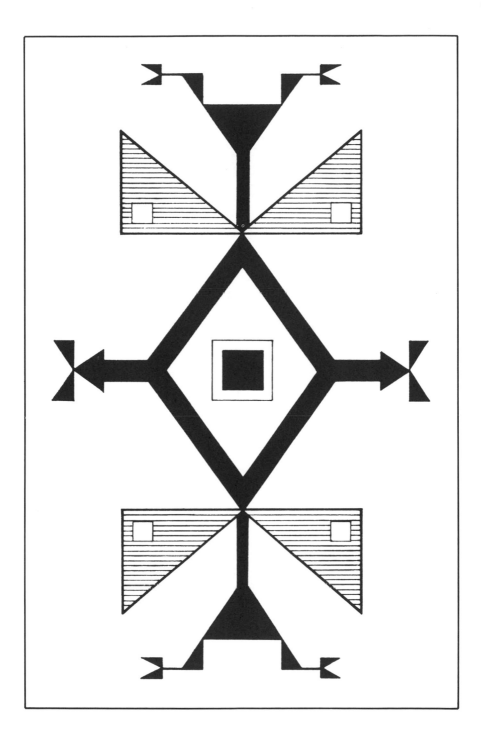

Chapter 9
Yuwipi and the Mass

In their daily lives, the leading participants of the Rosebud Medicine Men and Pastors' Meeting publicly performed the **Yuwipi** ceremony or the service of the Mass more than any other ritual within their respective traditions. So there was considerable interest in the discussion of these two most popular rites. The Lakota **Yuwipi** ceremony and the Christian Mass ritual are in many ways similar and in many ways different. In this chapter various aspects of these two ceremonies will be placed side by side so that the many ways they are comparable will be more obvious.

Yuwipi, and its sister ritual **Lowanpi,** are Lakota spirit ceremonies followed by a ritual feast. The origin of **Yuwipi** is regularly given by most Rosebud medicine men as around 1885 A.D. in Wanblee, South Dakota, by the renowned medicine man named Chips. The names of other early **Yuwipi** men are also given, like Moves Camp, Ashley, and White Lance. The details of the earliest form of this ceremony are very sketchy. One old medicine man remembers attending a ceremony by a Wanblee medicine man in St. Francis, South Dakota, in 1912. He said that it was then basically as it is now.

The Mass, which is sometimes called the Eucharist, is a Christian service which starts as a scripture service and climaxes with the consecration of bread and wine into the Body and Blood of Christ, which are consumed in a sacred feast. The first Eucharist took place the night before Jesus died in Jerusalem around 30 A.D. The details of the early Mass are sketchy, but it seems to have been a combination of the Jewish synagogue service and the Jewish **kiddush,** with elements of the Last Supper remembered. At a **kiddush,** a table is prepared in the home; the father of the family officiates. Wine is blessed, poured into a cup and shared with the family. A piece of bread is blessed, broken, and shared with them also. This "hallowing" action introduces every Sabbath and all great Jewish feasts.

The term **"yuwipi"** refers to one element of the ceremony in this most elaborate form. **"Yuwipi"** literally means "they bind him." At the beginning of this ceremony the medicine man's hands are tied behind his back with leather thongs in a special way. Then a star blanket is put over his head so that it extends to the ground. The sides are wrapped around tightly so that he looks like a mummy. Starting with a noose, the assistant systematically ties the blanketed medicine man with another long leather thong. Two men then grab the bound medicine man on either side and lay him on the stomach on the floor in front of his altar. Four hundred and five tobacco ties are made as an offering to the **Yuwipi** spirits, who in the dark in response to an unbinding song at the end of the ceremony, will release the medicine man from his bonds. The binding, **yuwipi,** is done for only the most difficult cases, such as extreme sickness. When the situation is not grave, the **Yuwipi wicaśa** (a medicine man who performs the **Yuwipi** ceremony) will perform a **Lowanpi** ceremony. Some medicine men do not have **Yuwipi** spirits but always **Lowanpi.**

A **Lowanpi** Ceremony is the ordinary ceremony of all men who are called "medicine men" on the reservation today. The word "**lowanpi**" simply means "They sing." Everything in a **Yuwipi** ceremony is in a **Lowanpi** ceremony, except there is no binding and no 405 tobacco ties are made to the **Yuwipi** spirits. Everything else in this chapter can be applied to either ceremony.

The earliest name for the Mass was the "Breaking of the Bread" (Acts 2.43) which refers to Christ's words and actions at the consecration, the central point of the Mass. Since the Mass in the early Church was in the Greek language, this ceremony is called the "Eucharist" because "Thanksgiving" is a main theme in the canon of the Mass, which begins, "Let us give thanks to the Lord our God." The term "Mass" comes from the closing of the ritual in Latin, **"Ite missa est,"** (Go, it is sent), referring to the sacrifice which was sent to God.

The **Lowanpi** ceremony takes place occasionally. It is usually directed toward an individual's felt need. The most common reason is for the healing of a sickness. When a healing does occur, there is usually a **Wopila** (Thanksgiving) ceremony, which is a **Lowanpi** at which the spirits are thanked for the cure. Other purposes for a **Lowanpi** are: finding a lost object, getting a person out of jail; asking guidance; helping to end a dispute; asking for help in obtaining food, clothing, a car or other necessities of life; asking to obtain a vision; requesting help in getting a job; finding a lost body or a lost relative; for answering spiritual questions; for help in raising children right and protecting them; for winning a competition; and for the avoidance of starvation or other calamities. The needs are very concrete and immediate. There is a tendency today to move from more material and physical needs into interpersonal matters like domestic feuds and personal problems.

Some medicine men have objected to this movement because it is not traditional. One can discern how very material and physical is their perception of the traditional domain of the Lakota ceremonies. While the Lakota ceremony is undergoing a change of purpose, the Catholic liturgy is undergoing a change of ceremonial form and involvement. Both are struggling to adapt to a rapidly changing world and congregation.

Even though the reforms of Vatican II have been in effect over 15 years now, I still hear complaints about the new liturgy not only from the old but also from those in their mid-20's. Turning the altar to face the people and changing from Latin to English or Lakota has changed what was once felt to be very awesome, mysterious, and sacred into something that now feels very profane, ordinary, and inconsequential. Previously the emphasis was upon worshiping the transcendent God; today the emphasis is upon relating religiously with one's neighbor. Previously the emphasis was upon silent presence; now the emphasis is upon verbal exchange. The active role of the priest and servers and the passive role of the congregation are now replaced with few or no servers and an increasing role by every person who comes. While priests grumble about a lack of whole-hearted participation by those attending and a lack of real sense of spiritual oneness found in the congregation, some older medicine men grumble that the people do not focus their prayers on the needs of a particular **Lowanpi.** This ceremony is a spiritual ceremony, and its success, in part, depends upon the faith and concentration of the congregation in that same direction. These medicine men point out that the person putting on the ceremony has made a considerable financial investment. All should be praying for the purpose for which the meeting was called. Some people, they say, bring tobacco ties and flags for their own problems and "come in on the shirt-tail" of the person putting on the ceremony. "Everyone is thinking about their own problems rather than 'throwing their thoughts' toward the one the ceremony is intended for." This person is given a special place in the room, often to the immediate right or left of the medicine man. In the old days all of the relatives of the person putting on the ceremony as well as many of the relatives of the medicine man would be at the ceremony. Today relatives find other things to do, like watch television, and there is not a united mind and heart within the family. In the old days, medicine men would accept only one Pipe for each ceremony. These days, because many people want the medicine men to pray for their needs, several Pipes will be accepted by newer medicine men, requiring him and the people to pray for several main intentions in a ceremony, rather than focusing on one main intention. Each petitioner brings food for the feast, and each petitioner is heard in his or her proper order.

In the Catholic Church, a distinction is made between first and second intentions. The Church only allows one first intention for each Mass. Usually this is announced so that the people can pray for that intention also. There are many second intentions from the people and the priest. These can be presented publicly in the Prayers of the Faithful or left unspoken in one's silent prayer. In the **Lowanpi** ceremony, there is a specific time about one-third of the way through the service where each person expresses the needs they want to bring to the spirits.

The **Lowanpi** ceremony brings many relatives together to pray with the Pipe to bring special blessings upon their people. The Sundance takes place only in mid-summer, and the sweatbath can only accommodate a few. The **Yuwipi** ceremony is the only ritual these days which brings many people together throughout the year when there is need. It brings the people together so that their united prayers are heard by the spirits, who in turn bring material assistance to the people.

The community Mass is held regularly on Sunday. This day is the traditional day when the Church gathers for instruction and worship, for this is the day of the Lord's resurrection to that new life all Christians share in. Just as the Lakota traditionally found sunrise, sunset, the time of the full moon, and the time of the high sun to be naturally appropriate for prayer, the Christian recalls the injunction of the Old Testament for religious observance of the Sabbath, which Jesus regularly observed (Lk 4:16). The apostles (Acts 2.42) and the early Church observed it. And the bishops still direct us to weekly attendance at Mass through their Precepts of the Church. Attendance at Mass spiritually unites the Christian with the leaders and members of the two thousand year old Christian community with the Sabbath Services thousands of years before that. Most of all, at Mass one is able to have a closer, more material relationship with the Lord Jesus Christ than anywhere else. At the Eucharist under the signs of bread and wine, Christ is present in Body and Blood upon the altar, and in that form, one is able to unite Christ's living reality with one's own body and blood. Throughout the Mass, one hears the joyful refrain again and again, "The Lord be with you," or more precisely **"Itancan kin kici niu[n]."** Oral Lakota expresses Christ's eschatological "coming" and his being "already present" more clearly than English.

There are so many people who are schooled by materialistic society to go to religious ceremonies to **get** something. Rather, the true Christian goes to Mass primarily to **become** someone. In joining oneself to Christ's sacrifice for sin unto resurrectional glory, disciples break their bondage to this confused, fragmented, vain, sinful world and partake in the sure, singular, fruitful, virtuous covenant with God in Christ. It is true that it is said that one receives ''sanctifying grace'' from going to Mass, but this gift of God's Spirit and Life is not a ''what'' but a ''who-in-relationship.'' At Mass the Christian becomes someone special through the relationship one has with Christ.

Similarly, the **Yuwipi** ceremony brings the participants as a group closer to that which is **wakan** and of **Wakan Tanka** than anywhere else. Here the spirits manifest themselves in physical ways to show their presence and concern. Here the Lakota religiously reaffirm again and again their unity and identity through the Pipe, the Lakota spirits, and **Mitakuye oyas'in.** All these elements unite the individual with all religious Lakota here and in the past. The presence of the Pipe unites the individual with all that is sacred since its coming centuries ago.

The physical location of **Yuwipi** ceremonies has changed over the years. Originally, when travel was very difficult, they were usually held in different people's homes, especially if the person was so sick that it was difficult to move him. As transportation improved, more ceremonies were held at the home of the medicine man. Within the last fifteen years, especially since children live at home rather than at a boarding school, about half of the medicine men have built separate frame buildings or log cabins which are used exclusively for religious ceremonies. Two medicine men have done several things to develop centers where people can come and stay for longer periods of time, learning about Lakota spirituality and ceremonies. This sequence mirrors the progress of locations for the Mass. At first, the Mass was celebrated wherever the missionary happened to stay overnight. Then the journeys of missionaries became organized and the missionary would visit each community in his ''band'' once a month, saying Mass for the local Catholics at the home of a chosen community leader or catechist. Afterwards, small district churches were constructed. As the people coalesced into larger communities, the district churches were closed, and the community churches expanded. Now a large, log-cabin Sioux Spirituality Center has been built for the training of Indian deacons and the giving of retreats to Indian people.

Just as the Christian Church initially was tolerated but then officially condemned, and the Mass had to be held secretly at night in individual homes and in catacombs, so too, the Indian religion was initially tolerated but then officially condemned so that **Yuwipi** and other Indian ceremonies had to be held in secret at night. But eventually the official persecution of the Church was lifted and the Christian religion increasingly flourished — but with members who were not as sincere or dedicated as in the time of persecution. Similarly when the suppression of the Lakota religion lessened, there has been a surge in the number of Indians practicing the Lakota religions — but while their ceremonies are more elaborate, their understanding and dedication to the Lakota religion are often not as deep or as dedicated as in former times. Certainly the suppression of the Lakota religion and the condemnation of its followers by missionaries were wrong, and atonement must be made for this sin done in religious zealousness and ignorance. This is similar to the suppression, persecutions, and martyrdoms experienced by Christianity soon after its encounter with "Western civilization."

Like the late evening **Yuwipi** services, the Christian Mass in the early centuries was celebrated at night, the beginning of the day for the Jews. The Lakota recognize night to be the time of intense spirit activity and the **yuwipi** services are performed in pitch darkness. Heavy blankets over the doors and windows keep any light from outside coming in so that the spirits are more apt to come. Darkness is a sign of the mysterious, unknowable side of God and all things **wakan.** It eliminates congregational distractions and helps the individual focus with faith on prayer. It is a sign of man's helplessness and pitifulness and ignorance before the all knowing and most wise spirits. As in the sweatbath, all eyeglasses and shiny surfaces are removed, probably because they would reflect and give a false image of any sparks which may appear in the room during the ceremony. To wear glasses in the dark is a statement of desire to see that which is unseeable and **wakan.**

In Christian services, candlelight has a special meaning, for it reminds the participants that Christ is the Light of the World shining in darkness to remove sin and ignorance. The dawn is a symbol of Christ's resurrection and the glorious coming of God's kingdom. It reminds the Christian of the special revelations God has already given man throughout salvation history, especially in his Son, Jesus Christ, in whom is the total, fleshed likeness of the Father.

Like the bare courts of the Jerusalem temple, the early Christian churches did not have any regular seating. Ordinarily a person at the early Christian ceremonies either stood or sat on the ground. If a person needed a chair, he/she brought it to the service. After the permanent installation of choir stalls for monks, pews for the congregation became increasingly accepted until in America all churches have pews. But in Europe the larger churches still do not have permanent pews. So free seating in the new church/hall combinations is actually quite traditional.

The tradition that Indians sit on the floor around the edge of a building or open area is very old, but gradually benches and chairs are being introduced at dancing grounds, traditional feasts, give-aways, and even at Sundance grounds. Now benches and chairs are being introduced by some medicine men in their **Lowanpi** ceremonies. Objections have been raised. It seems spiritually more meaningful that the Indian congregation humbly sit on the floor close to Grandmother Earth. Many families are not able to supply seating for a large group. The primary reason this is done, however, is because it is traditional, and chairs are a non-Indian invention. Increasingly older and younger people are finding it difficult to sit on the ground for long periods of time, so sitting on the ground is being replaced slowly with sitting on chairs. In the Catholic tradition kneeling is recognized as a posture of humility. With the emphasis shifting from an awareness of one's sinfulness to an awareness of one's dignity in Christ, many times of kneeling have been replaced by times of standing in the new liturgy.

The arrangement of religious things within the sacred space of the **Lowanpi** ceremony is different for every medicine man. Each medicine man receives a description of his altars in his visions. Still, there is a general pattern observable. Some type of covering is placed on the floor about six feet from a major wall in the room. It may be a buffalo robe, but more usually it is 3'x4' piece of canvas that is covered with sage. This bed of sage is brought in a roll and unrolled into place. This is the place where the medicine man will stand, kneel, and sit cross-legged during the service. Three-foot sticks, about 3/8 inch diameter, painted one or two colors, such as red on the top and blue on the bottom, are held upright in one of two ways. A **Yuwipi** man will usually have five small coffee cans of sand in which the sticks are set: four at the four corners of the sacred area, and one stick for the red flag before his altar. The 405 **Yuwipi** tobacco ties for the unbinding are wrapped around the rectangular area from flag to flag where the medicine man is laid. For **Lowanpi** men, a four-foot 2x4 with various drilled holes for all flags is often put about a foot in front of the bed of sage. Usually there are five tall sticks about 3 feet tall for holding about a yard-long cloth flag by means of a single, corner tobacco tie. The center pole may have special symbols from the medicine man's vision, for example, a black-tail deer tail, a medicine wheel, and an eagle feather. Smaller six inch sticks and flags may decorate the area.

The mole is the companion of Grandmother Earth. Ceremonial

dirt is taken from a mole's hill. A large leather bag of this dirt is dropped precisely between the bed of sage and the center flag. By stretching the single piece of leather, a circle of dirt naturally results. The head of a drum is pressed down on the pile of dirt, forming it into a flat circle about 9 inches in diameter. An eagle feather is used to smooth out any imperfection on this altar. Then strings of tobacco ties, made specifically for this service, are wrapped around the altar. For each spirit there is a different number of ties of a certain color, and a certain number of flags of a certain color. For example, the **Iktomi** ceremony usually requires 75 red tobacco ties. If a **Heyoka** spirit is to be called, a boiled puppy and 25 black and 25 white tobacco ties are often required. It is important for the person putting on a ceremony to ask the medicine man what are the correct flags, ties, and offerings for this ceremony. Every medicine man's spirits are different. At every ceremony, a pot of water is also put near the altar as a sign of and offering for ''life.''

Usually all these preparations are done by an assistant. He takes a bunch of sage and puts a piece on the pot of soup, one on the pot of water, one on each bowl of **wasna,** if there is any, etc. If the Pipe will not be held, a bed of sage is made for the Pipe beside the altar. Then the bundle of sage is passed around the circle of people attending; each takes a sprig and puts it behind one of their ears, blessing it so it will hear the spirit's message rightly.

There is usually a special woman who holds the Pipe during the entire ceremony. She is often the medicine man's wife and usually sits right in front of the altar. Once the Pipe is filled, a person should not pass between the mouth of the Pipe and the altar.

The medicine man always arranges to have at least one lead singer who knows the songs for his ceremony. It is good to have at least four singers and two drums, although this is sometimes hard to do. They usually sit in one location together. Everyone is invited to sing, as long as they know the songs. The lead singer usually sings the leading line, and the other singers repeat it. On the second line the women usually join in.

The person being doctored in the ceremony and/or the person sponsoring the ceremony sit in a special, prominent place, usually to the right of the altar. Everyone else sits wherever there is a place along the outside of the room. The ''circle'' is recognized as very sacred to the Lakota. Their teepees were circular; their encampments were put up in circles; cut trees and animals in the middle and one finds a circle; the world around the Lakota is seen as within one great, sacred circle. It bothered me to see **Lowanpi** ceremonies taking place in rectangular rooms. But watching the behavior and comments of people as they filled in large gaps on one wall or as they call things that were lopsided a "circle," it became clear to me that they did not mean an abstract, geometric circle as I had been schooled. Their world view is relational and concrete, pointing to real things. Verbs are more important than nouns. To make a circle to them does not mean make an abstract prototype; rather to make a circle means to "encircle" or completely "surround" a particular space — enclose it relationally. Thus sitting along all four walls of a room the people make a living encirclement, which will become **wakan** by the spirits soon to come. With everything and everyone in place, the helper lights some sweetgrass and incenses the altar, the pots, the medicine man, the singers, the sponsors, everyone, and everything in the room. A dominant theme of the Christian liturgy is instruction, so it is understandable that Christian Churches tend to put the people in rows facing the priest and teacher.

I find it interesting how the position of the altar has changed in both the Catholic and Lakota rituals. Originally the priest stood behind the altar and faced the people so he could speak to them of the mysteries as well pray to God with Christ in the midst of the assembly. But with the theme of awe before God the altar was turned around so that the priest no longer faced the people but only the Holy One. When the Lakota lived in teepees and the fire was in the center, the place of honor was opposite the door facing everyone. The Indian altar was scratched on the ground between the place of honor and the fire. When the Lakota moved into frame houses with stoves, the **Yuwipi** men began to occupy the center of the room, and the altar began to be placed near one wall. Recently the Christian altar was turned back to its original place facing the people. . .

In front of the Lakota altar is placed the central flagpole to which are attached various visionary symbols and medicines of the medicine man, who will act as an intermediary between the people and the spirits symbolized there. In a prominent place before the Christian altar is placed an image of the cross of Christ, who is present as the one Priest, effecting every Mass through his ordained minister standing before the altar. As ties, flags and offerings indicate the presence of other spirits, statues, paintings, and other artifacts point to saints and teachings which contribute to the religious significance of the mysteries being celebrated there. Sage and sweetgrass expel evil spirits and attract good ones in the Lakota ceremony; holy water and incense are used as sacramentals for the purification of one's sins and the lifting of one's prayers to God. Just as the Pipe and the jar of water are to be taken later by all present in a special religious way after being blessed by the spirits for "life" and "health," so too the bread and wine are there to be taken later in a special religious way by the Faithful as the body and blood of Christ unto a greater life in Christ.

Some Lakota have long criticized the priests for praying from a book rather than from their hearts; yet some medicine men rattle off prayers so routinely that there appears little heart in their prayers also. Some medicine men are now referring to books which describe the Lakota ceremonies of the past; some priests are moving away from the authorized texts to a more spontaneous prayer at Mass and in response to the many requests for prayers made in everyday life.

The Lakota surround their altars with color. The most sacred color is red. It is a sign of religious dedication and what is **wakan** . . .the Red Path. Red is the color of blood and the life and strength that comes from God. There are usually flags for the Four Winds. Black is the color of the West; it indicates the dark beginnings of things and the darkness of the rain clouds which give the rains that bring forth new life. Red is the color of the North; it points to the sacred Red Path of life and the sacrifices that must be made for the people as one walks the Pipe's **wakan** way. Yellow is for the East; it indicates the sun and intellectual enlightenment from the morning star and from visions. White is for the South; it indicates the final, joyful ghost gathering of all the relatives. Blue is the color of the Sky and the powers from above; green is the color of Grandmother and all the food she provides for her children.

Catholics use liturgical colors according to the time of the year. Purple is the time of penance and renewal. Red is for times of remembering those who have died for the faith and those inspired in a special way by the Holy Spirit. Green is for the times of ordinary growth in spiritual things. White is the joyful color of the resurrection and celebration for what great things God has done for us.

The drum cannot be used when a person is filling the pipe because he has only two hands. It is not used on vision quests. The steam stretches the head so it cannot be used in the sweatlodge. It is said that the drum is used at the Sundance because it is a dance. Outside of dances the most frequent use of the drum is at the **Lowanpi** service, which may indicate why it got the name ''They sing.'' The medicine men consider it crucial to have songs at the **Lowanpi** because their spirits will not come or give answers or go and do what they are supposed to do unless songs are sung. It is interesting that most Pan-Indian songs sung at powwows do not have words, but for religious ceremonies almost all the songs have very traditional words. These ceremonial songs cannot be composed by a human but must be given by a spirit in a dream or vision. In the Mass, music is strongly encouraged but, except in the Eastern Catholic liturgies, singing is not essential. Rather certain words and thoughts must be expressed for a Mass's validity and orthodoxy.

There are a variety of purification rituals that take place at the beginning of the Lakota and Christian ceremonies. For a **Yuwipi** or **Lowanpi** ceremony, the medicine men, singers and important male relatives usually take a sweatbath. For the others, hot rocks from the fire are sometimes brought to the door of the room where the ceremony will take place so that those who enter it may pour a little water on the rocks so that they can be purified in the rising steam. Sometimes a bucket of rocks is taken around after the people are seated. Sometimes leaves of Indian perfume are distributed or the leaves from a stem of sage are stripped off. These are rolled back and forth in one's hands and then wiped over oneself and one's clothing.

In the Catholic tradition significant participants in a Christian sacrament often go to confession just before taking part in a Mass of special significance. As the congregation comes into the church, they usually bless themselves with holy water. They also may be blessed with holy water collectively in the **asperges** ritual. They may also confess their sins in a general way, asking God's mercy and purification before the sacred ceremony begins. Incense is used at different times, indicating a desire that the prayers of the people may arise to God and be acceptable as a sweet fragrance.

Both the Lakota ceremony and the Christian ritual are divided into two parts. The first part involves primarily special verbal communications and blessings; the second part centers on blessed food. In the Lakota ceremony, the spiritual aspect of the first part receives the emphasis. In the Christian ceremony, the Eucharistic feast is seen as the unique element in the Mass. But both parts are seen as very important in the traditions for the people.

The Lakota have an essential opening ritual. When everything is in place, all the lights are put out except for a flashlight, which is focused on the Pipe. While the Pipe-filling song is sung, the Pipe is filled with prayers to the spirits for the success of the meeting. When the medicine man finishes his prayer, the Pipe is laid on a bed of sage or given to a chosen woman to hold throughout the meeting. Then the medicine man takes a small stick and marks the earth altar with the sign of his vision or his spirit. The flashlight is put out and the room becomes completely dark.

In special Christian Masses, a number of signs of Christ make a solemn entrance: the Christian people stand together, the cross leads the procession, the book of the Word of God is carried in with great honor, and the ordained ministers of Christ enter in their white robes. They reverence the altar, a sign of Christ in the Eucharistic sacrifice. Candles are often carried in and placed on the altar. As the entrance song is sung, all the participants take their places, each designating a special relationship and function with the sacred liturgy.

In total darkness, the medicine man welcomes everyone and thanks them for coming. He tells them why they are there, who is sponsoring the ceremony, and what things are to be especially prayed for by all. He reminds them that what is to happen is **wakan**, and that all must have good thoughts. Then he says his **hanbloglaka**, telling the people how he received his vision to be a medicine man from the spirits, strengthening the understanding and faith of the people. He tells them it is time to call these spirits so that they may help here. He may pray alone at first. He always prays to **Tunkaśila Wakan Tanka** (God the Grandfather) first, then to the particular spirits of the Pipe, and finally to his own particular spirits. In Christian Masses the congregation is welcomed and told if there is a special purpose for the Mass. The priest then says the opening prayer, always making it through Christ our Lord, in the name of the Blessed Trinity, and also perhaps through some saint being especially remembered by the Church.

Directed by the medicine man, the singers start singing special songs, calling the spirit friends of this medicine man. Usually after a short time, the spirits come in. Streams of blue sparks usually descend to where the medicine man is; then they may spark around the Pipe, the offerings, the water, the soup, and variously throughout the room. Often the medicine man has a set of rattles near his altar and usually these rattles begin to sound, knocking the floor, the ceiling, and other places through the entire room. These indicate the presence of the spirits. Sometimes there is heard the beat of an eagle wing or a blast of cool air fills the airtight room. Sometimes knockings seem to come from outside the door, the walls, the ceiling, or the floor. Sometimes a rattle will fly in front of a participant or touch his body in places. Sometimes there are touches of a paw or a hand. These are signs of the presences and doctoring of the spirits, and one should say, **Pilamaya, Tunkaśila,** (Thank you, Grandfather.). The means and understandings of these spiritual things will be discussed in the next chapter.

After the spirits have come and shown themselves in various ways, the singing ends and the phenomena settles down. The spirit talks through the medicine man, who tells the name(s) of the spirit(s) and why they have come. They speak about the great or little faith and generosity of those present there. After some religious teaching or advice, the singing begins and in the dark the sparks, rattles, and other **wakan** phenomena start happening again. When the song is finished the round of prayers begin. First the sponsor of the ceremony prays for the particular help the meeting was called for. After that person finishes praying, saying **Mitakuye oyas'in** at the end, the woman holding the Pipe prays and ends the same way. From her, every person in turn, going sunwise around the room, prays for the main intention of the meeting and then for any personal or family needs. Even if one does not have anything he wants to pray out loud for, each ends their prayer with **Mitakuye oyas'in.**

When everyone is finished praying, a song is sung, during which the spirits talk to the medicine man. Often one hears an affirmative **Hau** from the medicine man as the spirits tell him what to say next. Usually there are around 25 people at a meeting; for a significant individual there may be as many as 50. At a New Year's Eve Service I was at, there were 105. Sometimes the prayer of the people takes almost an hour. So sometimes the spirits' instruction of the medicine man takes the duration of two or three songs, but usually not more than one long one. When the song is finished the medicine man tells the people what the spirits told him to say. Starting with the sponsor, then the holder of the Pipe, and then every person in turn around the room, the medicine man tells each what the spirit said in reference to the prayer said. In a prophetic manner, the medicine man tells how the prayer of each individual person will be concretely answered. Sometimes the prayers are very general and at other times very specific; so too the answers are at times very general and sometimes very specific.

After that, special spirits may be called through various songs, e.g. the eagle, the prairie dog, or the clown. Each has his own signs. Besides saying things backwards from what is meant, the **Heyoka** (Clown or Contrary) will often lightly splash everyone with some of his dog soup. When all the spirits have finished, they are dismissed with special sending songs.

When everyone has been in the dark several hours, it is important to shade the eyes. Then one sees that the mark in the earth altar has been stirred up, and the flags and tobacco ties have been neatly wrapped and perhaps thrown to someone special as a blessing. If the **Yuwipi** man had been tied up at the beginning of the ceremony, his blanket and bindings will be neatly folded, and he will be seated unwrapped in front of his altar. All these actions are said to be done by the spirits. This completes the first part of the **Yuwipi/Lowanpi** ceremony.

In the Mass, after the purification, introduction, and opening prayer, the Liturgy of the Word is begun. Great respect is given to Sacred Scripture, which is believed to be God's word received through the Holy Spirit. Various hymns, refrains, psalms, verses, and alleluias from Sacred Scripture are sung intermittently through this part of the service. An instruction from a priest or deacon applies the message to everyone's life. Here the Spirit is recognized as touching everyone's heart in a different way, according to one's own special needs unto a fuller, holier life. The Prayer of the Faithful is said as a bridge between the first and second part of the Mass. While the Holy Spirit comes in a special way in the first part of the Mass, Christ himself will come in a particularly material way in the second part of the Mass, and the petitions are believed to have a special hearing in his special presence there.

In the **Lowanpi** ceremony, the second part is a feast. It begins with the sacred elements of smoke and water. The woman who holds the Pipe lights it, smokes from it meditatively, signs with it according to her devotion, says **Mitakuye oyas'in** and then passes it to the person on her left, who does the same, etc. If there are many people, several pipes may be filled and then sent to different places around the circle. The medicine man is the last one to smoke. This is seen as a spiritual communion with all that was sacred at the meeting. Drinking of the blessed water is very refreshing after several hours in the dark, hot room. It is a sign of both a good and happy material and spiritual life through the blessings of God and the spirits. The woman who held the Pipe is the first to drink from the bowl of water, after which she says, **Mitakuye oyas'in.** The bowl is then carried by a young man to the person to her left, and she/he drinks and prays the same way, etc. The medicine man is the last one to drink the remainder.

The flags, ties, and ribbons are gathered by a helper into one bundle. A sample of all the food is gathered, lifted to the Four Directions, the Sky, and the Earth in prayers and placed into the bundle, which is taken outside as a first-foods offering to any nearby ghosts who might be pitiful and in need. If there was a pot of dog soup **wahanpi** for the **Heyoka** or **wasna** (pemmican) for the other spirits, these foods are considered sacred and distributed first. Then the rest of the food is distributed. Special attention is paid to traditional foods like: **tatanka** (buffalo), **tinpsila** (wild turnips), **taniga** (tripe), **papa** (pounded dried meat), **wastunkala** (dried corn), **wahpe** (Indian tea), **wojapi** (fruit pudding), and **wigli on kagapi** (fried bread). All the food that was brought is distributed; there is always two and three times more food than one can eat in one sitting. Each person brings dishes and buckets. What is left over is taken home as **wateca** and the memory of the ceremony is celebrated for several days there after. Before the people leave, sweetgrass is shaken as incense over all the food and people as a final blessing, and the prayer **Mitakuye oyas'in** is said in turn by each. Then stretching their bones and muscles after the three to five hour service, all head home filled with hopes, blessing, and good food.

A "Liturgy of the Word" brings divine revelation from the Holy Spirit to all of the Christian sacraments — just as the spirits of the Pipe are present at all rituals of the Pipe. While it is the special coming of the Lakota spirits in sparks, rattles, and prophesies in the first part of the **Lowanpi** that provides its uniqueness, it is the Liturgy of the Eucharist in which Christ physically comes under the forms of bread and wine that gives the Mass its uniqueness. For the medicine man, this ceremony is not only steeped in Lakota spirituality, it is a living out of his own vision. For the priest, the ceremony not only capsulized centuries of Christian spirituality, but most of all it is a reliving of the Last Supper of Jesus Christ. As Christ has both an individual and a corporate aspect, so too, he is spiritually present individually in the priest at the altar and corporately in the people attending at Mass. The holiness and participation of the Faithful at Mass is in some ways similar and some ways different from the prayer and concentration of those in the Lakota ceremonial circle. While the Lakota throw their thoughts toward those in need in the presence of the Lakota spirits, Christians direct their intentions to God through Christ on behalf of those in need. While the Lakota emphasize material and family needs, Christians emphasize development of moral and religious virtues and needs on a regional or world wide level. The Eucharist not only proclaims what God has given to his people but also extols and worships God for his goodness. First comes thanksgiving for what God has done for us, then with reassured faith we turn to our needs as we individually see them. The Lakota are reassured by the **hanbloglaka** of the medicine man, but they express their concrete needs first, and once that has been obtained, the thanksgiving is made, not in general, but for the very specific help he has given to their relatives. The Mass recalls and prays with the saints in heaven for all who have died. While the Lakota make a food offering with very few prayers for the wandering ghosts who are not yet at peace, the Christian is confident that his prayers and sacrifices for the faithful departed will hasten their enjoyment of life everlasting. In the Mass, the Church throughout the world is remembered; we are one with them as we pray for their peace and salvation. In the **Lowanpi** the participants remember their relatives in a special way and pray for their health and life.

During the Lakota ceremony, the spirits come and bless the Pipe, the water, the dog, and the **wasna**. These are called a medicine for they will heal and physically strengthen the person who receives them. In the Mass, Christians believe that the bread and wine offered are transformed by the institution words of Jesus into his body and blood. When these are received there is a healing of the soul from the effects of sin and a transformation of the person more and more into Christ spiritually. The complementarity of these two rituals and religions can be clearly seen in the similar but different attitudes the Lakota and the Christian have toward the sacred foods of these two ceremonies.

After Communion, the Mass quickly comes to an end. In the old days, people took communion home with them so that they could receive it every day. But today many who wish to receive it daily have the opportunity to do it in their local churches. After a final benediction and song, everyone heads toward home. But for faithful Christians this is not the end for they continue to savor the spiritual message which they received in Mass and try to live daily until the next Mass.

Chapter 10
Questions on Yuwipi

In many ways I found this chapter most unpleasant to write. Discussions of negative things open old sores and are disheartening. I delayed bringing these questions up at the Medicine Men and Pastors' Meeting as long as possible, for these were matters which were behind the Catholic censureship of **Yuwipi** for so many years. These were matters about which the medicine men were extremely defensive. Only after years of openness and respect had a sufficiently peaceful and trusting environment been developed for the discussion of these sensitive matters. Hopefully the discussion of these things will reverse possible negative feelings and judgments into a positive viewpoint, as it did for the medicine men and pastors. There is so much beauty and sacredness in **Yuwipi** and the Mass, but there are some difficulties that must be realized and worked out.

It is very easy to lump many things together. The historic record is not that simple. It is easy to say that **everything** the missionaries said or did pertaining to the Lakota religion was wrong and bad, or that every law against Indian religion is to be blamed on the Catholic missionaries. The primary reason why the Sundance and other secret meetings were banned was military; the army did not want the Indians grouping together against the federal army in those early days of the reservation. The legal suppression of the Sundance and other Lakota ceremonies took place in or before 1883. It was not until 1883 that the Catholic Church began its first formal work with the Lakota. Some Eastern groups strongly objected to the breaking of flesh in the Sundance because it was "uncivilized." But the laceration of the flesh as a sacrifice has long been within the Catholic tradition — difficult, painful, and bloody though it may be.

1) Why was the Church's attitude toward Indian religion so negative for so many years?

Some people think that the Catholic missionaries had only one — negative — attitude toward Indian religions. Actually they had four different attitudes toward four different things:

a) Catholic missionaries have always been positively impressed by many of the characteristics of Lakota spirituality: their sense of awe and respect toward God; their sense of God's presence in all the things of the universe; their intense, deep, and concrete prayer; their dedication and sacrifice for the welfare of the people.

b) Because of the strong denominationalism of that day, the missionaries not only viewed their religion as superior, but they formally required the renunciation of all other religions, Protestant as well as Indian. Stories are told how Indians had to leave their medicine bundles outside of church or outside of the sanctuary when they came to be baptized. Medicine men were publicly permitted to continue giving medicine, but they were told to do it without **wocekiye** (ceremonial prayers).

c) But once the Catholic Faith was accepted, the missionaries pastorally tolerated the continued practice of the older, traditional Pipe ceremonies. Stories are told of how Catholics continued smoking the Pipe outside the Church on Sunday or at their homes, and the missionaries rarely commented either way. People had sweatbaths, and the missionaries did not tear them down or condemn people for taking them.

d) The missionaries strongly condemned attendance at **Yuwipi** ceremonies for three reasons: First, they felt that there was a lot of superstition attached to that ceremony. From these ceremonies, people sometimes got "spooky" about **everything** and "ran scared" over matters that could be spiritually interpreted more reasonably and peacefully otherwise. Second, there were many reports of medicine men hexing people or deceiving people or spiritually mixing people up through their **Yuwipi** ceremonies. Third, because of the priests' dualistic theology, they called these ceremonies the "work of the devil," and this was taken literally by some Indians as meaning that people prayed directly to Satan there — which was never the case and was not what the missionaries really meant. Regardless, with little direct investigation, the missionaries told their Catholic members that those who attended **Yuwipi** meetings where committing a serious sin, which they had to confess before they could receive Holy Communion.

These positions came from a time of denominational narrow-mindedness, blindness, and ignorance. The spirit of ecumenism in the world today and the discussions of the Medicine Men and Pastors' Meeting have severely altered that evaluation. In this chapter I will try to indicate why the blanket condemnation of **Yuwipi** has been replaced by cautious encouragement. Blanket approval is not given, but rather a discerning attitude is set forward — similar to the cautious and encouraging attitude that is traditionally found in the Lakota culture as a person approaches a **wakan** ceremony or a **wakan** medicine man.

2) For so long the Catholic Church condemned the Lakota religion, how can it change?

This change of attitude seems to be a natural progression of the Church's growing up on the reservation. At first the Lakota people and the Christian people lived in their own worlds, nurtured like little children in the traditional faith of the forefathers.

After childhood comes adolescence, when adventuresome individuals go out from the close security of their home to meet the enemy and fight, believing that ''Only I am right, and you are all wrong.'' The Church was in that kind of thinking when it came on the reservation; many young Indians are in that kind of situation now as they go off and attack the Churches and the federal government.

Today the Church is maturing on the reservation and throughout the world. It is seeking to unite whatever possible, rather than divide. The emphasis is not upon the things which are different but the things that are similar. There is a desire to bring together the best aspects of many, without being untrue to the uniqueness of each.

There are definite regrets and apologies toward the many people who were hurt by the extremes of our adolescent condemnations and zealousness. Still in many ways these seem to be part of growing up; so many errors were done in ignorance and religious dedication. Most Indians are aware of this and continue to be friendly and have great respect for dedicated missionaries who still earnestly seek the best for the Lakota people in this world and the next.

3) Are the sparks, rattles, and touches experienced in the **Yuwipi** ceremony really caused by the medicine man's spirits — or by the medicine man himself? This is one of the most frequently raised questions from new comers to **Yuwipi.** The answer is neither singular nor simple.

The story is told that Fr. Buechel went to visit someone one day. He found the man, a medicine man, having a sweat. People were standing around the lodge praying, and Father joined them. Inside, as the man sang, one could simultaneously hear an eagle whistle. (Now everyone knows it is impossible to both sing and blow an eagle whistle at the same time.) Everyone said that a spirit was in the lodge with him. After the man finished his sweat and received the words of appreciation from the people, who then left, Fr. Buechel asked the man how he could both sing and blow a whistle at the same time. The man said, ''Let me show you.'' At that the man pulled from the lodge a rubber ball with an eagle whistle stuck into it. As the man squeezed the ball, the whistle gave its call. Here the story ends. Was the medicine man deceiving the people? Were the people deceiving themselves? What did the medicine man and the people and Father individually think was going on? There are many questions here that are unanswered.

A medicine man said that he heard that some people had taken a flashlight into a meeting and during the meeting they turned it on, revealing the medicine man standing and shaking a rattle. Whether the incident **really** happened or is only gossip is unclear. But definitely the reaction of other medicine men was clear. "Such medicine men should not do those things. They give us all **true** medicine men a bad name."

In a Medicine Men and Pastors' Meeting a reliable Indian witness told how one night during a meeting a storm came up. The lightning revealed that one of the shades was not closed tightly, and the lightning filled the room with light so that everyone could see the medicine man sitting in the center. People moved to close the curtains, but the medicine man told them not to. He said that the lightning had a reason and a right for being there. Through the rest of the meeting, the sporadic lightning flashes showed that the medicine man remained seated in the center throughout the meeting; nonetheless, the sparks and rattles continued to appear elsewhere in the room. I have witnessed much of this type of phenomena. Although most phenomena are around the medicine man and could be done by him, I have witnessed some phenomena which, in my judgment, could not have been caused by the medicine man or a helper.

On the other hand, outside a sweatlodge not too long ago, a medicine man showed a priest a lighter without a wick. This medicine man explained that he liked this lighter more than other kinds because of the quality of sparks it gave. That was how he made the sparks in **his** ceremonies, and he was not ashamed to tell the priest. Still, in a good number of other ceremonies, the sparks are associated with the sound of two very hard rocks rubbing together; these sparks also appear different from the ones caused by a conventional lighter.

A number of medicine men told of spiritual phenomena and experiences in **Yuwipi** meetings that even startled **them.** With obvious alarm, a medicine man told of the first **Yuwipi** meeting he ever conducted. After the spirits released him and the lights were turned on, he discovered that his blanket, wrappings, and ties were gone! They had disappeared from the room. He said that he searched for a week trying to find them. This medicine man had in a variety of ways "twisted the arm" of the spirits to give him a **Yuwipi** vision. Through the help of several other medicine men, he finally got it. The disappearance of his **Yuwipi** paraphenalia in his first meeting so shook him that he never performed a **Yuwipi** after that — only **Lowanpi.**

The wife of a medicine man told this story about her uncle. He had been drinking and was sleeping it off on the couch. It came time for a **Lowanpi,** and he was still sleeping. All the furniture was piled up at one end of the room. They decided to let him continue to sleep, and they piled him on the couch on top of a table at the far end of the living room. If he woke up during the ceremony, there was a relative there to tell him to stay there till the end of the meeting. There were many people at the meeting. It was very crowded, so crowded that the people were shoulder to shoulder, and in many places two deep around the room. When the lights went back on at the end of the meeting, the women shrieked. The old man was lying on the kitchen cupboard, completely on the other side of the room. The reporter said that there was no way that anyone could have walked or been carried physically from one place to the other without disturbing many people during the meeting. The old man too was shocked to find himself on the cupboard and more shocked to hear that at the beginning of the ceremony he had been left on the couch on the other side of the room. It was a sobering experience, and the old man stopped his drinking. Such a scary, **wakan** thing would not have happened to him if he had been sober.

In one of the discussions on the various rattles, lights, and touching phenomena in the **Yuwipi** ceremony, a young but well-respected Full-blood stood and said that he found the questions the priests were asking perplexing. He never looked at these things the way the pastors' questions indicated one should look at them. He said that he never looked at these phenomena directly but always saw them within the context of the whole meeting. He said that his view was much more holistic than the pastors. From a Lakota point of view, he had real difficulty answering the highly analytical questions of the pastors.

The holistic view of the world and of events of the Lakota is quite different from the organized view of the Christians. The Lakota respect the independent and often incomprehensible behavior of individuals within their group. They are able to live with mystery in their ceremonies because they find so much mystery in their everyday lives. At first, I was perplexed and even angered when Lakota people repeatedly and nonchalantly answered many questions with a simple, ''I don't know,'' **Slolwaye śni.** My Western, academic background pushed me to find causality in everything conceivable. The Lakota recognize and are at peace with individual freedom, uniqueness, and various **wakan** and strange phenomena — provided they contribute to the life and welfare of their Lakota relatives. Unlike Christians, who formally speak much about what others do and little about themselves, the Lakota speak formally much about themselves and prefer to remain quite silent about others. That is one way that a Lakota shows respect for another person. The Christian is not at peace until one can causally trace everything back to fundamental principles. The Lakota is at peace when he says, "I don't know; it's **wakan.**"

This word, **"wakan"** (sacred), points to a language problem. The Lakota expression for "spirit" is **taku wakan kin,** which literally translates as "the mysterious thing." Westerners tend to divide reality into two main classes: what is concrete and visible and what is ethereal and invisible. The Lakota divide reality into two very different categories: what is **wakan** (mysterious, power-filled, extraordinary) and what is **ikceya** (obvious, pitiful, ordinary). Any number of times I heard Indians in a prayer meeting nudge a White person next to him and say in English, "You see those sparks? A spirit is making them." This statement leaves the White man with a wrong understanding. In ceremonies when Lakota-speakers are touched by a rattle they consider this a life-giving "medicine" and say, **"Pilamaya, Tunkaśila,"** (This pleases me. Thank you, Grandfather.). The term "grandfather" here does not refer to one's physical ancestor but rather says that the action indicates a grandfather-like relationship. While the English word "spirit" points to an inherent quality or nature of an agent, the Lakota word **wakan** points to a **relational stance** of the doer to the receiver of the action. So the Indian should have said, "You see those sparks? One who is spiritual toward you is making them." Metaphoric ambiguity is an inherent characteristic of the naming of and describing of things in the Lakota language.

In addition, the scientific method seeks to transform everything into the simplest of models, where everything is clearly labeled and defined. The scientific method works best when dealing with the lowest forms of matter where the degrees of freedom are few. But as an observer starts to apply the scientific method to phenomena of higher orders, especially human events, the scientific method increasingly loses its application. For example, if a person is hospitalized with ulcers and is healed, what part did the doctors play? the nurses? the hospital? the medicine? the prayers? the reconciled peace in the heart of the patient? God? Who really is responsible for the effect of the medicine on the stomach? The patient who digested it, the nurse who served it, the pharmacy that supplied it, the doctor who prescribed it, the government who supervised its production, the laboratories that made it, the scientists who discovered it??? Who or what causes anything? That is a very complicated question. . .always. A religious person knows that everything originally comes from God, **Wakan Tanka.** In a Lakota healing ceremony, whoever the healer is, he is "an angel from God," and is, in a figurative way, **taku wakan kin.**

Modern science pulls things apart to examine integrated living things with the critical eye of the skeptic. One hears, "Turn on the lights so we can see if it is the medicine man or the spirits who are making the sparks." Yet even if the lights were turned on and one saw the medicine man shaking the rattle, the question still remains, for the spirit may be not only shaking the rattle but also shaking the medicine man as well — in a state of spirit-controlled ecstasy. But turning the light on would be a sign of disbelief, and one would expect disassociation with the spirit in that action.

In "cause-and-effect" situations, Christian theologians concentrate upon the cause; Lakota people concern themselves with the effect. Things are judged and named by their fruits. They concentrate upon the end and trust that God, the spirits, or a medicine, or the offerings will supply the things necessary for the need of the ceremony. A thing is judged **wakan** (sacred) and **taku wakan kin** (a spirit) not because it originates from one who has a particular nature but one who produces some phenomena, healing, or message that will be extraordinary and awesome.

The question whether it is the medicine man or really a spirit who makes the sparks, rattles, and other things in a **Lowanpi** is becoming one of increased importance because today's young Indians are being trained academically in Western-style schools, so they are beginning to think and talk with analytic categories. One expects a "yes" or "no" answer, but the data is too mixed. Some medicine men showed no hesitancy in explaining to priests how they produced certain phenomena themselves. Still others claimed that in their meetings all such phenomena were produced entirely by a spiritual being other than themselves. Consequently, there seems to be a number of legitimate possibilities:

a) The phenomena are caused entirely by exterior spirits with the medicine man remaining completely still and only praying in the center. This is the prototype and the most **wakan,** spiritual form.

b) The medicine man can go into a state of ecstasy where the spirits control the body of the medicine man, who becomes the material, unconscious agent of the spirits. One medicine man said that when he first became a medicine man he "blanked out" during the meetings. He remembered the inviting songs and then the closing songs, but what happened in-between he could not remember. He had to ask the people what was asked, and what the spirits had said and done. He also said that this "blanking out" only lasted for a while; gradually he became conscious of what was going on during the whole meeting.

c) As the prophet in the Old Testament said, "Thus said the Lord...," the medicine man says, "The spirits said this...". The medicine man, like the prophet, is usually the conscious human agent of that which is **wakan.** Hearing the prophet's words, the Jewish people said, "The Lord has spoken." Hearing the medicine man, the Lakota people say, "This is what the spirits said." Out of respect, one does not say that the message given by a messenger is the messenger's; that idea gives an entirely erroneous idea. Every spiritual message, as spiritual, is only of the spirit from which it came. Words are symbolic sounds communicating spiritual messages. Sparks, rattles, touches, and winds are symbolic actions communicating spiritual messages. While the spirits can **cause** certain actions directly, the spirits can also **direct** certain actions to be done indirectly through the medicine man. In this latter case, although the action is physically done by the medicine man, its spiritual and symbolic message is entirely the spirits'. If a spirit tells a medicine man to speak certain words which have **wakan** significance, then the message of those words is of the spirit in its **wakan** quality. If a spirit tells the medicine man to shake a rattle which has **wakan** significance, then the message of that rattle is of the spirit alone in its **wakan** character. If the spirits direct a medicine man to touch a person for **wakan** reasons, the medicine man is only acting as the instrument of the spirit. The person who receives the touch as **wakan** can properly say, "**Tunkaśila, pilamaya,**" (Grandfather, thank you), identifying **Tunkaśila** as the spirits, because the **wakan** power of the action is not really from the medicine man but from the spirit.

On this level, even if the lights were turned on, a person could not know whether the medicine man's words or actions were caused by the spirits through their instructions, or whether they were really initiated by the medicine man himself. Is there an advantage here in having the lights on? Rather there is a disadvantage. With the lights on, the mind concentrates upon visual image, which could be confused with the real cause. The darkness closes the visual image and makes the participants more conscious of the hidden, **wakan** side of reality, which is the operative side in the Lakota healing ceremony. Contrariwise, it is religiously better that the Mass takes place in the light so that people can see in the priest, in the Eucharist, and in the People of God, the incarnational blessing and life of the Son of God, who came not in an invisible, mysterious way but in a clear, ordinary way.

d) The fourth possibility is that the "medicine man" is faking it. The Lakota are aware of this possibility. A number of them have pointed to this or that medicine man as being fakes. There were different motivations for their making such a remark: a previous disagreement, jealousy, self-promotion, sincere interest to communicate the truth. If a man was a fake the people would say, "He doesn't have any power." If a medicine man is **wakan,** people will be healed, prophesies will be accurate, and prayer requests will be answered. Many beginners are fascinated by the sparks, rattles and touches, and fakers love to put on a great show of these. After a short time, a person is not really impressed by the "external theatrics" of the ceremony. Very quickly one's mind focuses on the needs of one's relatives. Personally I find that when there are few sparks and rattles in a ceremony, my mind begins to wander from the hours of prayer in the darkness. The sparks, rattles, touches, and sounds help me to keep focused on the needs of the people towards whom these mysterious, **wakan** phenomena are directed. Unfortunately, most priests, sisters, and White people who attend the ceremonies do so out of interest in the ceremony rather than out of concern for the relatives in their pitiful state. Consequently, they are not able to enter into the ceremony properly to experience its spiritual value.

When a person does enter into the ceremony for "health" and "life" of the relatives, one very quickly becomes aware of a pervasive "spirit" in the meeting. Using a "sixth sense," a person just **knows** whether a medicine man is real and sincere or a fake and show-off. So in the short-run, a perceptive person is able to distinguish the **heart** of a real medicine man from that of a fake. More convincingly, in the long-run, a perceptive person is able to distinguish a real from a fake by the success or failure of his healings and prophesies.

4) Do hexings really take place in **Yuwipi** and **Lowanpi** ceremonies?

The medicine men and Lakota people recognize that the medicine man with the help of his spirit can hex [**tehmuga**]. However, investigations of these hexing reports indicate many false reports, rumors, and neurotic fears. Rather Investigations indicate that there actually are **few** such hexes. With these ceremonies becoming publicly accepted, they are increasingly publicly attended, and there is increased public pressure against doing such things. So today if the medicine man is going to actually hex someone, it must be in very small, private meetings where the full **Lowanpi** ritual is usually not followed.

Medicine men and others closely associated with Indian medicine point out that there are many temptations to use the

wakan power for one's own advantage or to someone else's advantage for a large fee. They are aware that those things which are **wakan** have a powerful kick-back, and those who indulge themselves in these things end up getting themselves or other family members hurt. So as with evil spirits, they are said to keep the good side out for the benefit of the people and keep the evil side down low. This same criterion is to be used by ordinary people in deciding which medicine man and which ceremonies to go to.

If the sponsor of a ceremony or a medicine man prays that some harm or misfortune comes to someone, one should leave that medicine man and ceremony as soon as possible and seek the help and protection of an experienced, good, spiritual counselor. They should not be afraid to approach a person trained in the area of spiritual discernment to help them interpret and correct the source of their spiritual unrest — be it from ignorance, fear, superstition, alcoholic DT's, real spirits, or whatever. If the sponsor's and medicine man's intentions and prayers during the ceremony are for the benefit of the sick, the needy, and the people, attendance is not only allowable but encouraged.

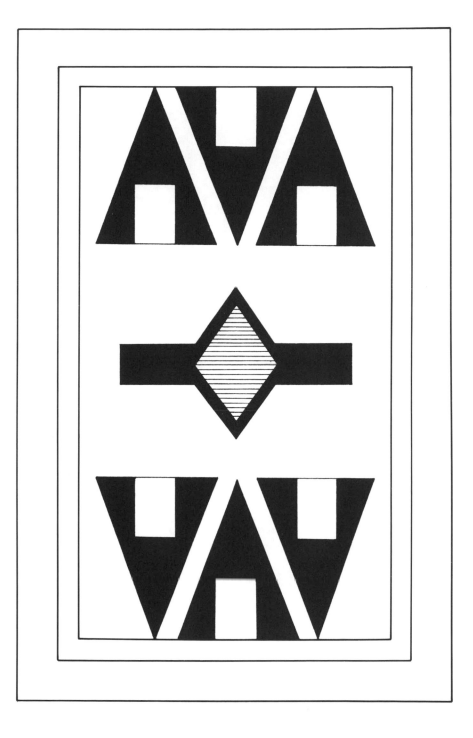

Chapter 11

Sundance and the Paschal Mysteries

The Sundance is the great, annual religious ceremony of the Lakota people. Similarly, the celebration of the Paschal Mysteries, from Holy Thursday through Easter Sunday, marks the high point in the Christian liturgical year. Entire books have been written describing each set of ceremonies. In this chapter the discussion of these two sets will focus on their comparative elements, as seen through the eyes of the members of the Rosebud Medicine Men and Pastors' Meeting.

Mid-summer was the Lakota's time for renewed social contact, storytelling, and great councils. The central religious focus, which dominated preparations and activity, was the Sundance, the most public, elaborate, and community-forming ritual of the Lakota. Similarly, the events and ceremonies leading up to Easter were the most public, elaborate and community-forming rituals among the Christian people. Special songs and musicians, noted speakers and addresses, elaborate fasting and purification, and singular preparation of the ceremonial areas marked these celebrations far above all others.

The sun plays a symbolic role in both the Lakota and Christian traditions. The early Christians associated the rising of Christ from the tomb on Easter morning with the rising of the sun. They compared waiting for the coming of Christ at the End of the World with a man waiting for the rising of the sun at dawn. The Christians chose Christ's birthday as December 25th; this was the octave day of the Roman Saturnalia celebration of the rising of the sun after winter solstice. The rising of the sun is a symbol of the transforming work of Christ, who brings man from a world of darkness and sin into God's kingdom of light and life. Easter takes place in the first month of the Jewish calendar, Nisan, when the Jews celebrated their leaving the bondage of Egypt to pass through the Red Sea as God's redeemed people on their way to the Promised Land of Milk and Honey. The Paschal Mysteries celebrate the Christian's transformation from a state of sin and darkness, to the resurrection promise and glorification. The Main Easter service is a long vigil ceremony. It originally began at night and ended with dawn. Today the services are shorter, the coming from darkness into new light is symbolically expressed in the lighting of the people's candles from the Easter candle, which is lit from a fire started from flint rock. Sometimes there are special sunrise services commemorating Christ's resurrection from the tomb at the break of that first Easter day.

The Lakota call the Sundance, **Wiwan[yank] wacipi,** (They dance watching the sun.). It takes place in the "month when the chokecherries are ripe" (August). This is the time when the sun is the highest and the days are the hottest, between the busy times of spring and fall, during a time of leisure and prosperity. While the **rising** of the sun is observed with solemnity at some Sundances, it is the **presence** of the sun that is more important. If it is cloudy or rainy, the breaking through of the sun is seen as a special blessing. Before the recent renewal of the Sundance, there was only one Sioux Sundance, and it was at Pine Ridge. The dancers would come into the sacred area shortly after sunrise, and the dance would climax around noon, **wicokanhiyaye** (the sun comes to the middle). Today dancing often goes till almost sunset. "When the sun is overhead at midday, even the smallest thing in the deepest valley is seen." People take part in the Sundance to complete a vow, to seek a vision, to come to an awareness of one's Indian self-identity, to sacrifice for the healing of a loved one, and for the life and health of the people. There is an undercurrent which craves strength and power for the people. Talks, actions, prayers, and songs are done by many people. The expectations are much more positive and confident than at any other Lakota ceremony. In many other Lakota ceremonies, the orientation is inward, passive, and receptive. While these are not abandoned, the orientation is more outward, active, and aggressive — even to the point of being occasionally militant.

Some White people ask whether the Lakota worship the sun at the Sundance. The word "worship" refers to the special recognition given to a spiritual person, recognizing that person as divine, or of the highest spiritual order. One Sundance chief said, "So many people have asked me about the Sundance. Do we worship the sun? I tell them, No. We worship almighty God. We admire his work. Without the sun we wouldn't be able to see one another or recognize one another. We would not be able to recognize the different colored people of the world in the four directions of the Sundance." Again this quotation accentuates a key concept of the Sundance: through the sun and the Sundance, the Lakota people obtain a clear perception of the Lakota's world, and relationships can be realized to their fullest. The ability of the sun to expose, enlighten, relate, unite, and heal makes it awesome and great, **wakan**. Consequently, the sun is "something sacred" or **taku wakan kin** or a "spiritual being" or a "spirit." During the dance the dancers will periodically raise one or both hands toward the sun and look only at the rim of the sun. This is right and respectful, for to look upon the sun directly, as looking upon God directly is dangerous, if not impossible. With raised arms and heads, the participants blow their eagle whistles, a higher and more penetrating prayer than ordinary words. Before the modern revival, the dancers only occasionally faced the sun and prayed to/through it. In the modern revival, some sundance chiefs have the dancers facing the sun all the time, moving only as the sun moved. Most, however, still have the dancers constantly moving to the four directions most of the time. They wear specially made wraps, often with Indian symbols on them. They are purified and anointed to be **wakan** and strong.

In the center of the great Sundance circle, marked with sacred colors in the four directions, a special cottonwood tree is placed. Here the tree becomes a symbol of the **wakan** "man" standing in the center of God's **wakan** universe. This tree has fallen, but it was caught so that it never touched the ground. It is dead and yet it is still in leaf. It is surrounded by leaves in the shape of hearts. When the sides of the leaves are rolled together, they look like teepees. If a person cuts through a limb, one finds a star. The central tree stands alone at first, but then the dancers are attached to it by means of rawhide strips or ropes. Through these dancers all of the relatives and people are joined to the tree and God above. In the crotch of the tree is set a bundle of cherry sticks in which a food offering is placed, a nesting place of the **Wakiyan** spirit. In the branches are put leather symbols of the buffalo, the sun, the moon, and man. To the uppermost branches are attached large flags of the colors of the directions. The pole extends from Grandmother Earth and lifts all these signs and gifts of the four-legged and the two-legged to **Wakan Tanka Tunkaśila** (the Great Grandfather Spirit above), who will send his power and blessing to the people through the pole and the attached dancers and to the surrounding people [**oyate**]. During the dance, the dancers periodically raise their hands to salute this pole from a distance or touch it at close range, for this pole is a **wakan** intermediary between the dancer and God and gives the dancer courage and strength.

The primary artifact of the Paschal mystery is the Easter (or Paschal) Candle. It is marked with a cross, filled with sweet incense, marked with universal symbols indicating the universal effect of Christ's salvific act, and lit by a fire started from flint. The Easter Candle is the symbol of the Easter resurrectional glorification of the Good Friday Cross. The Easter Candle is not only a symbol of the resurrected Son of Man, Jesus Christ; it is also a symbol of the universal Christian. The participants at the Easter Vigil Service have their own candles, which are lit from the Easter Candle. The Easter Candle is made of bee's wax, made from pollen gathered from all points of the compass. So too, all of God's people are gathered from every nation into the one People of God in Christ and His Church. Just as it is the nature of a candle to express itself by giving of itself for the enlightment and warmth of others, so too Christ gives of himself to the world through his Spirit of Light and Truth. All Christians are united to him and likewise spread light and truth into the world to the extent that they are able to. Christ is like the central wick that penetrates the candle from beginning to end, even though only a small part of the wick is showing at any one moment. Christians are like refined bee's wax, uniting themselves together through the warmth of Christ's love, to give themselves in ways similar to but different from the sacrifice of Christ. While a few Lakota carry the central tree and are physically tied to it, only one carries the central Easter Candle. Still there may be some who have prepared themselves through instructions or a catechumenate for their own baptism or their child's baptism, and all Christians there unite themselves to Christ through their own candle lit from the Easter fire as they renew their baptismal vows. In the Easter vigil service, the Church recognizes that this particular congregation is both one of the many churches throughout the world on that particular day as well as one of the many groups of God's people whom He has blessed through all of salvation history — from the beginning of the world until now. While the Lakota in their talks stress the importance of this people within the sacred traditions and history of their people, the Christians speak of God's **universal** plan of salvation in the death and resurrection of Christ.

Besides honoring the rising sun, the Easter candle, and the incensed nails, and recounting salvation history, the Christians honor the lamb. Similarly, besides honoring the glorious sun, the Sundance pole, and the cherry-stick skewers, the Lakota honor the buffalo. The buffalo saved the people from starvation, provided all the material things they needed for survival, and was the sign through which the Pipe was received. The sacrifice of the lamb is associated with the Jew's deliverance from the hand of the Angel of Death and the slavery of pharaoh. It was the sign of the Jewish Passover and covenant with the Lord in the Old Testament and a sign of the new covenant achieved through the sacrifice of Jesus, the Lamb of God who takes away the sins of the world.

If a person is going to take part in a Sundance, one often makes a pledge with a pipe one year before the event so that one may prepare for it thoroughly. One should stay away from fighting and wrong living throughout that year as well as pray with the pipe and take sweatbaths regularly. In the Sundance after the daily, early-morning sweatbath, male dancers wear an ankle length wrap around their waist over shorts, and female dancers wear a traditional styled dress of calico. Ribbons usually decorate them. After the sweat they tie bands of sage around their ankles, wrists, and head. The men place two upright eagle feathers into either side of their head wreaths.

The Sundance chief leads them through the east gate of the Sundance area. Depending upon the number of dancers, they either circle the central pole on all directions or face the pole from each of the four directions in turn. While traditional Sundance songs are sung, the participants dance quietly in place facing the central tree. During the first round they carry pipes in the sacred area and pray with them, but they are then placed on a pipe rack on the west side in front of the buffalo skull. During each round they at times rush toward the tree, touch it, and pray to God for strength. Then they return to their former position to dance for a good length of time. When the Sundance chief decides, one dancer is taken to get a pipe. It is taken to the direction of the current singing group. There the pipe is offered in the ceremonial four-fold way. When the pipe is taken, the music stops and the dancers have a rest period for a time in a shade to the west of the dance circle.

When the pipe is completely smoked, it is returned to the sacred area and the dancing begins again. After a number of rounds, the sundance chief may decide to begin the piercing. Male dancers are brought one at a time to the center and lay down on a buffalo robe or a bed of sage. They give the sundance chief two skewers and their rope, one end of which is tied high in the center cottonwood tree. Usually they are pierced through the skin above the pectoral muscle. After medicine is placed on the spots, two slits are cut in the flesh and a skewer is forced through. Then the rope is tied to either sides of the skewer. The dancer stands and returns to his spot to dance in place until everything is ready. Meanwhile, relatives come into the sacred area through one of the flagged gates and stand behind their sacrificing relative to encourage him and pray for him.

At the direction of the sundance chief, those who have been pierced move forward to touch the central tree and pray for strength. Then the dancers move suddenly backward and sacrificially pull on the rope with only their flesh until the skewers tear through the skin, releasing the dancer.

A number of young Indians said that as they hung from the pole, they found themselves identifying themselves with Christ, asking Him for strength, drawing encouragement from his example. In that physically demanding act, they gave themselves completely, body and soul to God in ways that they had never done before. They recognized their failings and their weaknesses. They found their limitations and their strengths. They discovered the love they had for their God and their people. The Sundance was a total faith experience to them.

Depending upon a dream or a spiritual desire, the dancer may be pierced in the back on the shoulder blades so that he can pull a string of buffalo skulls around the sacred area. Sometimes they may desire to be hung from the central pole. There are various ways a person may be called to sacrifice his flesh for the health and help [**wicozanni na wawokiye**] of the people. Women in the circle are not pierced but rather ''give flesh.'' Often relatives and friends around the outside of the circle will support the piercers by ''giving flesh.'' Medicine is rubbed on their upper arms, and a certain number of pieces of flesh are cut off with a knife or razor blade in sacrifice for the people.

Some people have great difficulty understanding and appreciating the tearing of flesh that takes place in the Sundance. Even today one hears statements and questions directly or indirectly considering such practices to be ''savage,'' ''barbaric,'' and ''pagan.'' Modern Americans are very health-conscious, and many cannot understand that there are higher values for which health is to be sacrificed. Many Americans live pampered, sheltered lives. Most never have seen an animal slaughtered. Modern processing, packaging, and eating utensils set blood and meat at a distance. Natural, organic fluids are quickly washed off and soon become repulsive to them. With a strong emphasis of mind over matter, the symbolic aspect of things replaces the reality of things.

The Lakota still live very close to nature ''in the raw,'' the way it is. They personally kill most of the meat they eat. They eviscerate it, skin it, and butcher it with their own hands. They know personally that animals must be killed that they may live and be happy. They also are well aware of the criss-cross character of the material and spiritual orders. Spiritual prayers request favors from God, and He helps them in material ways. Sacrifices made in a physical way strengthen and fulfill spiritual relationships.

American Catholics not only tend to separate Church and State, they tend to separate the material and spiritual orders too much. They shy away from physical penances and prefer the "neater" spiritual kinds. Most penances today are diluted materially into the normal practice of Christian prayer and virtue. Material contributions come primarily from one's surpluses and left-overs, rather than from one's livelihood. Modern Christians generally have little appreciation for the early Christian's eagerness and joy in material penances, persecution, and martyrdom. The Lakota can easily ask those individuals who are confused by material sacrifices the same question that Jesus asked his disciples on Easter, "Was it not necessary that the Christ should suffer these things and enter into his glory?" (Lk 24.27)

People who physically struggle together to survive and achieve something meaningful have memories and feelings seared upon their souls. Similarly, Lakota individuals who have been pierced together are bonded together in remembrance, love, fidelity, and mutual self-sacrifice. Similarly, Christians who have struggled together religiously — like Jesuits in a forty-day retreat — have a deep affection and mutual dedication because of it.

As it was said earlier, persons who are going to take part in a Sundance usually make a vow to that effect one year before the event. During that year they increasingly stay away from wrong doing and take part in spiritual things. The four days just before the Sundance are days of special sweatbaths, prayers, material preparations, and perhaps even some fasting. The next four days of the Sundance proper are now observed as days of total fast from food and even water, despite the fact that one is dancing eight to fourteen hours a day under the hot August sun. For the Christian, the forty days of Lent before the Sacred Triduum (Three Days) are prescribed to be days of more intense prayer, abstinence, and fasting. The more dedication that a person puts into these days of preparation, the more spiritual benefit will be given to the individuals and the people.

Vows are associated with both the Sundance and Easter vigil rituals. For the Lakota, vows are made usually in relationship to a request of God for a healing, for special help, for receiving a vision, for an insight into one's Indian identity, for the success of a particular project, or for perhaps safe return from a tour of duty as a soldier in a war zone. The Sundance is the **fulfillment** of a vow. For the Christian, the Easter Vigil is a time for a **renewal** of one's vows. The Lakota know that the spirits are with them in a special way up through the ceremony. The Christian knows that Christ will be with him in a special way henceforth from this ceremony. For the Lakota the period after the Sundance is a time of settling down into the traditional ways, to the chores preparatory for the harsh winter ahead. For the Christian, there is a joyful eagerness to step out of the springtime feast into new activities, to be bold in the face of difficulties.

The Lakota emphasize the **material** obligation of fulfilling a vow. This was humorously illustrated by this Full-blood story. "A son made a vow that he would Sundance if he came back alive from (military) service. He did, but he delayed the Sundance because he was scared of it. Finally the father corralled him into the Sundance. After he was pierced, his three sisters were standing behind him. . .but he didn't pull. His father got two horses, and he tied the thongs to the two horses — he would give them away after the Sundance. He slapped the horses. . .and the boy ran off behind them!!! He wasn't going to let them tear **his** flesh." (The Full-blood audience who heard the story roared with laughter.)

In a similar way, the Christian emphasis upon **spiritual** dedication resulted in this humorous situation. One day an inactive Catholic Lakota stopped by for coffee. In the course of the conversation I asked him, "John, do you believe in God?"

"You bet. I believe everything they taught me in catechism."

"Tell me. Is there a difference between **believing** a man and believing **in** a man?"

"Oh sure. If you believe a man, you know that what he says is true. If you believe **in** a man, you're going to go out and do something about it."

"So, John, when was the last time you went to church, even on Easter?"

He paused. One could tell the gears upstairs were turning. Suddenly he jerked his head up. He looked me straight in the eye and said, "Listen, Father, I already **have** the Faith. Why should I get all hung up **trying** to be faithful?"

All I could do was groan.

At the Sundance and the Easter Vigil there are **many** stories, most of them serious rather than humorous, but each one telling of the traditions, ways, and history of the Lakota and Christian people. At the Lakota ceremonies, the emphasis is upon oral tradition and more recent times. In the Christian way, the emphasis is upon scriptures and the time of Christ. Except for the very beginning where the blessing of the sacred tree and area is important, and for the very end when the Sundancers bless the sick and the people, the Sundance ritual is basically the same throughout the four days. Spiritual realities associated with the Pipe dominate: The Four Directions around the Sacred Pole, songs to **Tunkašila Wakan Tanka** for blessing, Grandmother Earth, the buffalo skull, the Pipe, sage, and sweetgrass. In the

Christian way the services are different each day; they commemorate the different events of Christ's life from the Last Supper to the resurrection. Spiritual realities associated with Christ dominate: the cross, the Easter Candle, Easter songs, the theme of the lamb of sacrifice, baptismal water, the Eucharist, incense.

Both the Sundance and the Paschal Ceremonies emphasize the gathering of the people around sacred, tradition-filled sacrifice for the life and welfare of the people. But in terms of external forms the four day Sundance ritual and the four days of the Passover Services are quite different. Still a person receives much appreciation of the two sets of rituals by comparing and contrasting them.

Chapter 12

The Pipe and Christ: Their Comings

Because of the importance of the Pipe and Christ in the Lakota and Christian religions, the members of the Rosebud Medicine Men and Pastors' Meeting spent considerable time studying and discussing their comings.

The stories of the Comings of the Pipe and of Christ are not myths but legends. They do not speak of events which happened near the beginning of time using highly symbolic figures. These stories take place in recent historic times; they are publicly recorded in Winter counts and in Gospels. While the variations in the stories point to a certain amount of human idealization and invention for the sake of instruction of the hearers of these stories, thus making these stories "legendary" in terms of their literary form, still the content and consistencies of these traditions point to definite, historic events. These in turn give each religion a solid, historical origin. Founded not in vision or word but in historic deeds, these legends describe how the sacred and the human orders were linked together in special ways. In many ways, the legends concerning the comings of the Pipe and of Christ are comparable. In the first two sections of this chapter each legend will be individually summarized. In the third section the legends will be compared and contrasted. In the fourth section, other stories and data related to origins will be presented.

Through the centuries, the Sioux people have told and retold the story of how they received the Pipe in a special way from a Maiden. There are as many variations of this story as there are story tellers, for each person tells the story in his own spiritually significant way. Still each story has the same central elements. All the story tellers point to the coming of the Buffalo Calf Pipe at the beginning of a new spiritual relationship with God for the Sioux people. The story goes like this.

Two young men were walking one day. They were looking for food because the people were in need. These two hunters saw something in the far distance, walking in a marvelous, **wakan** manner. As it came closer, they realized it was a woman coming toward them. She was very beautiful. She was carrying a bundle in her arms. One of these young men had evil thoughts. He wanted to lay with her, but when he reached out to grab her, a fog enveloped them. All one could hear was a humming noise. The maiden then stepped from the fog, and the fog lifted. All that remained of the young man was his skeleton on the ground.

The other young man was very scared. The Maiden said, ''Go home and tell your people and your chiefs to prepare a teepee and to wait for me there. I have something for them, and I will bring it to them.'' The young man went home as fast as he could and told his people and the chiefs. They made a great teepee and waited for her inside.

Very soon someone said, ''She is coming now.'' She came singing into the teepee where the chiefs and the people were waiting for her. She told them, ''I have brought you this Buffalo Calf Leg Pipe so you can pray to God. With this you will not starve, your children will grow, and your people will be healthy, and you will have life. Whenever you are in danger or in need of anything, you must respect this Pipe and pray with good intentions, and your prayers will be answered.'' Then singing, she left again. Going off into the wilderness, she turned into a white buffalo and galloped away.

There are many minor variations to the story. Some say that she came from the center of a herd of buffalo. Some say that the young men were standing on a hill when they saw her coming. Some say she bore the Pipe in a bundle on her back when she met the young men. When the cloud lifted, it is said that there were snakes crawling among the bones. Some say that the Maiden appeared suddenly within the teepee and afterwards disappeared just as mysteriously. Some say the woman also gave the chief a flat, round piece of pipestone, which had a series of seven small circles carved on it — these represented the Pipe's seven rites, which would be revealed in dreams and visions among the people. In most stories her words are not exactly the same, but the message always points in the same direction. Some say that when she left the teepee, she rolled over and became a black buffalo, rolled again and became a red buffalo, rolled over again and became a yellow buffalo, and finally she rolled over and became a white buffalo. (This is the current color sequence of the Four Directions indicated by the Pipe ceremony.) Others say simply that she left in a **wakan** manner.

Each of these details adds its own religious dimension to the basic narrative. Since folk people have a special reverence for the religious things they have received, they do not diminish what they have traditionally received but rather make their own additions, usually for the spiritual edification of the hearers. These additions bring out some point which matches a particular historic need or interest. Therefore, it should be possible to gather the many variations of this story from different Sioux clans and learn from the additions and variations some useful information about the Sioux's local religious history. In general, the more common an element is, the older it may be considered to be. The above narration is one of the most common and therefore one of the oldest accounts of this religious event.

Attached to the legend of the coming of the Buffalo Calf Leg Pipe are instructions concerning the care and use of the Pipe. It is said that it was the Maiden herself who instructed the chiefs in the right use of the Pipe and instructed them how to make their Pipes thereafter. She also gave her Pipe to one worthy person, who was to be the first of a long chain of Keepers of the Pipe. The first Pipe Keeper was Standing Buffalo, a chief of the clan called **Itazipco,** (Without Bows), or Sans Arc. Some say that there have been fourteen Keepers of the Pipe; others say that there have been eleven so far. The current Keeper of the Pipe is a young man named Orville Looking Horse. He said that the original Pipe was received far up river near Devil's Tower, and he can trace the movements of the Sacred Pipe in stages to its current location. The Pipe has been kept now many years at his family's place at Green Grass, South Dakota, west of the Missouri River on the Cheyenne River Reservation. Many Indians have made pilgrimages there in recent years to pray there and even at times to see and pray with the Pipe.

At one of the Medicine Men and Pastors' Meeting, one pastor asked how it was known that the story was really about an historical event rather than an Indian's dream. This question greatly incensed the medicine men, because the speaker was implicitly saying that words of the Indians were not sufficient since they always presented the legend as an historic fact rather than as a dream or vision. Although imprudently phrased, the question was asking for supporting data pointing to the real historicity of this story. First of all, the tradition says that it was an historic event and not a dream. The medicine men constantly demanded (because their spirits also demanded). "Don't speak above it; don't speak beneath it; speak it as you hear it." To change a description from a dream to an event would be a grave violation of one of their fundamental religious rules of spiritual transmission. Secondly, Lakota spiritual experiences are predominantly non-physical, except in fulfillment of healings and prophesies. It would be normal and acceptable to communicate the origin of the Pipe in the same genre as the story of the origin of many Lakota ceremonies — in individual dreams and visions. Actually, a dream is a more **wakan** genre than an historic event, in the Lakota way of thinking. Thirdly, this legend did not originate from an experience of an individual but of a clan, and it would be difficult to state something as a great experience of a clan without it being so. Fourthly, the legend is attached to the appearance of a special material object that has been in the care of a relatively short line of Keepers.

A number of accounts point toward the specific date of the appearance. While one Winter count gives a much earlier date, most of the winter counts give descriptions of a god-woman, [**winyan wakan**] or a woman dressed in white, coming among the Teton Sioux between 1785 and 1800 A.D. For example, the "Sioux Calendar" by Jos. Chief states, "1792. **Winyan wan ska wanyankapi Pte hincala canumpa toka yuhapi.**" (They see a woman [in] white; they have first buffalo pipe.) Anthropologists once examined the Pipe at Green Grass and said that it bears a striking resemblance to several Arikara bowls on display at W.H. Over Dakota Museum at Vermillion. Historical records indicate that the Sioux first contacted the Arikara on the Missouri sometime between 1722 when they were near the headwaters of the Minnesota River and 1743 when the La Verendrye brothers met them north of Pierre, South Dakota. This is the period when they first acquired the horse. Weakened by smallpox, the Arikara were driven from the South Dakota Missouri River valley in 1792. Stanley Looking Horse, keeper of the Sacred Pipe, says that the Buffalo Calf Woman brought the Sacred Pipe to the people near Devils Tower. A winter count says that the Sioux first came to the Black Hills in 1775-1776 and by 1805 the Sioux had overcome both the Kiowas and the Cheyennes and were in control of the Black Hills. There have been 14 keepers of the Sacred Pipe. If one speculates that on the average each keeper cared for the Pipe one generation (20 years), then the Pipe would have to have come after 1700 A.D. So a variety of data points toward the late 1700's for the White Buffalo Calf Woman bringing the Sacred Pipe to the Lakota. (1)

The Lakota medicine men call the original Pipe **Ptehincala Hu Cannunpa** (Buffalo Calf Leg Pipe). At the meeting there was

(1) See: John L. Smith, "A Short History of the Sacred Pipe of the Teton Sioux," University of South Dakota Museum Notes, (28:1-37).

considerable discussion about the tradition that says that the original Pipe was made from the leg of a buffalo calf. Many of the participants had been to Green Grass and prayed with the Pipe there, but this Pipe looked like the Pipes that are in use today — ones which have wooden stems.

Then John (Lame Deer) Fire, a well-known medicine man, told his story. In 1935, before anyone else at the meeting had done it, John said he went to Green Grass. There he met the old woman who was the Keeper of the Pipe. She said that she had expected him and that she had something to tell him. She knew that he came to see the Pipe and to pray with it. The Pipe was **lila wakan** (very sacred), and only a few could pray with it. They went to an old shed, and she got the bundle. He cut the string and opened it. Inside, wrapped in much sage and with other things, were **two** Pipes. She pointed to the oldest Pipe; it was the most sacred. It was a little one, about a foot long. Its stem was made from one of the left front leg bones of a buffalo calf; the bowl was made from an ankle bone or something. The bowl was strapped to the stem with a leather thong. On either side of the bowl were little wing-like things protruding downward. The stem was very dry. A person had to be very careful or part of the bone would flake off. The bowl was filled and capped with sage. The old woman said she was going to bury this Pipe to protect it and that only a few would know where she'd hide it. (John said that he knew, but John is dead now. He didn't indicate any others who knew.) John said the woman told him that when the Pipe would have a good permanent home they could dig it up again and put it there. The woman said that it should not be handled or moved from place to place. It should be put into a place where no one could take pictures of it directly. In addition to the small bone pipe, John said there was a second Pipe. This one had a wooden stem about two feet long. It looked very much like the Pipes used today. The old woman told him that this was the first Pipe, the one made the way the maiden told the chiefs to make it. This is the one after which all other Pipes were to be modeled. This is what Lame Deer said.

This testimony raised considerable discussion at the Medicine Men and Pastors' Meeting. Some medicine men could not believe that the original Pipe — the one the maiden carried — would ever begin to dry out and flake away with use. Many found it difficult to accept the distinction between the **original** Pipe that the Maiden brought and the **first** Pipe which the Maiden taught how to make. Still, other Lakota thought that the Sioux had not used a similar Pipe before the coming of the Buffalo Calf Woman and the Buffalo Calf Leg Pipe. Some maintained that the first Pipe had the image of a buffalo carved on the bowl. The more traditional medicine men definitely held to the tradition that the pipe that the Maiden brought was called **Ptehincala Hu Cannunpa** (Buffalo Calf **Leg** Pipe). In a spontaneous comment in Oglala, Max Blacksmith, who grew up on the Cheyenne River Reservation said that in the 1920's his father, John Blacksmith, told Max that he saw the original Pipe at Green Grass. "And you know what it looks like? It looks like a buffalo calf leg and its hoof." It is reported to me that others have more recently seen the sacred Pipe that is made from a buffalo leg at Green Grass. Still other people report being shown a more traditional-styled pipe at Green Grass. Perhaps, as John (Lame Deer) Fire said, "There are two pipes, the original and the first, each being shown at different times for different spiritual reasons." Regardless, it is important to remember the words of Black Elk who said, that any pipe that is made as the Buffalo Calf Woman taught and is used in the correct sacred manner is **wakan** like the original and will bring blessings, visions, life, and health for the people.

Historical investigations can easily get confused and raise much dust to cloud people's clear religious vision. The Pipe at Green Grass is being shown more often than in the past, and more questions are being raised about it. In the old days when there was little travel and gatherings were smaller, the Pipe was seldom shown, and the Pipe religion was the strongest. It is good to recall Black Elk's words: "Any Pipe used as the original Pipe was meant to be used is as sacred as the original Pipe given by the Maiden. Indeed, to one who understands they are the same." (2)

The story of the coming of Christ has had its historical criticism too. Similarly one must have patience with the investigators interested in drawing out all the material details that are knowable. After that, one must return to the basic spiritual message given by God to the people in the birth of Jesus.

The story of the coming of Christ has been repeated again and again with multiple variations from inspired artists and church leaders. This is true even in the Gospels themselves. Matthew, Luke, and John each emphasize his own special concerns as they describe Christ's entrance into this world. They all agree on the essential theological points: that a special gift of God, the Son of God, became man in order that He might bring salvation to everyone and establish God's reign over the entire earth, in

(2) **The Sacred Pipe,** Joseph Epes Brown, University of Oklahoma Press, 1953.

fulfillment of God's plan formed long ago. Luke's account is the most complete, the most popular, and from internal evidence, the most historical.

Much has been written about the meaning and historicity of the Infancy Narratives. I will say only a few things here. First of all, the question of historicity was faced by Luke himself. In the introduction immediately before the infancy narrative, Luke tells of the care he exercised in compiling his account precisely as those events were transmitted to us by the original eyewitnesses and ministers of the word. The unity of the text of the infancy narrative indicates that there was one primary source behind its many episodes. The special Aramaic quality of the first two chapters is unique; it does not occur elsewhere in Luke. It would seem that the one from whom this section originated was close to those events, as Luke says it, one of "the original eyewitnesses." The source of the infancy narrative then would be one close to the families of Zachariah and Joseph. The original source displayed both a deeply authentic yet personalized understanding of the Old Testament. In addition to loyalty to Jewish spirituality, the author showed the loftiest understanding of Christology found in any of the Synoptic Gospels. In the prophesy of Simeon, even the role of Christ as Suffering Servant for the salvation of many was indicated. The words of the angel to Mary pointed to the prophet Daniel, and it was from Daniel that Christ took the title, Son of Man, a corporate identity who was to suffer and come to a divine destiny in heaven and then on earth. Luke suggested that Mary was the source of these stories because the infancy narratives closed with the statement, "His mother meanwhile kept these things in her heart." At least it would have to be someone very close to her. If Mary was the original source behind Luke's infancy narratives, then one finds her to be a woman well educated in scripture, truly Jewish and truly Christian. One can sense the joy and depth of her spirituality. Clearly these historic events are seen more from their theological meaning than their historic detail; still their relevance is grounded on the reality of those events. At least it can be said that the infancy narrative in Luke expresses the very traditional and religiously sensitive environment of the extended-family in which Jesus grew up.

Luke begins the story of Christ's birth in the temple in Jerusalem. There was a priest named Zachariah. He was old, and he and his wife had no children. They were both good people who tried to do everything God told them to do. One day when Zachariah went into the temple to pray, an angel of the Lord came to him and told him his wife would have a son, and that they would call him "John." John would prepare the people for the coming of

Christ by taking a vow, by living a very poor life, and by vowing never to drink any alcohol.

John would be filled with the Holy Spirit even within the womb. He would bring all back to God. He would turn the hearts of father to their children; he would direct the rebellious to the wisdom of the just; he would make people ready and well-disposed for the Lord. John was to preach a baptism of repentance to prepare the people for the coming of Christ. All these things the angel told Zachariah.

But Zachariah was frightened. He could not believe that he and his wife could have a son in their old age. The angel said, "I am Gabriel. I stand immediately before God to do his command. I was sent to tell you this good news, but since you did not believe me, you will be speechless until the birth of the child." Everything happened as the angel had said. John prepared the people for the coming of Christ.

The angel Gabriel also came to Mary in Nazareth. The angel told her that God was with her in a special way, that she was blessed among all women, that she would have a son, yet remain a virgin. The Holy Spirit would come upon her and the son she would bear would not be the son of a man but the Son of God himself. The child's name would be given by God, and it would be "Jesus" because he would save all people from their sins. He would be great in dignity. He would receive the throne of David his ancestor and would rule over God's people forever. Mary responded, "I am the servant of the Lord. Let it be done as you say." So according to the word of the angel, Jesus was conceived in the womb of Mary by the power of the Holy Spirit.

An angel told Joseph not to hesitate to take Mary as his wife because her child was the Son of God. An angel announced the birth of Christ in Bethlehem to the shepherds, and they came and saw the savior of the world, lying in the manger. A star in heaven directed the magi to Bethlehem, and they presented gifts of gold, frankincense, and myrrh — gifts symbolic of a king, a priest, and a prophet who would die for the people.

This legend is very familar. It at first appears to be very different from the story of the coming of the Pipe. Yet there are a surprising number of similarities and differences, which point out to the general religious values and the unique religious characteristics of the Pipe and Christ.

First of all in the comparison of the comings, the Buffalo Calf Maiden who came to the young men, is like the angel Gabriel who came to Zachariah. Both came in holy, spiritual, wonderful ways. Both announced a special gift from God to his people. Both the maiden and the angel told men to get the people ready. The two are different in that the angel came from heaven and returned there, but the maiden came walking on the earth and returned the same way, turning into a buffalo. They both came twice with different but related messages concerning a new spiritual order to be realized through the Pipe and Christ, respectively.

One of the greatest mysteries of the Christian religion is the fact that Jesus Christ is both God and man. This results in a wonderful combination of things both in heaven and on earth. For this reason, we can begin to understand how the maiden who brought the Pipe is also very much like Mary. Both were very holy. Both were very humble and said only a few words. Both gave what they received to others and then walked away. Still they are very close to their people and are still pictured carrying sacred bundles forever. The maiden left in a mysterious way, walking on the earth and turning into a white buffalo to be special among all of God's buffalo people; when Mary died, she was assumed in a mysterious way, body and soul, into heaven to be reckoned beside her Son as the most blessed woman of God's chosen people. Some very traditional Lakota-Christians have said that the Buffalo Calf Woman **was** Mary. While I admit that they acted similarly, there is no data that would substantiate that identity. Since the Buffalo Calf Woman definitely came and went as one of earth, and visionary appearances of Mary always present her as one from heaven, such an identification would be wrong in my eyes.

There is punishment in both stories. In one story the young man had bad thoughts and was killed; in the other, the man did not believe the angel and was struck speechless. The sin of the first was a sin of the flesh; the sin of the second was a sin of the spirit. The bones of the young man are a lasting instruction on the consequence of disregard for the **wakan** power in women and an unbridled release of one's passions. After Zachariah miraculously recovered his speech at the birth of his son, he proclaimed God's praise and covenant of love to his people. His canticle has been sung through all the ages of the church. In some ways, the young man with bad intentions is similar to Zachariah with his weak faith, but in other ways they are different.

In some ways, the good young man and John the Baptist are alike. They both told men that God would give them a special gift. They both became bearers of spiritual messages and the beginning of a new order. The hunter told the people to prepare the tent; John the Baptist told men to prepare for Christ's coming by changing their lives.

The Lakota band is like the shepherds. They gathered for the coming of God's gift. The first included all the relatives joined in blood; the second included only men of good will joined together in God's Spirit. St. Joseph is in some ways like the chief of the band who prepared the lodge and got things ready for the coming of the gift to the people. Both stood in the background. One was the head of his tribe, chosen the normal way chiefs were chosen; the other was the head of the family, directed to be such, not by the will of flesh or the customs of man, but according to the directions of an angel.

Two things especially make the Pipe and Christ different. First, the Pipe is made of rock and wood; tobacco and eagle feathers are added. These things are of the earth and remain here with us. Christ is of flesh, blood, bone, and spirit, and they have been transformed in the resurrection, and he is in heaven — to be truly with us, but under the signs of bread and wine. Both the Pipe and Christ are sacrificial; in the Pipe, tobacco is consumed for the life of the people; in the poverty of his birth and on the cross, Christ gave his life humbly for the salvation of those faithful to his heavenly Father's revelations. The tobacco was offered at the hands of a religious Lakota person for all the relatives; Christ was slain at the hands of unbelievers and foreigners; he was cast out by his own, for the salvation of all.

The magi do not have a parallel in the story of the coming of the Pipe, and with good reason. These wisemen from the East are related to the universal proclamation of the coming of Christ. The Lakota revelation was meant mainly for the Lakota people and those close to them; the coming of Christ was especially for the poor, outcast Jews, symbolized by the shepherds, and for the wise people of the world, symbolized by the magi.

The Keeper of the Pipe and his descendants are like St. Peter and the popes after him. Both were to guard and protect the gift of the Pipe and the Eucharist as well as the sacred revelations that have been given them. The keeping of the Pipe was to be done within the same physical family; the responsibility of the gospel, however, was given to the apostles and their descendants in a spiritual family. In the Lakota religion, the leadership would be held by medicine men who received their powers in a visionary, charismatic way; in the Church, the leadership would be chosen juridically by the laying on of hands. While the traditions of the latter were passed on broadly by learned people in a written tradition, the traditions of the former were passed on restrictively by spiritually wise men in an oral tradition.

There are other stories concerning origins that were given at the Medicine Men and Pastors Meeting. One participant asked two questions: From where did the Maiden come? How did she get the

Pipe? He answered his own questions by giving the following story. A number of other participants agreed with his answer. The following story was said to be very old and known by only a few.

A long time ago a band of Lakota went down near Denver and were massacred. It is said that only a woman and her child escaped. It was a girl-child, still sucking at the breast. One day the woman was lying with her daughter sucking at her breast when, unexpectedly, she felt something shake her shoulder. When she turned to see, it was a starving buffalo calf. She had pity on it and let it suck beside the child. It is said that the child and the calf grew up together. When the girl became a maiden, the buffalo calf grew up to become the chief of the buffalo, and he gave himself to the maiden in the form of the Pipe. It is said that she lived with the buffalo and traveled north with them in the summer. That is where she came from.

From the early church, there comes a story about Mary's early life. Mary was a very holy child. Joachim and Anne were her parents, but they died when she was very young. Consequently, Mary was sent to live and pray near the temple. Because she was such a holy person, people wondered who should marry her. All of the eligible suitors were told to come and put their staffs in a designated room. They locked the room and prayed outside. When they opened the door, they found that God had provided a sign. The staff of Joseph had bloomed with many flowers, indicating that God had chosen Joseph to be Mary's husband. To this day, many statues of Joseph show him holding a flowering staff because of this story.

Although these stories do not have the same religious weight or acceptance as the legends of the coming of the Pipe and Christ, the truths and symbols of these stories show how the Lakota and Christian people dearly love and honor the sacredness of the Maiden who brought the Pipe and the Virgin who gave birth to Christ.

Many Lakota think that the first time that they received the Pipe was from the Buffalo Calf Woman; this is because this Pipe was the first Pipe of the current Lakota religion, which has developed since the Lakota came on the Plains. The Lakota had used Pipes, however, in a religious way long before the Maiden brought the Buffalo Calf Leg Pipe to the Sans Arc. At one of the earliest meetings, the medicine man, Arthur Running Horse, told this story of how the **Lakota** (which here may be translated as "the Indians") first received a Pipe.

This is what he said. There was a Lakota man. He prayed, but he didn't know how to pray well. One day he was walking, and he went on a hill. On the top he stood there praying with his arms stretched up. Suddenly, he felt something resting in his hands, but he was afraid to close them. After praying some more, he closed his hands and lowered them. In his hand he held a Pipe. The man realized that he didn't know how to handle this Pipe. He set it against a rock and went home. When he got there, he told his wife about it, and they discussed the matter. His wife made a Pipe bag to put the Pipe in. He took it and went back to the hill. He put the Pipe in the bag and brought it home. When he prayed after this, he used the Pipe. The man's name was said to be Standing Growling Bear. This is what Mr. Running Horse said.

A Pipe can be made from different colored stone from different places. For example, the Lakota community called "Black Pipe" receives its name from the black pipestone found nearby. But the stone most respected by the Lakota is the red catlinite found near Pipestone, Minnesota. A story is related to the red color of this stone. It is said that long ago, there was a battle in that area and many Lakota died there. Their blood soaked into the earth. The ghosts of many brave warriors were honored there for a long time, but they are gone now. The sign of their sacrifice, however, remains in the red stone.

Today, that area is a National Monument. Only Indians can get a permit to dig out pipestone there. Occasional trips from the reservation are made there for rock. With pick and sledge hammer, it is necessary to go through six to eight feet of stone now to reach the real pipestone vein. It is said that people are often not doing it right; they are not showing proper respect. When people take pipestone out of the ground, they should put something back, usually a tobacco offering, especially at the Three Sisters, stone guardians of the area.

Both the Lakota stories and archeological evidence indicate that the Indians smoked pipes long before the coming of the Buffalo Calf Pipe. Careful study shows that pipes for smoking tobacco first appeared in Central United States and in California around 2000 B.C. (around the time of Abraham). By the time of Christ, pipes and tobacco were used through most of North, Central, and South America. Gradually, the use of the Pipe decreased and even disappeared in many American areas. In the northern Mississippi and Ohio River valleys, however, the ceremonial and cultural use of the Pipe increased. The use of the Pipe and tobacco for healing, visions, prayer, recreation, ritual, decision-making, and council agreements is well documented for many tribes throughout North America at the time of the coming of the White man. The northern tribes of the United States used the Pipe more extensively than in other areas. During this period, the Pipe was used both for the benefit of one's friends and for the destruction of one's enemies.

The Pipe was highly respected; it gave the bearer protection and safe passage. It was a key element in ratifying the decisions of councils. For the Indians, the smoking of the Pipe at councils was a spiritual pledge to live according to the decisions of the council. If one could not go along with what was being presented, one did not smoke the Pipe but rather turned and went one's own way. (In a way, it was like putting one's hand on the Bible and swearing to keep one's pledge.) The Pipe is properly called the Sacred Pipe [**cannunpa wakan**]. In the old days it could be used for things both good and bad — not morally good or bad but physically good or bad. When the Pipe was circulated among leaders to gather allies for a war, it was sometimes called a Pipe of War. When it was circulated for the purpose of harmonious activities, it was sometimes called a Pipe of Peace. Because the Pipe was smoked at the signing of treaties at the end of Peace Treaty Councils between Indians and Whites, the Pipe became popularly called the "Peace Pipe" by the Whites.

Although the Pipe long ago was used for both peace and war in different parts of the United States, nonetheless, among the Lakota, the Buffalo Calf Leg Pipe and its ceremonies had a particular universal quality of harmony that extended to the limits of the world. The sharing of the Maiden's Pipe and offensive warring did not mix. This Pipe was for health and life in the broadest sense of those terms. This Pipe can invite a Lakota to adopt within their families people who had been their enemies — as in the story of the Rees in the first Making-A-Relative ceremony. The approach of the Pipe, even in the hands of one's enemy, would call forth cooperation and mutual respect. Thus it became an effective instrument in the hands of the U.S. Government officials who sought treaties, agreements, and cooperation from the Sioux. The Buffalo Calf Leg Pipe gradually and spiritually moved the Sioux from extreme animosity against their enemies toward a tempered, tolerant, universal relationship with outsiders.

From this context, one can perceive a religious dynamic working in the repeated attempts of the early Lakota chiefs and elders to bring the Black Robes and Catholicism onto their reservations and among their people. That same dynamic seems to have been moving the pastors from a level of animosity to a level of temperance, tolerance and harmony. With God as our Grandfather and Father, all men are called to be children and relatives through the Pipe and Christ. Because of their universalizing aspects, the Pipe and Christ have been approaching each other from the beginning. Perhaps they are now close enough to shake hands religiously — in mutual respect, harmony, and sacredness before God from whom both have come.

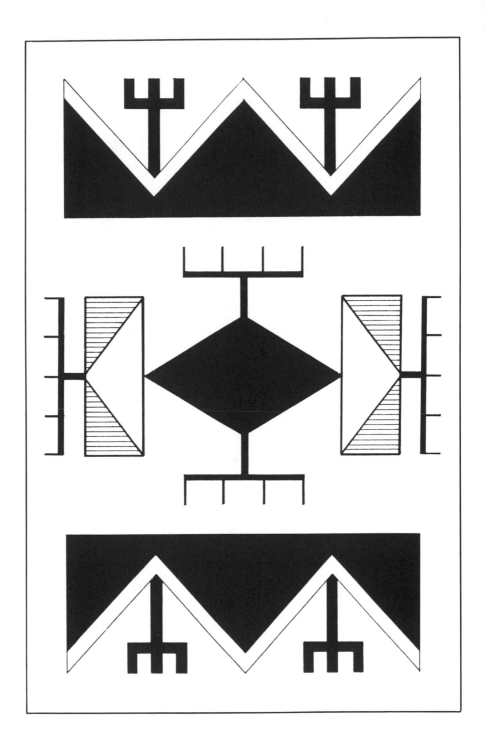

Chapter 13
Lakota and Christian Views of God

At the Rosebud Medicine Men and Pastors' Meeting, considerable time was spent in actual prayer as well as talking about prayer, for to the Lakota the primary aspect of religion is prayer [wacekiye]. While there are some common terms for God that are used in the ceremonies of both religions, there are some terms whose use is limited to one religion or the other and some commonly used terms have different meanings in the two religions.

Most terms for "God" are very abstract. This is seen in the roots of words. "God" = "the invoked One." "**Wakan Tanka**" = "the great spiritual One." "Deity" = "the brilliant One." "**Theos**" = "the stormy One." "Yahweh" = "the One who is."

Immediately attached to these words is usually a description of the power of God. In the Lakota religion [**wocekiye**], God is **iyotan waś'ake** (most powerful), but in the Christian religion, God is **omnipotens** (all-powerful). These expressions are similar but also different. Each religion has a very different understanding of the primary distribution of power in God and the world. The Christian view emphasizes participation; the Lakota view emphasizes individuation.

The Lakota world view is very existential. Lakota are concerned primarily with human birth, life, suffering, and death in the current situation. They have only a few myths about origins and end-times, and these play only a small part in their religious consciousness. The Lakota view of God is highly influenced by their conception of their Lakota society and their immediate, natural world. Every person has a right relationship with every other thing in this world. Each has a role, a responsibility, and an honor. The grandfather has a special and powerful **moral** role. In the realm of the Sacred, God [**Wakan Tanka**] and the Four Winds [**Tatiye Topa**], and the Lakota spirits [**Taku Wakan kin**] are each special and powerful in their own individual ways. Still there is a hierarchy of **wakan** individuals according to power. The Great Spirit who dwells above is the most **wakan** and powerful of the spirits. All other spirits are beneath him. The Lakota realize that there is some communication of power between spirits just as between spirits and humans, but the nature and extent of that communication is **wakan** and unknown. Their daily immersion into the vicissitudes of real life does not draw them to think in terms of "logical necessities." They firmly believe that things **wakan** (supernatural) can willfully alter what is **ikceya** (natural) in response to prayers, and they fear and respect the free will of each individual. These concerns turn them away from an absolute understanding of material causality, from which a reflective thinker can be moved toward seeing every creature as ultimately from one Creator.

The relationship of spirits [**taku wakan kin**] to the Great Spirit [**Wakan Tanka**] is understood differently by different medicine men — just as the relationship of spiritual persons to God is understood differently in the Christian world. At least one medicine man sees **Wakan Tanka** as a term which applies to all the **taku wakan kin** collectively. For him, the "whole" [**Wakan Tanka**] was the sum of all the willful, powerful "parts" [**taku wakan kin**]. Addressing God is like addressing a family which lives and works tightly together — just as some Christians picture the Triune God as a family of three people. This is not the generally accepted position. Most medicine men view **Wakan Tanka** as a distinct, single person, who is the Great Grandfather over all. He is the most powerful "Other" who lives above the heavens. Each **taku wakan kin** is personally distinct from him and is freely and personally empowered by **Wakan Tanka** to be truly free and personal. One medicine man indicated that he thought of **Wakan Tanka** as the "whole" which is greater than the **taku wakan kin** "parts." When the spirits do a healing, it is **Wakan Tanka** who is thanked because all that which is **wakan** originates from Him and is an expression of his power and life. Concentrating on **wakan** power he considered the individual spirits as merely particular figures through whom **Wakan Tanka** communicates his power to men. There are groups of Christians who hold each of these positions in similar ways. However, religiously interested more in spiritual experience than logic, the Lakota focus primarily on **wakan** things coming from **Wakan Tanka**. It is toward these **wakan** (not **ikecya**) things that the Lakota are looking when they think of God as **iyotan was'ake.**

Christian tradition focuses not on the personhood and the volition of the individual but on the individual's material foundation. The creation stories in Genesis tell how God made the ordinary, natural world. In this world, material sequences are firmly recognized and focused upon. The Jewish people recognized their value not from their existence but from their immediate family's lineage, possessions, territorial inheritance, which they said they ultimately received from their God. To the Jews, origin myths and stories are very important. Historical records of distributed authority are very important religiously and were kept meticulously. While Christianity moved away from the physical aspects of material succession, it applied the same outlook to the spiritual aspects of reality — in things like apostolic succession and the receiving of grace or theological virtues.

The Lakota are matrilineal, and their relationships are very broad and open. The power of God is often visualized as power coming in from all directions toward the human individual in the center. The Jews are patrilineal, and their relationships are very tight and closed. God is visualized as a Middle Eastern benevolent despot who holds all possessions as his own and disburses his favor to the people who surround his throne. Christianity maintains this emphasis in its hierarchy and theology. Consequently, Christianity emphasizes that, except for sin, God is the ultimate source of all that is or happens in the world.

From both the Lakota and Christian perspectives, humans of themselves are not really very **wakan** or holy. In the Lakota perspective, humans are not **wakan** because they are sick, weak, powerless, or incapable of doing important, great things. They are onsikapi (pitiful). In the Christian perspective, humans are sinners; they do not do what the Father wants and are therefore relationally apart from Him and His blessings. Most of all they become outcasts from the Lord's presence when they do not do his will. These negative, low views of humans are the consequence of having such great and powerful images of God. God is always conceived as the "Other." It is interesting to note that while the Lakota have a great natural sense of interrelationships, they approach God as one from whom they can obtain power and material goods. For the Jews, power and material possessions were everyday commodities, and they found their interpersonal relationship or covenant with God as the greatest good.

Even on the reservation I have run into some people who object to the presentation of God in human terms, in what are called anthropomorphisms. They often want God presented in strictly abstract, philosophical, and theological terms, which are third-order abstractions from reality and thus are always deficient of some reality. They often think that the more simple and abstract a term is, the more spiritual it is — which is a totally false assumption. They fail to realize that cognitive distinctions really examine the materiality rather than the spirituality of a thing. That's one of the reasons why cognitive examination of God always ends up in paradoxes. God is a living God. He is best considered in terms of the living realities in which He is actively presented. Christ is the model of all Christians. He is the incarnation of God. He is the total, real anthropomorphization of God. Since every man and woman is made by God and thus express his image, they too are walking anthropomorphizations of God. Thus it is legitimate that God be described as an anthropomorphization of the perfect man. It was through parables taken from human life and natural events that Jesus gave the greatest teachings concerning God our Father and His Kingdom. In my opinion, systematic disdain for theological anthropomorphisms is anti-incarnational, unChristian, and unLakota.

Both the Lakota and Christian religions apply terms of endearment to God, namely Grandfather [**Tunkaśila**] and Father respectively. At the Medicine Men and Pastors' Meeting some medicine men said they thought that in speaking about God, the term **Tunkaśila** was older than **Wakan Tanka,** which they said was rather recently adopted. Regardless, the term **Tunkaśila** was the most common and the most familial.

In traditional Lakota culture, a man became a grandfather around the age of 40 years. By that age he had "sown his oats" and was settling down. By then he had experienced most things of life; he had struggled with his own identity and no longer had to do rash things to prove himself. A Lakota man in his mid-thirties once spoke of how members of his community wanted him to become a medicine man, but he knew how much community responsibility would be given him, and he was still not settled down. "Maybe after I'm forty; that's the usual age for seeking such an office." Around that age, a man's own children are reaching maturity, and he begins to take interest in the welfare of the clan as a whole. In the traditional Lakota culture, there were two major groups of men. The younger men were aggressive warriors and police; they carried out the decisions of the elders. The elders were recognized grandfathers, who discussed in greater depth, circumspection and experience, clan affairs and made the major decisions for the group. Anyone with considerable relational respect and authority was admitted to the council of the elders as a **tunkaśila.** The President of the United States as well as the local government agent, were called **tunkaśila.** Spirits gave directions and helped fill the major needs of the people, and so they were called **tunkaśilapi. Tunkaśila** is more a social and relational term than a biological one. When **Wakan Tanka** is called **Tunkaśila,** this refers to his knowledge and his attentiveness to the cries of the people, helping them in their needs toward a better life. This term refers more to his concerns and status within an extended family than to his material relationship through blood.

The Lakota term for one's male parent is **ate**; this Lakota term cannot be simply translated as "father" because the term **ate** refers also to one's father's brothers, that is, one's uncles on one's father's side. Thus a Lakota youth probably will have several **ate.** The **ate** were gone from the camp much of the time, helping each other on hunting trips and warring expeditions. When in camp, the **ate** spent little time at their wives' teepees, but rather spent considerable amounts of time at the Dog Soldier lodges with their friends of their warrior society. The grandfathers usually stayed closer to the camp, maintaining the order there and making decisions pertinent to the clan from the information coming in from different directions. It was the grandfather who did much of the instruction of the boys. Especially at night, the grandfathers would tell ancient stories by which Indian cultural traditions and religious values were carried on. It is not by accident that, even today, men active in the Lakota religion say, "My grandfather was a medicine man." Only a few will say that their father was a medicine man, for while the child is in the formative years, fathers are still normally out of the house doing things.

Contrariwise, the term "Father" which the Christians apply to God has a strong cultural basis, especially in the old Jewish culture. Unlike the Lakota who were hunters, the Jews were shepherds, farmers, and tradesmen. The Lakota had no real property that was handed down from one generation to the next; their very nomadic life militated against that. The man had very few personal possessions, and when he died, these were left at his burial site, and his wife abandoned and gave-away all the material possessions she had acquired during their marriage. She simply left all to return to her blood relatives. In the Jewish culture, the survival of the clan depended upon the maintenance of family wealth, e.g., one's flocks, tents, and golden treasures. Having a male heir to whom one could give one's material and religious inheritance was very important. If a man died without producing an heir from his wife, his brothers had the responsibility to have at least one son in his name. In this way the male family line was not broken.

The Jewish attitude toward material property must be understood in order to appreciate adequately the father-son relationship. All the tents, sheep, and land in the family were considered

to be the father's. Out of self-identity and love, the father identified himself with everything material around him. To hurt his
property was to hurt him. The Lakota have a sense of relational
identity, but it is built on an extreme form of mutual independence
and respect and does not extend itself to material property, which
mostly was the possession of the women — not of the men as in
Jewish society. Among the Jews, people were put into the same
category as property, and property was under the same family
protection as the members of the family. A wife was considered a
piece of property, but in a special way. Genesis 2 speaks of woman
being taken from the rib of man, saying that they are to be,
therefore, two in one flesh. As Paul writes, ''Treasure your wife
as you would your own body.'' A son was said to be the ''seed'' of
the man, the fruit of his loin, the one made by the father in his
image and likeness. When a son was a minor, he maintained the
legal status of a slave — material property in a very absolute
sense. Unlike many other peoples, the Jews were very good to
their slaves because Scripture reminded them that they too were
once slaves in Egypt. The Jewish slave had rights and protections
under the Law. The interrelationships and thought patterns of the
Jewish people in general were very materialistic, and this despotic
materialism was the context of much of their religious thought.
They were the seed of Abraham, so materially they were of **one**
flesh. This provided a cultural framework understanding the Old
Testament commandment ''Love your neighbor as yourself,'' for
you are both from the seed of Abraham. Because of the organic
relationship of father and son, for a Jewish father to disown his
son was as to cut off his own arm. When a son legally lost the
status of slave at the entrance into adulthood at his bar mitzvah at
the age of 13 years, the ideal son would willingly continue to take
that attitude upon himself. A true Jewish son was to act exactly as
the father would act or would want him to act. He was totally
obedient to what the father asked, willing to take the attitude of a
slave, totally dedicated to protect and even give up his life to save
the inheritance of the father. The image of the Mystical Body of
Christ in which Christ is the head and the Christians are his members is a typical Jewish, organic image of material descent of
wealth, power, and life from the patriarchal father-figure.

Within the Jewish culture, there was also another father-son
relationship. A rabbi was a Jewish teacher of Sacred Scripture and
tradition. In a culture in which reading was limited to a few, and
religious observance was linked to a written document, the role of
the teacher was very important. He was the one who preached the
Word of God and His promise to the people. These instructions
helped the individual grow spiritually, thus making them heir to

the inheritance given by God to Abraham insofar as they observed the statutes of the Law. The inheritance of the promise made to Abraham depended upon the faithfulness of the seed of Abraham to keep their side of the covenant. Thus the Wisdom of God given through the Law became a living, growing reality within the hearing man, **adam**, earth. Jesus reaffirmed this in the parable of the sower. Students of the Law called their teachers "father," who in turn called their students "sons" because they were made true spiritual sons of Abraham by letting the seed of Scripture enter and grow from within them, being fertile sons of Adam (Earth) as well. Thinking in this way, it was easy to see how God was the Father of the people Israel through the Word of God entering into them and giving them the life that finds its fulfillment in the Kingdom promised to Abraham, David, and all who follow the Law given to Moses.

Figuratively the term "son" was used with qualities, for example, "sons of thunder." This is related to the tendency in the ancient Mediterranean world to personify any noun, like psyche, into divine-like reality — either as a god or as a perfect reality attached to the divine. Although some took these substantializations seriously, often predications such as these were taken in jest as nicknames.

After Christ came and the Church expanded away from the Jewish and into the Hellenistic world, the notion of material descent from Abraham was spiritualized. As a rabbi or religious teacher, His words (seed) were planted in the hearts of His disciples or students, promoting a new Father-son spiritual relationship between His hearers and God. Christ went beyond this and spoke of God as not only his spiritual Father but also as his Father in an intimate, immediate, material way. Therefore, Christ claimed that it was not the Jewish people but himself that was the bearer of the promise and inheritance of God's people. He was one who could establish a new covenant in his blood. Christ effectively said, "What was collectively yours is now personally mine." Not only did he raise to another level the notion of God's spiritual Fatherhood, but he also perfected the notion of kingdom, so that God's people would come to share not so much an earthly Kingdom but a heavenly one. In Christ, the material, spiritual, and figurative notions of sonship were combined.

The important thing to realize is that when Christians speak of God as Father, they are not speaking of the father-son relationship found in the Lakota society or the contemporary White society. This father-son relationship is not simply a warm, kind, supportive relationship of two respectful but unequal people — that describes the notion of "friendship." A true Christian understanding of the father-son relationship can best be found in an organic interpretation of the expression, ''You are mine.''

The contemporary White view of a grandfather is one who is old, feeble, and retired. In the old days when true Lakota spoke of a grandfather they thought of one in full health and knowledge, who had shown his ability to provide materially for the people and who was engaged in community organization, and who, by his word, was able to effect the welfare and happiness of the people in multiple and surprising ways. At the age of about 30 years, Jesus spoke of his Father, who then can be pictured as someone around 50 years of age. The Lakota apply the term ''grandfather'' usually after 40 years of age. Both of these figures point to someone who is middle-aged, mature, and politically active in contemporary society. The Christian term ''Father'' and the Lakota term ''Grandfather'' point toward the same level of social development, but each term points to the social values associated with full maturity. The Christian background emphasizes God as the material source of all grace and strength and as the Master and Lord, who directs his children, as if they are his servants, in every use of His possessions. On the other hand, the Lakota background emphasizes God as one who is materially detached, whose interaction and directions are relational gifts, who is but one of the many individuals in the camp, who is most responsible, wise, helpful, and patient, and who has the respect and resources of the people in the camp at his disposal because of their respect for and cooperation with Him. So is God **iyotan waś'ake** or **omnipotens**? As the Lakota would answer — Yes. The descriptions one uses of God depend upon one's focus. He is best described as most-powerful when one is focusing on the freedom and personality of someone individually other than God. He is best described as all-powerful when one is focusing on the material foundation and energy that an individual has in order to act in God's world.

Despite their differences, the Christian notion of Father and the Lakota notion of Grandfather point to God as a rescuer in behalf of the material and spiritual needs of the people. Both see God as a wise person who makes decisions, instructs the young, corrects what is wrong, guides the people on right paths, and has a special interest and care for the poor pitiful. He has a special interest in providing for a full and happy life — but in His own way for each religion according to their cultural and traditional backgrounds. In both religions there is a place in which God can correct, give hard instructions, and even ask for total sacrifice for the welfare of the people. He is always first. Everything is beneath Him. He hears prayers and answers them. In both religions, God is a loving, generous person who expects right order and right conduct. In the Lakota culture reverential fear is more immediate; in the Christian religion His judgement is usually perceived as being fully realized only in the End Times. Still He is happiest when His children and grandchildren are respected and when there is peace and joy among the people. So a number of people on the reservation find it fitting to address God under both titles. They pray, "Father, Grandfather, have mercy and pity on your people." In so doing they bring together the best spiritual understandings of God and religious values of man from the patriarchal, authoritarian Judeo-Christian culture and from the matriarchal, relational Lakota culture.

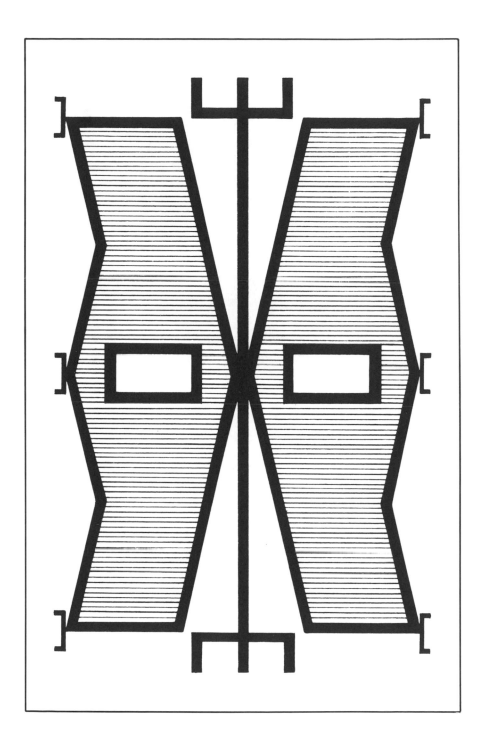

Chapter 14

The Pipe Ceremony and the Sign of the Cross

The Pipe and Christ are the central intercessory elements in the Lakota and Christian religions, respectively. The Rosebud Medicine Men and Pastors' Meeting spent considerable amounts of time studying ritualistic acts which regularly referred to them.

In the Lakota religion, almost every major ritual begins with the Pipe ceremony; here the major Spirits in the Lakota world are invoked. In the Catholic religion, most ceremonies begin with the Sign of the Cross; here Christians renew their baptismal consecration in the Name and power of the divine Persons of the Christian God. Lakota ceremonies usually end with the smoking of the Pipe, and similarly, Christian rituals usually end with a benediction in the name of the Trinity.

The Pipe Ceremony and the Sign of the Cross express several things. They are traditional and rudimentary professions of faith in the primal Spiritual Beings from whom all life and blessings are said to come. These acts intimately link the people present to the central revelations of each religion. In the Lakota religion this is the gift of the Pipe by the Buffalo Calf Woman for the health, welfare, and happiness of the Lakota people, and in the Catholic religion it is the sacrifice of the Son of God upon the cross for the salvation and glorification of mankind. These are public acts, engaging individuals spiritually and bringing them into the mainstream of the life and struggles of an entire people. They reaffirm and renew the active presence of these Powers here and now with the individual and the group and prepare the people in faith and action as they enter into the realm of the Sacred of these Spiritual Beings.

In this chapter an examination and comparison will be made of the principal spiritual beings associated with the Pipe Ceremony and the Sign of the Cross. The theology of the Pipe directs the Lakota to look at the things of the world in terms of "four" since there are four great Spirits in the four cardinal directions which watch over all the affairs of the world. The Sign of the Cross is a Catholic ritual invoking the names of the three Persons of the Trinity. Realizing that it is the Triune God who is behind everything that happens in the world, Christians through the centuries have had a preference for analyzing the things of this world in terms of "three." Comparing and contrasting the Lakota "four" and the Christian "three" brought forth considerable theological insight.

The "medicine wheel" is a common religious sign in Indian religion, not only among the Lakota, but among many other American Indian tribes as well.

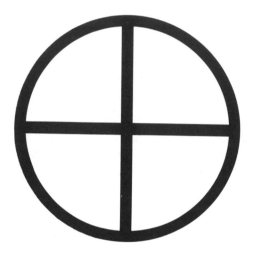

Strangely enough, there is no common Lakota expression for "medicine wheel"; it is simply described as **cangleska na tate topa** (hoop and four winds). Still it is a very common, highly regarded sacred artifact on the reservation, second only to the Pipe. The medicine wheel consists of a circle, through the center of which are drawn a horizontal and a vertical line, to which an eagle feather is usually attached at the center. The circle represents the sacred outer boundary of the Earth; the horizontal and vertical lines represent the sun's and man's sacred paths, respectively; the crossing of the two lines indicates the center of the Earth where one stands when praying with the Pipe; the eagle feather is a sign of **Wakan Tanka**'s power over everything. The medicine wheel is often marked with sacred colors, especially red, which is the color for something truly **wakan.** Only a few things are made of porcupine quills today; of these the medicine wheel is the most common. The medicine wheel is hung from the rear view mirrors of cars, worn as a necklace, hung as a wall decoration, attached to pipe bags, and used as a most sacred marking in Lakota religious ceremonies.

The circle has great religious and cultural meaning to the Lakota people. The Lakota teepee, its fireplace in the center, the sweatlodge, its pit, the Sundance grounds with its pole in the center — all are in the form of a circle. Whenever possible, the Lakota formed their camps into circles. When the elders gathered in council, they sat in a circle. In the **Yuwipi** ceremony and other ceremonies, the altar is made of or on the earth in the form of a circle. Not only the physical world but also the life of the Lakota people are considered to be like a hoop. When a person cuts through any living thing in its middle, he finds a circle. If the circle is broken, it is said that the person will soon die unless it is quickly healed. When the Lakota people are dying as a people, it is said that the hoop of the Lakota people is broken. In a circle, there is equality for all, rather than the superior/inferior attitude found in lines, opposites, classrooms, and most White churches. In a circle, there are mutual responsibilities, sharings and respect. In the circle are found abundance, harmony, and tranquility. Religiously, the earth is conceived to be circular with a great, sacred hoop as its boundary.

The "center of the Earth" is not a geometric center. The "center of the Earth" is the center of life as realized in the heart of each individual. The "center" is wherever the believer stands, especially with the Pipe. As the Lakota walks the Sacred Red Path of the Pipe, he/she is always at the center. Only in death does the faithful one make that **wakan** passage to the Sacred Rim. The "center" is where the Four Winds are affecting and guiding the individual. Because the power of the Four Winds are always beyond the mountains that edge the world, they can never be reached by ordinary people in this life; this place is extraordinary and **wakan.** West is **always** west. Those who understand, know that West is beyond geometry, geography, climatology, and weather; these are but messengers of the West to the believer. The one holding and walking with the Pipe is in the center of the activity of the major forces guiding and shaping all major events on the Earth. Over this spot the eagle flies.

For the Lakota, the sacredness of the circle is extrinsic and secondary. Many Whites tend to find an intrinsic, primary holiness in the circle. When an area of the ground is cleared for an altar, not just anyone can draw the circle, only a medicine man is able to do this. His relationship to his spirits is communicated to the circle as he draws it. That is **his** altar because his spirits will come to it. Many people associate the Pipe Ceremony with the circle. Rarely is the word "circle" used in the Pipe Ceremony prayers. Rather the ceremony is directed toward the spirits in the cardinal direction. These four sufficiently **encircle** the one who prays and determines the magnitude and the **wakan**-ness of the Great Circle. The hoop of the Earth marks the boundary between the ordinary domain of men and the **wakan** domain of the **Tatiye Topa**. This hoop is sacred because of its relationship to those great **wakan** powers. One medicine man drew a circle. Pointing to the inside of the circle he said that this is where **we** live. Using his pointer to sweep around the entire area outside of the circle, he said that this was where everything **wakan** has its home. This was a very clear way of illustrating the smallness of our ordinary, **ikceya** world and the otherness and greatness of the **wakan** world. In the Pipe Ceremony, although the mouth of the Pipe is only swung through three quadrants between the four directions, it is still said that the Pipe has been moved in a circle because it has pointed at the four directions which define the "encirclement." At the Sundance, the sacred area is considered a circle, even though it is marked out ritualistically by only four pairs of flags placed in the four directions. In the vision quest, the seeker is surrounded by the flags in the four directions. The sacred area is **encircled** by the tobacco ties, even though the physical shape of the area is a rectangle.

Many different sacred and secular relationships produce Lakota circles. A particular circle is "ordinary" or **wakan** depending upon whether the relational elements making the encirclement are "ordinary" or **wakan,** respectively. When a medicine man redraws the circle, he is repeating a sacred action that is part of the religious tradition of the Lakota people. By redrawing the circle he calls for the re-actualization of the previous, **wakan** relationships. If the people do not wish to re-establish their **wakan** relationships, the leader says that the sacred hoop is broken. The medicine man could not say that the "circle" was broken if the circle was a paradigm of the Lakota universe. The circle is not a sign of a prescribed, **wakan** order, implying that it is the circle which **orders** right relationships. Rather, the circle is **a** symbol of **their** moral order. The frequency of the circle in nature and Lakota life makes the circle an awesome figure, but a secondary one. The encircling by the relatives is a sign of the virtue of the relatives. Therefore "walking the straight Red Path" is not inherently contradictory to "doing things in a circle" because value is not found in the physical form of the straight line or in the circle but in the practice of righteous, interrelational virtue. The circle is not an archetype or a paradigm for the Lakota but a concrete consequence of their righteous social and religious virtues, especially respect and generosity. Respect is a virtue laced with fear that keeps the individuals in a society at their righteous distance from one another. Generosity is a virtue that shows itself especially in the filling of pitiful emptiness. From the practice of these two virtues alone, one can understand most of the circular distributions, actions, and figures of the Lakota. In summary, it is Lakota relational values that establish Lakota archetypes, paradigms, and geometries, and not the other way around.

In the Christian religion, the most common physical sign of faith is the cross. This can be seen everywhere among the followers of Christ: on walls, around necks, on books, but most of all, over every Christian church and altar. While the medicine wheel is most at home flat upon the Earth, the cross is most at home in a vertical position. The medicine wheel speaks of the blessing a person receives from the Sacred Powers of the Earth for his earthly survival; the cross speaks of man's being lifted up to God through the incarnation, death, and ascension of Jesus Christ. Through him, earth and heaven are united in a special way. Besides the vertical axis of the cross, the Fathers of the Church saw a special meaning in the horizontal axes of the cross. They saw in the open arms of Christ the beginning of a great circle, embracing all mankind in his death for the salvation and sanctification of all sinners. However, while the cross emphasizes the redemptive work of Christ, it does not of itself, incorporate the Trinity symbolically. It is only when the Christian marks himself in the form of the cross in the name of the Father, and of the Son, and of the Holy Spirit that he makes a miniature profession of the Christian creed. By this act Christians renew the blessing of the Trinity upon themselves. This blessing recognizes and sanctifies Christians, making themselves holders of divine life. The Sign of the Cross divinizes Christians and makes them part of the Church which Christ will raise to heavenly glory on the Last Day. By this action, Christians place a cross upon themselves, as Christ did.

The Lakota believe that there are really distinct personal powers in the four directions. These are called **Tatiye Topa,** which is usually translated "Four Directions." The Lakota word for "strong wind" is **tate. Tatiye** is probably a contraction of **Tate-o-uye** (He sends the wind.). Rather than being the wind itself, the **Tatiye Topa** are the cosmological powers **behind** the physical winds; they are the ultimate causes of the four-fold, significant events of the Earth. They are **wakan.** They know everything that happens. God put them where they are. He gave them their power, and this power is really their own to use, but they use it as God would use it. The lyric of a Lakota song says, "God is with you, beside you, and you are holy, but you are not the same as He but beneath Him." In a very respectful, indirect way, this song reminds these powerful spirits that they should use their **wakan** powers rightly, for our righteous God is greater than each and nearer to each of these **wakan** spirits than He is to ordinary persons. The words of this song quite clearly indicate the Lakota's belief that these spirits are free persons.

In the Pipe ceremony, a person takes the pipe bowl and pipe stem from a pipebag, which has been kept away in a respectful location. Sweetgrass is usually lit, and the pipe is incensed in its sweet smoke. Then a pinch of tobacco is taken in the fingers, incensed, and extended as an offering in turn to one of the spirits of the different cardinal directions: the West, the North, the East, the South, toward **Tunkašila Wakan Tanka** above, and to **Unci Maka** below. After each spoken or unspoken prayer, the tobacco is placed in the Pipe. If the Pipe is not filled by the six offerings, the remainder of the pipe is filled prayerfully but silently. Sometimes a Pipe-filling song is sung while the Pipe is filled. Once the Pipe is filled it may be pointed in the different directions so that the one praying can "shoot" their prayer and petition to the spirit(s) in that direction.

Several priests who use the Pipe have told me they do not believe in these major spirits as persons. One said that they were nothing but personifications of the physical forces in the world. Another said they were only expressions of the primal, Jungian archetypes within us. Another said that they are only anthropomorphic expressions of the actions of God — just as angels are but expressions of God's grace to us. My response to them has been two-fold. Just as priests consider it sacrilegious for people to receive Holy Communion when they consider this sacrament to be only bread and wine and only symbolically Jesus, so too the medicine men consider it "playing with the Pipe" if the person who points it toward the directions says they're not real persons but only some kind of aspect of God. In taking part in the Pipe ceremony, participants should believe (or want to believe) in the Spiritual Beings which give this ceremony power, in the same way that the Lakota believe in them. Otherwise, they are not following the ways and the "rules of the Pipe." Secondly, one must seek to grow in this understanding through the ceremonies and in particular from the spirits themselves. "Seek and you shall find." This seems to be a Catch-22 situation. One must become like a child, trusting the medicine men as parents while they teach and lead one carefully to places and people unknown. One must put aside the tendency to trust the mind before spiritual experiences, and be willing to place oneself in a more primal situation, seeking direction through visions as the medicine men do.

Because of their traditional fear of evil spirits, the priests probed deeply at this point into the possibility of these spirits participating in hexing. Since they were free, could these spirits of the Pipe do something that was not right? Some medicine men said simply that the Pipe and the Four Winds ''can't do it'' [**okihipi śni**]. By this they meant that it could happen materially, but that it would not be done morally. It was morally impossible because of the intelligence of the Four Winds and their closeness to the source of all order and righteousness, **Wakan Tanka.** Another group of Lakota medicine men responded differently. From the standpoint of the obligations of Lakota relationship, the Lakota spirits would agree to help the person. At the same time however, these spirits would demand the ''kick-back'' that comes with unrighteous deeds, they said. In their own way, the Lakota offered explanations which recognize the righteousness of the spirits in both actions: first, in giving material assistance to a relative, and second, in establishing a right relationship between the wrongdoer and **Wakan Tanka.** The unrighteousness is to be found only in the wrongdoer. The assistance of these major cosmological spirits is relationally righteous. They fulfill their part of the spiritual Pipe relationship even when what is given is misused. In many ways their answer appeared to match the Christian response to the question: In what ways does God willingly participate in a person's sin? Since the Lakota consider **Wakan Tanka** and the Four Winds to be the source of righteousness in the world, just as the Christians consider the Triune God to be the source of all goodness in the world, the discussion of this question was most difficult and painful.

According to the theology of the Pipe, the Four Powers are distinct from one another but are also similar to each other and frequently work together, even though their ways differ greatly from each other. Lakota sometimes compare them to angels (perhaps to the order of Powers). They have intelligence and wills of their own. They are strong like rock, swifter and mightier than all things experienced on earth. They are as ancient as the world and full of wisdom. They care for the people and indicate to the people their ways, but they usually do this through messages carried by lesser spirits and by medicine men. They direct and teach what must be done for a full life. If people do anything wrong against them, they will punish. Usually people respect them, and in return, they send good things. They deserve to be called ''Grandfather.''

In the old days, there were many stories which helped children to picture these powers and to learn about them in an enjoyable way. Today there are few stories. The night habits of families and the education of children have changed so drastically that the religious stories are told only to adults in ceremonies or in private. As a consequence, most of the imaginative details have been dropped. A real demythologization has taken place. The barest outline of the Lakota cosmology remains today.

The Lakota say that the homes of the Four Winds are in the mountains in the four quadrants of the Earth. More is meant here than physical mountains; these spirits have a special closeness to God so that while their feet are upon the Earth, they are closer to God than all others on Earth. Besides the wind, an ordinary rock is a sign of their presence. They sometimes "speak very fast" through the rocks in a sweatbath to a medicine man. When they are viewed as angels assigned by God to the four directions for the guidance and correction of the major events on the Earth, there is little incompatibility with Christian revelation. However, it is still important to appreciate appropriately the symbolic side of their descriptions and manifestations.

According to the theology of the Pipe, there is a Sacred Power in the West, and he and his companions are ancient. From the West comes the purifying water of the sweatbath and these powers guard the water that washes away evil and gives strength. From the West comes the companion, **Wakiyan.** The word **kinyan** means "to fly"; the word **kinyanpi** is usually translated as "the wingeds." The **Wakinyan** are said to be the spirits who give men and women dreams and visions of lightning and thunder. So the name **Wakinyan** is variously translated as "The Flying One," the "Winged One," the "Thunder Beings," and most commonly the "Thunderbird." In Lakota mythology it is said that the **Wakinyan** comes in the thunderstorm as a bird. When his eye blinks, the lightning flashes. When his wings beat, the thunder claps. He is strong and frightening like the thunderstorm. He is at the beginning, and the beginning is always sharp and hard, but then comes the innocent joyful, early, tender growth. He guards against and corrects religious evil. He sees to it that the Pipe is used rightly. In the West, a sacred stone looks on and is black, which is the color of the West. There the Horse People are his companions. The black eagle is his messenger.

In the North, there is a sacred power. Some picture him as a great man who tests the people. He guards the health of the people. **Waziya** is his name, and he has become confused with Santa Claus in recent times. The Power of the North helps the people to grow right and tall, like a pine tree. He straightens out the wayward. God has placed him in the North to watch those who enter the Red Path that leads from north to south. The Red Rock looks on, and his color is red. The Maiden who brought the Pipe is there as well as the Buffalo People who pray and sing. The baldheaded eagle is his messenger. It is on the north side of the sweatlodge that virgins sit.

In the East is a Power that resides where the sun rises. He watches over wisdom and understanding. The Morning Star that gives wisdom and the Moon that gives guidance come from there and bring many spiritual things, especially just before the dawn. For the East comes the sun that enlightens and enlives the world. Through him, especially when a person is on the hill, one is able to see how different parts of the world fit together. From there a yellow stone looks on and yellow is his color. His companions are the Elk People. His messenger is the golden eagle.

In the South there is a Sacred Power who guards the place toward which humans always face and the generations walk. He controls the final destiny of all things. Some say there is a river there that only the good can cross. His breath gives life. He watches over the joy and happiness of the people whose ghosts gather there in the **Takte Makoce,** the Deer Killing Country ("Happy Hunting Ground" to the Whites). There the souls of deceased Lakota are peaceful relatives with all the animal people, **Wamakaśkan Oyate.** In the South there is a Sacred White Rock, and so the color of the South is said to be white, the color of the brilliant fog. Its messenger is the white crane.

In the Bible it is significant that the four-directional spirit motif appears in apocalyptic passages pertaining to the End Times. Speaking about the Last Day, Jesus said, "Then the Son of Man will appear in the sky, and all the clans of earth will strike their breasts as they see the Son of Man coming on the clouds of heaven with power and glory. He will dispatch his angels with a mighty trumpet blast, and they will assemble his chosen from the four winds, from one end of the heavens to the other." (Mt. 24.30-31) In (Rev. 7.1) one finds, "After this I saw four angels standing at the four corners of the earth; they held in check the earth's four winds so that no wind blew on land or sea or through any tree." In the prophet Zechariah (6.1-3) the four winds of heaven are seen as chariots.

Again I raised my eyes and saw four chariots coming out between two mountains, and the mountains were bronze. The first chariot had red horses; the second had black horses; the third, white; and the fourth chariot spotted horses — all of them strong horses. I asked the angel who spoke to me, "What are this, my lord?" The angel said to me in reply,

"These are the four winds of heaven which are coming forth after being reviewed by the Lord of all the earth."
This passage speaks of the winds in a fairly unimportant servant role.

There are other scriptural passages which speak of a different type of four-fold being, very close to God. Similar to this passage, the Lakota hold that each element of the "four" also is in "four," etc.

As I looked, a stormwind came from the North, a huge cloud with flashing fire (enveloped in brightness) from the midst of which (the midst of the fire) something gleamed like electrum. Within it were figures resembling four living creatures that looked like this: their form was human, but each had four faces and four wings, and their legs went straight down; the soles of their feet were round. They sparkled with a gleam like burnished bronze. The faces were like this: each of the four had the face of a man, but on the right side was the face of a lion and on the left side the face of an ox, and finally each had the face of an eagle. Their faces (and their wings) looked out on all their four sides; they did not turn when they moved, but each went straight forward. (Each went straight forward; wherever the spirit wished to go, there they went; they did not turn when they moved.)

Human hands were under their wings, and the wings of one touched those of another. Each had two wings spread out above so that they touched one another's while the other two wings covered his body. In among the living creatures something like burning coals of fire could be seen; they seemed like torches, moving to and from the living creatures. The fire beamed, and from it came forth flashes of lightning.

As I looked at the living creatures, I saw the wheels had the sparkling appearance of chrysolite, and all four others looked the same; they were constructed as though one wheel were within another. They could move in any of the four directions they faced without veering as they moved. The four of them had rims, and I saw that their rims were full of eyes all around. When the living creatures moved, the wheels moved with them, and when the living creatures were raised from the ground, the wheels also were raised. Wherever the spirit wished to go, there the wheels went, and they were raised together with the living creatures, for the spirit of the living creatures was in the wheels. Over the heads of the living creatures, something like a firmament could be seen, seeming like glittering crystal, stretched straight out above their heads. Beneath the firmament their wings were stretched straight out, on toward each other. (Each of them had two covering their body.) Then I heard the sound of their wings, like the roaring of mighty waters, like the voice of the Almighty. When they moved, the sound of the tumult was like the din of an army. (And when they stood still, they lowered their wings.)

Above the firmament over their heads something like a throne could be seen looking like sapphire. Upon it was seated, up above, one who had the appearance of a man. Upward from what resembled his waist, I saw what looked like fire; he was surrounded with splendor. Like the bow that appears in the clouds on a rainy day was the splendor that surrounded him. Such was the vision of the likeness of the glory of the Lord. (Ez. 1.4-28) NAB

Later in (Ez. 10.8-21) these creatures are identified as cherubim.

In the Old Testament, the first commandment ordered that "You shall not crave idols for yourselves in the shape of anything in the sky or the earth below or in the waters beneath the earth." (Ex. 20.4) Still God commanded that cherubim be carved and placed upon the ark. Strange!? In ancient sculpture, cherubim were usually hybrids: e.g., a creature with the head of a man, the front quarters of a lion, the hind quarters of an ox, and the wings of an eagle. In non-Jewish cultures, these images indicated the protective spirits of places, temples, and city gates. Despite the many negative commands forbidding Jews to become involved in pagan religions, a most ancient Jewish law directed that these hybrid spirits should be mounted on top of the most sacred object in the Old Testament.

There was one other image that God ordered Moses to make. When the people sinned, seraph serpents were sent to bite the people so that many would die. In response to Moses' prayer, God ordered him to make a bronze image of a serpent, mount it on a pole, and lift it up for all to see. Those who looked on it were healed (Num. 21.4-9). This image, which the Jews kept for a time but finally cast away in embarrassment, was a pre-figuration of Christ, who was raised on the cross to bring salvation to those who turn to him. As the serpent on the pole, Christ on the cross was unacceptable, unorthodox and rejected by the Jews also.

Now then. . .If the serpent which God specifically ordered the Jews to make was an indication of a future, universal, salvific reality, then one is seriously moved to consider the cherubim on the ark to be also indicative of universal, naturalistic, hybrid realities around his heavenly throne. I maintain by this argument that the apocalyptic passages in Ezekiel and Revelations are not only talking about something symbolically, but they are also pointing to something real!!!

In the book of Revelations, John speaks of four living creatures immediately around the throne of God.

At the very center, around the throne itself, stood four living creatures covered with eyes front and back. The first creature resembled a lion, the second, an ox, third had the face of a man, while the fourth looked like an eagle in flight. Each of the four living creatures had six wings and eyes all over, inside and out. Day and night without pause they sing, "Holy, holy, holy." (Rev. 4.6-10) See also (Rev. 5.6-8, 7.6-8) NAB

These scriptural passages from Ezekiel and Revelations are apocalyptic, and it is most difficult to know absolutely the realities indicated by these colossal descriptions. Obviously they were written in times of religious suppression, and the great visions were given to spur hope more than anything else. But images expressing hope must have some basis in reality. Each image had meaning; some were known only in local religious circles. Still there are four levels of interpretation of any scriptural passage: 1) the original historical meaning, 2) the meaning in reference to Christ, 3) the meaning in reference to the church and the individuals in the church today, 4) the meaning in reference to the final judgment. It is experience that fills out the details of any kind of vision, be it covenantal, vocational, prophetic, or apocalyptic. A person familiar with Lakota symbolism is immediately drawn to many meaningful and coherent religious understandings that are most difficult to put into words. While it cannot be said that the above Scripture passages **prove** that there really are four-sided creatures around God's throne now and at the ends of the earth, one begins to wonder when the same type of imagery emerges from the revelations of other religions. At least the Lakota and the Christian religions are compatible on this point. Still, a more profound comparison can be made.

When a Catholic makes the Sign of the Cross, he says, "In the name of the Father, and of the Son, and of the Holy Spirit. Amen." This formula renews the triune blessing spoken at baptism. There are two ways of looking at the persons of the Blessed Trinity. First, one can look at the persons of the Trinity from the standpoint of salvation history. In the Old Testament, the first person to dominate was God the Father, although the other persons of the Trinity were present and active. To the Father primarily are ascribed the creation of the world, the calling of Abraham, the giving of the Law on Mount Sinai, the blessing of the Temple, the correction of the people when they went astray, and the material blessing of the people when they were true to the covenant. (Still the Son was present as Wisdom in creation, and the Spirit is noted as moving over the waters of creation.) Jesus Christ, the Son of God and the Son of Man, dominated through the time of the Gospels in his birth, teachings, suffering, resurrection, and ascension into heaven. (Still the Father was always there indicating His will, and the Spirit led Jesus.) Starting at Pentecost it was the Holy Spirit that dominated, leading the Church through the centuries. (Still the Father supported the life of every person in the church, and Christ gave each his life in the sacraments.) In this "economic" understanding of the Trinity, all three persons of the Trinity work together, but from the human point of view, the work of the Father appears to dominate first, followed by the Son, and lastly by the work of the Holy Spirit.

In an "imminent" description of the Persons of the Trinity, theologians try to speak of God in terms of internal interrelationships. They speak of the Father, who is first through all eternity, who generated before all time the Son as the perfect image of the perfect Father. They speak of a human's knowledge of himself as different from oneself and incomplete, but of God's self-knowledge as so perfect that it is a Person: the Word of God. These are not two, for the second is totally within the other, of the other, and is the other — and yet somehow distinct and subsequent from the other. The Spirit is described as the total love of the Father and the Son. This love is so total, so personal, and so perfect that it too is a perfect expression of each and consequently a Person. The three are not distinguishable in their perfections, for each shares fully what the other has. Still there are distinctions possible in their relationship to one another: God, the Word of God, and the Love of God in relationship to Himself.

Many Indians have great difficulty with the doctrine of the Trinity. As one full-blood put it, "They say, 'In the name of the Father, the Son, and the Holy Ghost.' Now they cut off the 'Ghost' part and they say 'Spirit.' They say there are three persons in one God. To us Indians, God is not like a can of sardines, one head sticking out here, another there, and a third one there — three heads for one God." Many people have great difficulty with the notion of the Blessed Trinity because they are strongly influenced by the drawings in their catechisms where the Father is pictured as an Old Man in one corner of a triangle, the Son as a young man is pictured at another corner, and the Holy Spirit is pictured as a dove at the third corner. When this picture, made for children, is carried over into adulthood, it leads to the heresy called "tri-theism." It is wrong to imagine the Trinity as a family of three different people. There are not three gods but only One. The Lakota people are very strong monotheists. "We all believe in the same God (singular)." The Jewish people were trained by God to be very strong monotheists. Every Christian is a monotheist. If it is wrong to picture the Trinity as three separate people, how then can it be explained? I have presented the following illustration to many on the reservation, and it is very meaningful and understandable to most.

The Trinity can be likened to one man extending his hand in friendship toward another. First of all, the decision to shake hands begins deep within a person, in his heart, in a place totally invisible, the source of his creative energy. (This is like the invisible, loving, creative Father.) Secondly, this invisible love comes to express itself in the world through the man's body in the extension of his hand out into the world. (Jesus Christ, God's Son, is the extension of the Father into the world. If the hand is true, it will do exactly what the heart wants it to do.) Thirdly, invisible light rays go from the hand of the man in all the directions of the world, especially to the eye of the person's friend, telling the friend of the person's hand coming to him/her in love and friendship, stimulating a response. (The Holy Spirit expresses the actions of Christ and the disposition of the Father much like the light from the hand tells of the approach of the hand and the sentiment of friendship that is clear in its approach.) In summary, the light expresses the hand, which expresses the heart — much like the Spirit expresses Christ, who expresses the Father in the world. All three are "organically" one in sequence and meaning but multiple in relationships and modes of expression.

Still the analogy is not complete, for the extension of the hand — although complete in itself — anticipates the response of the other person's hand. The analogy above indicates a fourth moment when two hands are joined in friendship. But we're beginning to jump ahead.

From the beginning of my interest in the Lakota and Christian religions, I realized that if the two religions were to be recognized as truly compatible, they had to be compatible on the most fundamental level. The primal spiritual beings of the Lakota religion had to be clearly compatible with the primal spiritual persons in the Christian religions. The comparison of the Four Winds of the Lakota religions and the Three Persons of the Trinity in the Christian religions demonstrated significant similarities.

First, the Spirit of the West is like God the Father. They both mark the beginning of all things and help make them grow. The Father's work is pre-dominately creative; the rains from the West bring new life. The **Wakiyan** and the God of the Old Testament reveal their will, especially on mountains amidst lightning and thunder. They establish definite rules concerning religious things. They strongly enforce ritual and religious traditions. When things are "done wrong," they both show their anger so that many people fear them. The Spirit of the West is feared most of all. The fear of God in the Old Testament and the fear associated with the West are very similar. They are both strong and demanding. They are just and will not let the evil doer go free. They require much purification especially before ceremonies, although the formal rules that each prescribes and the modes of purification that each orders are different.

Secondly, the Son of God, like the North Wind, shows what good comes from a life that is obedient and straight. Respect for the directives and teachings of one's elders are essential for a good straight life. They both show the tremendous good that can be accomplished by sacrifice for the sake of the people. Here **woman** has a special place, for the Maiden is pictured carrying the Pipe and Mary too is always pictured with her Son. The Pipe is the primary intercessory instrument in the Lakota religions. Through it prayers are sent to **Wakan Tanka Tunkasila** for the temporal welfare and material life of the Lakota people. Christ is the primary agent in the Christian religion. Through him prayers are sent to God the Father for the eternal salvation and spiritual life of all God's people. Jesus is called the Lamb of God who takes away the sin of the world so that we may live eternally with God in heaven. Similarly, the buffalo provided religious meat to the Lakota people. By the death of the buffalo the Lakota people overcame physical death and hunger. Each points to a straight and narrow path; for the Lakota it is the Sacred Red Path that leads to union with one's relatives in the South; for the Christian it is following Christ, carrying one's cross unto establishing God's heavenly Kingdom.

Thirdly, like the Power of the East, the Holy Spirit is associated with the obtaining of wisdom. He raises up leaders within the sacred community and gives to ordinary men understanding, courage, ability to pray, and effective communication in the spiritual order. Both spirits are related to "enlightenment." Charisms and the exercise of spiritual power, however, are received according to the religious and cultural tradition to which one belongs, for wisdom perfects and unites that which has already been given by God. The harsh, humble and personal outlook of the first direction is now replaced by a lofty, living and universal outlook. Strict obedience to traditions is now enlivened by one's own spiritual experiences and familiarity with what is **wakan**/holy.

What of the fourth stage to which we referred earlier? There is no fourth person in the blessed Trinity obviously! This presented a great impasse for a time in the comparative study of the two religions. Some felt that perhaps the character of the fourth element in Lakota religion would give a clue to a fourth element in Christianity. In examining the Lakota mythology, it was noted that the peoples of the first three directions were very specific: the horse people, the buffalo people, the elk people. But in the South the Lakota spoke of all the animal peoples, **wamakaśkan oyate**. It is to the South that all faced, **Itokagata**. The South is the **takte makoce** where one will live in ghost form in an earthly happiness with one's relatives and all animals. The south was different from the others in that it was more corporate and dealt with the after-life more than with the present. Comparatively, the question arose immediately: Is there any divine Christian reality that will be universally corporate in the after-life? The immediate answer was: Yes, the Mystical Body of Christ!

So there are now, and will always be only three individual divine persons in God. But because of the incarnation there will be a corporate reality, the Mystical Body of Christ, united to the Triune God in the End Times. Christian revelation points to some kind of divinization of believers within that corporate entity called the Mystical Body of Christ. Revelation says that in the final Kingdom, the faithful Christian will see God "face to face." There is definitely an aspect of equality indicated in that expression. In the Sign of the Cross, the Trinitarian formula is not expressed in a vacuum but **over** someone. When a person is baptized, he is marked in the **name** (singular) of the Father, and of the Son, and of the Holy Spirit. To be marked with a Jewish name is to be declared to be of the same "stock" and "household." Receiving a new name spiritually changes a person. By the power of God, man comes to have God's life in him somehow by gift; he is united to God, he is one with God. In the Mystical Body of Christ, Jesus, under the aspect of his humanity, becomes the head of a corporate entity, with the Spirit sanctifying and raising all the members to the nature of their highest and pre-dominant member, the God-man Jesus Christ.

In the Lakota medicine wheel the West and the East are united in a special way. This is similar to the close relationship of God the Father and the Spirit of God, who have always been recognized as clearly active in the world in imminent and extrinsic ways, respectively. In the Lakota medicine wheel the North and the South are closely connected through the Sacred Red Path, which all are called to follow. This is similar to The Way that Jesus walked from the particular time of his incarnation to the particular time of his return at the parousia. Since the fourth element is transcendental, eschatological, and corporate, it is qualitatively different from the first "three," which are more established, existential, and individual.

Certainly the Lakota four-directional Spirits are not divine. The Lakota primarily speak of them as operating in the physical domain where they assist humans, animals, and Grandmother Earth. These spirits, like all the other Lakota spirits, act both as intermediaries between us and God and as independent agents of special but limited **wakan** powers. So there are many differences between the Lakota "four" and the eschatological Christian "four." Still despite their differences, this three-plus-one comparison indicated a compatibility between the two religions on a most fundamental religious level.

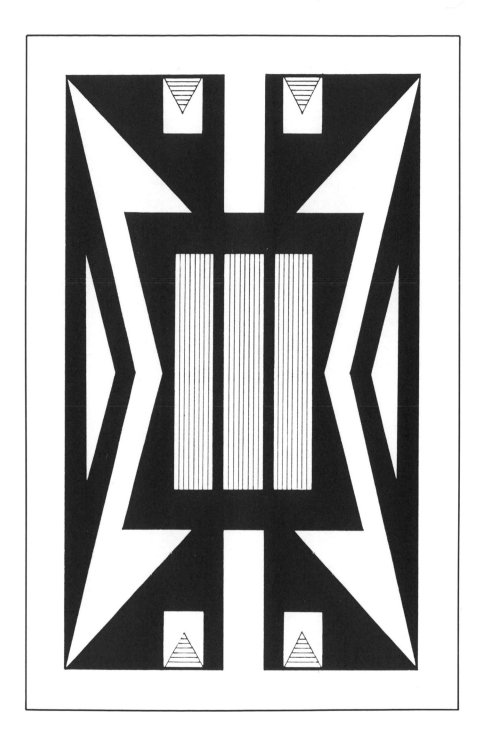

Chapter 15

How Are the Lakota and Christian Religions Related?

In its many examinations of rituals and beliefs, the members of the Rosebud Medicine Men and Pastors' Meeting found the similarities and differences between the Lakota and the Christian religions to be legion. Repeated patterns of similarities and differences have long been seen by many people on the reservation. Not everyone has the same response to them however. Generally, people take four very different theological positions with regard to relating the two religions.

One group says that they see no difference between the two religions. (Many in this group feel themselves very weak and pitiful and want to keep peace and harmony between all parties. So there is often much suppression and denial here.) One often hears them say, "We all pray to the same God." In the Lakota language, the word for "religion" is **wocekiye,** which is the absolute form of the Lakota word for "prayer." These people disregard differences of prayer forms and the revelations that spiritual beings have given to different individuals and groups. They feel that it is the act of saying prayers — any type of prayer-petition — that is important. This group is very interested in miraculous cures and material assistance, and they will support any verbal request to almost any one to achieve that end. They often invite one religious group after another into their homes to make intercessory prayers. When the cure or request is granted, they thank God and do not concern themselves with distinguishing whose prayers it was that really helped. Distressed by inter-religious disagreements and criticism, they like large, sociable interdenominational meetings where differences are deliberately put aside and there is much fellowship and theistic spirituality. One's religious denomination is very much determined by one's family ancestry and upbringing. However, they will make changes toward some friendly minister, or away from some unfriendly minister. Their involvement is at most occasional, and then primarily in terms of external actions. They really do not understand what the discussion of religion is all about. They see no positive values but only negative, displeasing differences emerging from these discussions. For them, the particular revelations and beliefs of each religion have no spiritual meaning to them. Consequently most of the religious instructions of medicine men and priests mean little to them; they are only concerned that everyone pray for **their** needs. They are self-centered, for many different reasons. They proudly proclaim that they can go to services at any church, but in fact they attend few or none. For them there is no real spiritual difference between the Lakota and Christian religions; they both are **wocekiye.**

On the second level, people focus on the differences between the two religions. Some point to externals like Indian tobacco offerings, the outdoor prayer environment, the language differences, etc., as proof that they are different. Others point to the different social and religious values found in the Lakota and **Wašicu** words. Indian militants and other strict separatists suppress similarities. Anthropologists often separate Christian and White accretions from descriptions of Indian society, dismissing them as spiritually and culturally insignificant and harmful to the Indian people. Although they will live and work with different groups, the people in this group often say that everything Indian and Lakota is good, and everything White and Christian is bad. In many ways they desire to return to the idyllic period between the coming of the horse and being confined to the reservations, that is, the period of hunting on the Plains and the Indian Wars between 1650 and 1850 A.D. Desiring to return to the Old Days, yet finding that they have lost contact with that life style, they often go to college classes or read books to try to recreate the "authentic" form of Lakota life and rituals that existed before the reservations. Here an unfortunate thing sometimes happens. This aggressive group of idyllic, younger people frequently comes in conflict with the older generation, who are living the traditions as it has developed and come to them through the years. (In a number of ways the conflict of those propounding an ideal culture versus those who have evolved in a lived tradition is like the Protestant and Catholic conflict of centuries past, where the first group focuses upon the original texts while the latter focuses upon living tradition.) Angry, separatist ideas often result in dismissing Indians as well as Whites. Name-calling comes easy; for example, any Indian they judge to be too acculturated is called an "apple," — red on the outside and white on the inside. Another common split is according to "blood." Some categorically deny that it is possible for a Mix-blood to become a medicine man or authentically take part in any Lakota religious ceremony. Such people say that Lakota ceremonies are exclusively for the Lakota, and all Whites should go back with their Christian religion to the place from which they came. While focusing on troubles and difficulties, this second group is antithetical.

On the third level, peace-seeking and religiously concerned people blind themselves to the many differences between the two religions. They only see the similarities. This group is quite reflective. They have a deeper understanding of religious things and a wide range of religious insights. They often comprise a large portion of the active core in a religious group. They deliberately mask over differences for the sake of harmonizing interreligious activities. For example, one medicine man said, "You **mniakastan** (pour water on) in baptism. I **mniakastan** in the sweatbath. We **mniakastan** in both religions. Therefore there is no difference between the two. We are both purifying the people and bringing God's blessings upon them in their needs for a better life." Hence, what is seen to be quite similar is said to be the **same.** In the Medicine Men and Pastors' Meeting, as the discussions brought out more and more similarities, one regularly heard the comment: "See, they are the same." How quickly these people would be deflated as the discussion was redirected to corresponding differences.

There was a very long, difficult meeting on the relationship of Christ and the Pipe. After the participants were most careful to express the traditions as they received them and the spiritual insights as they had them, one visiting priest stood up and said, "Let's slice through everything that has been said tonight and get to the heart of things. **Wanikiya cannunpa kin he e.** (Christ is the Pipe.) Upon hearing that, one wondered if this man had heard the many ways in which the Pipe and Christ functioned differently?! This man reasoned to a mystical union between Christ and the Pipe insofar as Christ is **the** source of all that is true and good, and the Pipe is **a** source of truth and goodness. This statement focused on only one side of the Christian theology of divine participation in the world. By similar reasoning it could be said that Christ is the air, Christ is a tree, Christ is you. There is in this thinking a lack of respect for the material and historical side of divine participation in which an individual is truly an individual and not God. There are a great many people in this group, some quite simple and others quite sophisticated. Regardless of the level of education, they are good people, bent on trying to establish harmony between religions. However, in so doing they often destroy the uniqueness of revelation that gives each religion its strength and place in religious history.

On the fourth level are found individuals who are able to appreciate both the similarities and differences of both religions and keep them in their respective places. Like the pivot of a teeter-totter, these people find fulfillment by first going to one side and then to the other and back again. If all the weight is put on one side, they feel unfulfilled because there is another side that has its time and place. Thus the two traditions are always in constant relationship with one another. Many medicine men were repeatedly concerned — and justly so — that the combination of the Lakota and Christian religious ceremonies would result in the subjugation and ultimate suppression of the Lakota spirits, with the medicine men losing their spirit-contacts and their **wakan** powers. The priests likewise were hesitant about combining the two religions. At the Meeting, Moses, the vice-president, repeatedly said, "We are not here to combine the two religions. We are here to understand one another and to respect one another."

It seemed apparent that the two religions already were harmonious on a most fundamental level in the lives of many of the participants. What was needed was not combination but explanation, and in that explanation both similarities and differences had to be simultaneously recognized. The similarities pointed to a spiritual unity, which found its origin in the same God and our same basic human nature and similar spiritual sensitivities. The differences established the uniqueness of each religion. It was from the differences that each religion was able to contribute to a fuller life for each individual and people. The differences made each religion special and pointed to the unique ways each was to be respected. Just as two people do not have to be exactly alike to marry — so too, two religions, like the Lakota and the Christian religions, need not be made equivalent to be brought together in a fruitful interrelationship.

In the Medicine Men and Pastors' Meeting, the Lakota used the word **ikoyake** to describe the relationship of the two religions as they experienced it. The Lakota and the Christian religions **fit.** They "fit" as a hand and a glove "fit." The hand is like the Lakota religion, natural and close to the things of this world. The glove is like the Christian religion. With the glove a person is able to do things a bare hand cannot do, like touch things that are hotter or colder than a human could naturally deal with. The gloved hand is in a way capable of "super"natural deeds. When the hand and the glove "fit," then at every point the hand and the glove touch, but wherever they touch they are different and separate.

The two religions "fit," as a horse and wagon "fit." The Lakota religion is like the horse. It is very natural, continually touching and feeding off the earth. The wagon is man-made, and it can carry more people and things than the back of the horse can. Jesus is the driver. He sits on the wagon, and the leather reins go from his hands to the front of the horse to direct it wherever it goes.

While a person does not try to put the glove in the hand or the wagon in the horse, he may put the hand in the glove and the horse between the poles of a wagon. This is not done destructively but carefully so as not to damage it in its original, healthy form. While the Christian religion welcomes pre-Christian enrichments, the Lakota religion does not welcome them. Why this is so, will become clearer when we consider the difference between second-level, national, folk religions and third level, international, cosmopolitan religions.

What is the **theological** relationship between the two religions? If a relationship is to be truly **theo**logical, it must be based in God, **Theos.** There must also be a logical consistency between the character of God and Salvation History, of which the Lakota and Christian religions are a part. This is a very large topic, and there is space here for only the barest outline of a theological model which can effectively link the two religions together respectfully.

The Lakota medicine men repeatedly said, "All things are in four." In the previous chapter it was indicated how the Lakota descriptions of the Four Winds and the Christian description of the four-stages of the eschatologically fulfilled Trinity are very similar. Because of the great mythological, symbolic, and cultural qualities of these descriptions, however, it is very difficult to build a theological argument on them.

I decided to take the words of the medicine men seriously to see if "all things are in fours." Because of the limitation of space, and the comparative religious content of this volume, I will present only a taste of what that search for a $(3+1)$ paradigm produced. In physics there are four-dimensions: x, y, z, and t, of which the fourth parameter is uni-directional. There are four fundamental forces in the universe: gravitation, electro-dynamic, strong nuclear force, and weak nuclear force. In mathematics one generates a circle using the x and y coordinates which determine both its place and orientation, the radius, and the moving arc that sketches the circle. Scholastic philosophy long recognized four fundamental types of causality: material causality, efficient causality, formal causality, and final causality. Turning to more recent times, Hegel saw history as a dialectic composed of a thesis, antithesis, and synthesis, which were driven by and toward the universal Spirit. Today some analysts extend the Freudian triad of the id, Ego and super ego to include a spiritual element. Jung's study of symbols, myths, dreams, and archetypes brought forth the four-fold theme repeatedly. Major stages of pyschological development are frequently put forward as: childhood, adolescence, adulthood, and old age. As one can see, I have extended some classical sequences and combined others. A detailed comparative analysis would be needed to justify such alterations. It likewise would be necessary to demonstrate that systems associated with the numerologies of 1, 2, 3, 5, 6, 7, 8. . ., are all contained in the typology of the "four." This must wait for another time; our concern here is only in the area of theology.

If the relationship of the Lakota and Christian religions is to have a theological basis, it must be based on **Theos** (God). An imminent, process understanding of God as "Lover" reveals four moments: 1) The pre-existence of the lover, 2) The lover's affirmation of another as his beloved, 3) The lover's gift of himself to his beloved, 4) The lover's openness to the love of the beloved — thus closing the circle of love. In Scripture an economic understanding of God as "Covenant-maker" is given in four-phases: 1) The establishment of an individual and family covenant with Adam and Noah in pre-historic times, 2) The establishment of a tribal and national covenant through Abraham and Moses, 3) The establishment of an international and universal covenant through Jesus and his Church, 4) The establishment of the eschatological and divine covenant through the second coming of Christ on the Last Day.

The comparison of the Lakota and Christian religions in the Medicine Men and Pastors' Meeting repeatedly showed the ways the Lakota folk religion is like the Jewish religion in its world view, its emphasis upon the material side of things, its concern about the members of the tribe, etc. It is also true that there are revelational differences in God's special closeness to the Jewish people, especially as they were prepared for the coming of Christ, the Messiah and Son of God. The Lakota religion was also close to God and the missionary record shows that they were, in fact, open for the revelation of Christ and the formation of the Church, since almost the entire Lakota people was converted to Christianity within a generation after they came on the reservation.

Rather than consider the Lakota people to be in a covenantal relationship that is parallel to the Mosaic covenant, some Fundamentalist Christians consider the Indian people to be children of God's covenant with Adam and Noah because of their harmonious religious relationship with God, as expressed through creatures of the world and natural signs such as the rainbow. Either way, the four-fold model still stands.

If one accepts God [**Theos**] as an eschatologically-oriented four-fold Lover, and if one accepts that the divine four-fold love process is reflected in everything in creation, and if one accepts that the eschatalogically-oriented stages of Salvation History reflect God's four-fold Nature, and if one accepts that the Lakota religion is an expression of a second-stage revelation and the Christian religion is an expression of a third-stage revelation in Salvation History, then some very important **theo**logical conclusions can be made regarding the relationship of the Lakota and Christian religions.

First of all, just as a Lakota does not value the North over the West and a Christian does not value the Holy Spirit over God the Son, so too a person should not value one's private, personal relationship with God over one's Lakota (or folk) religious relationship with God or over one's Catholic (or universal) religious relationship with God. By their places in God's Plan, Christian revelations and rituals are subsequent and more universal than Lakota visions and ceremonies, which providentially preceded Christianity and prepared the way spiritually for Christian missionaries. Each has its proper time, place and purpose in the life of the people — even now.

There is a tendency to consider history as a smoothly advancing reality. The four-fold model, however, finds the events of world to occur in quantum steps so that there are enduring, distinct stages in Salvation History as there are in the "spiration" of Triune God and in the four-fold aspects of **Wakan Tanka**. Therefore, as the Persons of the Trinity and the spirits of the Four Directions remain enduringly distinct, so too are the levels of revealed religion in Salvation History to be recognized as enduringly distinct — of which the Lakota religion and the Christian religions are from two distinctly different stages of revealed religion and should be respected as such and remain enduringly distinct.

In saying that the material universe and Salvation History are ordered, one must be careful of the word "ordered." Some Lakota wrongly may become angered by this word; some Christians unjustifiably may become proud and censorious in their use of this word. The word "ordered" is really ambiguous in value. There is a time and a place for the emergence of each stage (in salvation history as in the Triune God). The emergence of a subsequent phase advances but never totally replaces the need for the presence and action of the previous stage. Thus, the model easily justifies and illustrates the principles of participation and subsidiarity, in which one element can be totally contained in the next without its being destroyed in its unique independence.

"Two" is contained within "three" but "three" is not contained within "two." Throughout the history of Christianity, there has been the tendency for its thinkers and liturgists to use philosophical, social, theological, and ceremonial elements from pre-Christian cultures and religions. This mode of enriching the Church from secular or pre-Christian history has been formally endorsed by Vatican II. There is a constant tendency within the Catholic Church on the reservation to bring traditional and local elements within its liturgies, churches, and sermons. On the other hand, the medicine men have been very resistant to bringing formal Christian elements into the Lakota religious world view and ceremonies. Forcing Christian values and elements into the Lakota religious realm has the effect of disrupting its religious cosmology and the place of the familial spirits found in that religion.

The model also indicates some degree of individuality and independence in the interrelationship of the different levels. In the four-fold way for human beings, there is a time delay between the establishment of "otherness" in the second stage and the establishment of "oneness" in the third stage. Therefore, it is understandable that differences within and between levels should exist for a time. The limitations of the human heart are such that often an individual is not able to take all of God's revelation upon himself, and so there is a tendency to adhere to one or the other rather than to both and all. When a person is able to concentrate upon only one religion, Christianity's eschatological orientation says that the individual should answer Christ's call and follow all the teachings and practices of the Christian Church. On the other hand, Lakota nativists say that one must first remain faithful to the more ancient and familial revelation and ceremonies. These attitudes create a real dilemma. If a handicapped person were to choose to pray to only one, would a Christian pray to the Father, to Christ, to the Spirit, or to the Communion of Saints? There are many values to be weighed here. It would seem that God's plan is directed toward growth and those practices which promote a gradual expansion of beliefs and practices are to be advocated. Nativists today tend to be reactionary and conservative and this position seems to be designed to save them from spiritual disintegration. Those who practiced Lakota religion in the past, however, were inclined toward an expansion into Christianity, just as Christianity today is open to recalling and re-activating our religious folk foundations. The ideal is the invocation of all relevant spiritual beings. When the limitations of the human spirit of an individual are such that only one revelation is possible, it is important to discern spiritually with the person as to which revelation is bringing this individual closest to God, His people, and things Sacred.

. It is also important to realize, not only the imperfections of the individual, but also the imperfections of both the Lakota and Christian religions. Frequently, at the sight of another's imperfections, people become critical and angry, especially when the failing pertains to the leadership or their teaching of religions. Instead of allowing this to happen, we ought to recognize that placing ourselves in the hands of God and dedicating ourselves to Him will produce a new life, a new revelation and a new relationship with God beyond our current, limited world. Active immersion in both religions is a sign of a more total dedication to God. Comparative study and involvement help point out deficiencies and weaknesses in religions. Thus, both religions together provide a stronger ladder with which to ascend toward the Sacred.

In summary, the theological legitimacy of this position is grounded in a Lakota-Christian's respect for the Unity of God and the progressive distinction of Persons in the Trinity as well as the four Sacred Powers placed by God in the Four Directions. From a theological perspective, there is one-to-one typological relationship between elements found on three levels: namely, a) the imminent Trinity where God is known as Father, Son, and Holy Spirit; b) the economic Trinity where God successively reveals himself in history as Creator, Redeemer, and Sanctifier; and c) the progressive covenants of Salvation through Adam and Noah, through Abraham and Moses, and through Jesus and his Paraclete. Consequently, one may conclude that it is theologically true, holy, and God-like for a person on the Rosebud Reservation to participate authentically and wholeheartedly in the revealed religious ceremonies of the Lakota, and exercise Lakota moral values and attitudes whenever a folk situation arises. Similarly, it is theologically true, holy, and God-like for a person to practice authentically and whole-heartedly Christian religious beliefs and rituals whenever a Catholic, universal situation arises — error and sinfulness in both religions notwithstanding.

In many ways, there can be Lakota Christians just as there are monastic Catholics. The first term in these word combinations describes the respect paid to one's local religious community and its spiritual traditions. The second term describes the respect paid to the universal Church and its religious traditions. There is, in addition to this example, a more fundamental level — that of individual spirituality. Every Lakota or monk has their own distinctive personal relationship with God and other spiritual beings. There are occasional conflicts between these levels, but people are able to work and establish harmony between them. Harmony is not to be confused with identity, however. The four-fold way implies that these levels of spirituality and religion are meant to be distinct, harmonious, and interrelationally fulfilling, leading a person to a more sacred existence.

A number of people have pointed out that the world views of the Lakota and of Christians are radically different. The Lakota regard the Earth as personal while Christians view it as impersonal. The Lakota spirituality is very concerned about physical health while Christian spirituality is more concerned about the health of one's soul rather than one's body. The question is therefore raised: Is it intellectually possible to be a Lakota Christian? How can one attempt to maintain two radically different world views without becoming schizophrenic? Many young people become torn between the traditional values of the Lakota culture and the progressive values of the Christian culture. Here is the key: A person cannot think or function in two radically different world views **at the same time.** Rather, one must totally put oneself into one situation at a time. There is no error here since both world views have a share in the truth. The truth known from each perspective is simply incomplete because of our multifaceted nature. One must be careful not to be negative about what is unobserved but should remain silent until one learns more from another aspect. There is nothing wrong in being ''silent'' about one realm of experience while operating in the other. Switching from one world view to another is called a ''paradigm shift.''

The term ''paradigm shift'' is taken from nuclear physics in which the prime example is the complementary relationship of particle and wave mechanics. The Lakota world view is, in many ways, like wave mechanics. It has been noted that in the Lakota world, things are seen in circles. The world is also perceived in a very existential, static sort of way. Things are known in terms of relationships and continuities. The Christian world view is like particle mechanics in which a primary concern is the transfer of energy from one point to the next, usually with a scattering of effect. In the Christian world, the transfer of power from the ''head'' is carefully watched as authority passes along through history. The splintering effect of heresy is of great concern; the spread of Christ's Spirit and the Gospel throughout the world is praised. Wave and particle aspects of matter are complementary. Their world views are inherently distinct and cannot be derived one from the other, yet each yields valuable information for the service of people. Similarly, the Lakota and Christian world views are complementary and harmonious. One is not historically derivable from the other. Although there are many common aspects, each religion deals with its own religion revelations and insights into God's creation. Each has its own particular way of dealing religiously with the world. If these religions are of the one true God and **Wakan Tanka,** the different ways of these religions should be distinct but not incompatible, just as the different ways of the Persons of the Trinity and the four **Wakan** directions are distinct but not incompatible.

The optical exercise on the next page demonstrates how a person's internal perception of the world is bifurcated: A person is able to focus mentally on only one thing at a time. Whatever is not in focus recedes to the periphery of consciousness, while still serving as an essential complementary background to the main object of focus. Another exercise shows how quickly a person can make the paradigm shift.

Many people have found the following illustration very helpful in understanding how a person is able to switch quickly between personal and universal world views, as well as between the Lakota and Catholic religion. In psychology, transactional analysis demonstrates the importance of effective paradigm shifts for healthy living. Its primary model describes three basic psychological complexes: Child, Parent and Adult. The following simple story will illustrate the desired point: While a man works during the day, he must act as an adult, taking responsibility for community affairs and projects involving people. This adult tries to treat everyone respectfully so that peace and harmony reign in a swirl of activity. At the end of the day when he goes home to relax and is with his children, he plays but for no other purpose than to have fun. Since this man is psychologically healthy, he is able to push his ''adultness'' into the periphery of his life when he acts as a ''child'' while playing with his children. When the children get out of hand and start hurting each other, he immediately switches to a ''parental'' role. When the situation is corrected, he is able to return to play or perhaps back to adult concerns again. Unfortunately, many people get stuck in a rut and can think and act in only one way. Some feel that they must always act as an ''adult'' and that it is wrong for them to act as a ''child.'' Some people try to combine two or even three of these levels together, and thus, act as an ''integrated'' person rather than a ''layered'' person. Experience shows that the blending of these psychological states produces great confusion. Transactional analysis shows the importance of a person reacting successively on different psychological "plains," depending upon the needs of a situation.

FOUR-FOLD PERCEPTION EXERCISE

1. Thesis

2. Antithesis

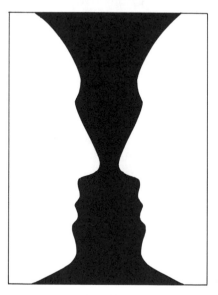

3. Synthesis

4. By concentrating alternately on the face figures and then the vase figure, one experiences a "paradigm shift" which makes one figure stand out against the background of the other. Similarly, concentrating upon Lakota things, Catholic things fall into the periphery of consciousness, and concentrating on Catholic things, Lakota things fall into the periphery of consciousness. By concentrated effort, a person can learn to switch easily from one to the other, being totally immersed in each, one at a time. The concentration on one implicitly affirms the presence and form of the other.

When we analyze social levels of activity, we find that it is right and loving to dress to the hilt for a public dance and to dress most casually when with personal friends. It is right and loving to be formal and careful in one's speech in public and to jabber spontaneously amongst one's family and peers in local slang. It is right and true for a court judge not to express his own private opinion and judgment in court but only speak in the manner prescribed by law while sitting on the bench. These things have been known and practiced for centuries. However, some people are uneasy about this switching and feel like a hypocrite when they are not always acting the same and the best way. Some people say that there are no standards and that all morality is strictly relative. The four-fold way advocates a pluralism that is restricted in its relativity. Because the divine/human interrelationship is easily recognized in the four-fold way, acting in a multi-leveled way according to the social situation is easily realized as being both moral and **God-like.**

In summary, the four-fold way indicates the God likeness of practicing the Lakota religion in a Lakota community context for the life and health of Lakota people, and in practicing the Christian religion, in the context of universal needs unto eternal salvation. In this way, a person can practice the Lakota religion in a totally orthodox way and also practice the Christian religion in a totally orthodox way — each at its appropriate time — both with a faith and interrelationship that encompasses the real situation of the individual, bringing blessing from God, **Tunkašila** and Father, for **mitakuye oyas'in** and the People of God through the Pipe and Christ.

Chapter 16

Closing Remarks

The participants of the Rosebud Medicine Men and Pastors' Meeting sought to promote mutual understanding and respect for the Lakota and Christian religions. Our discussions showed that there were many similarities and differences. Different people related them in different ways. While one group saw no difference between the two religions, another group emphasized the differences and encouraged a separation of the two religions. Most of the Indian participants of the dialogue, however, were living in such a way that the two religious traditions found a spiritual harmony. The participants worked for long hours in an effort to clarify these interrelationships and to resolve the various theological difficulties. They wanted this book to become a tool for the young to help them on their spiritual journey as they agonize over the tensions between traditional/modern, folk/urban, Indian/White, Lakota/Christian values.

Sadly enough, every major Lakota elder who participated in the meetings is now dead. Some traditional people might be inclined to say that the reason they died was because they took part in the meetings and spoke of **wakan** matters wrongly. However, it would seem that if what they did was wrong, the spirits would have punished them sometime **during** the meeting when they were saying these things rather than keeping them alive until the dialogue was finished. We are blessed by their testimonies, for they showed how the modern Lakota is able to have, as in generations past, respect for the Christian religion as well as for the Lakota religion. It is the traditional Lakota way to seek and use from **any** source whatever serves the welfare of the people, and to turn their back on and bury whatever hurts the people.

At the beginning of the Civil Rights Movement, the younger people were very critical of Christianity and every White institution. They are now less militant but maintain a stance of respectful aloofness, desiring to develop their own cultural way and their own Indian identity. They are now increasingly admitting that there are some worthwhile things in the non-Lakota culture, but they are stating verbally and non-verbally that they want to do it their own, traditional way.

A primary value of this book is the ability to show clearly that there really are radical differences between the Lakota and Christian way, **and** it is possible for a person to draw spiritual good from both traditions without sacrificing one's authentic participation in either religion. In this way, a person is able to receive and share **all** the revelation which God has given to those whom He has called to be spiritually and culturally one with the Lakota people, as blessed by both the Pipe and Christ.

To make the two ways function together and form one better, fuller life is a most difficult task. . .but it is more natural than one may suspect. It is similar to having two "opposing" hands. As infants, we have difficulty grasping with only one hand at a time, but as we grow up, we learn how to use these "opposing" hands together. . .with greater ability and capacity for a fuller, better life for ourselves and our people. We know it is very difficult for opposites to fit together, **ikoyake.** But it is through the conjugal union of opposites that children are born and a new generation and new hopes emerge.

The medicine men say that all things are not in two, but in four. I have touched briefly on how the Pipe and Christ (the Lakota religion and the Christian religion) are but the second and third elements within God's four-fold way of the world and salvation. An in-depth study of the Lakota-Christian Four-Fold Way must wait for another time, however.

For now, let us remember that because of the nature of God and all things holy, life and history are pluralistic. Often, there are more spiritual gifts and promises from God in this world than we know about or want to encounter. It is not we who establish and define true religion but it is God and His spirits. Our duty is to grow in patience, respect, reflection, prayer, sacrifice, and willingness to accept **all** that God has given to humanity. May God bless you and help you in your search for spiritual wholeness in this pluralistic world which God has made for all our relatives in the Pipe and Christ. **Mitakuye oyas'in.**

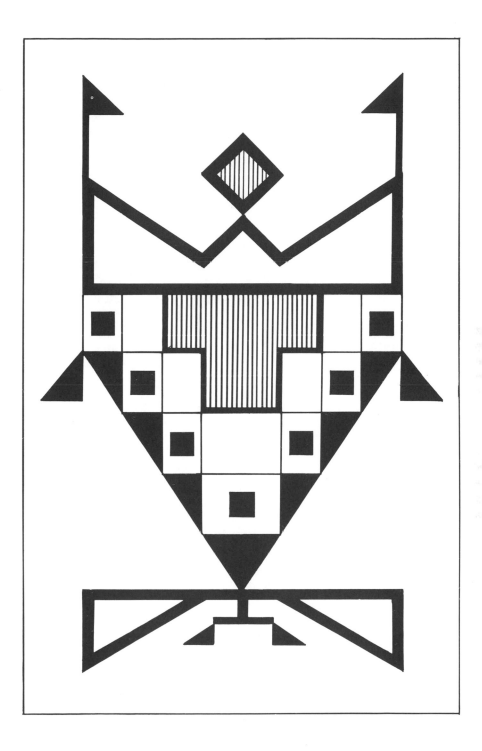

Appendix
Pronunciation Key to Lakota Words

Here are a few rules to help the beginner approximate the correct pronunciation of Lakota words in this book. For a more comprehensive treatment of the Lakota language consult: **Lakota-English Dictionary** by Eugene Buechel, S.J. and Paul Manhardt, S.J. and **Lakota Grammar** by Eugene Buechel. Both are available from: Indian Museum, St. Francis Mission, St. Francis, South Dakota 57572.

Accent is usually on the second syllable. The first syllable is accented in some words. A few of the major words in this book that are accented on the first syllable are: hunka, onśi. . ., śica,'' topa, taku, tanka, winyan. Please note: Many people mispronounce the Lakota word(s) for ''God,'' that is, **Wakan Tanka,** which is pronounced as a single word with an accent on the second syllable in the first word only.

An apostrophe (') within a Lakota word indicates a glottal stop. It decisively separates the previous consonant from the subsequent vowel — as in (k-ettle).

The letter (n) at the end of a word or before a consonant usually is silent and indicates that the previous vowel is nasal. The letter (n) at the beginning of a word and before a vowel is usually pronounced as the English (n).

Vowels, in general, are pronounced classically:
a — as in father
an — as in blanc (French)
e — as in they
i — as in machine
in — as (in) in ink
o — as in obey
on — as (oo) in soon
u — as in rule
un — as (oo) in soon

Many consonants are pronounced as in English. Note the following:

c — usually as (ch) in chair
g — usually as in rig
j — as (s) in fusion
š — as (sh) in ship

There are three or four ways of pronouncing: c, g, h, k, p, s, t. The following are noteworthy. (t) is pronounced as (d) in the following words: taku, mitakuye, mitakuyepi, toka, tokeca, and the ending — takiya. (k) is pronounced like hard (g) in the following words: kin, tunkasila, hunkayapi, wakiyan, taku, takuyapi, mitakuyapi, canku, itokagatakiya.